Introduction

This book is dedicated to God,  and Earth who knows and sees Christ.

John 3:16, 17: "For God so loved the world that He gave His one and only Son, that whoever believes in Him shall not perish but have eternal life. For God did not send His Son into the world to condemn the world, but to save the world through Him."

God first loved us so that we could love one another. The greatest gift that our LORD has given us is His love. We can love because He first loved us by sending His only begotten Son to die for our sins and us.

My mission statement:
Father, I vow with the divine help and power of my LORD and Savior, Jesus Christ, that I will strive to be Christ-like in thought, word and deed. I will endeavor to be Your vessel making sure Your love and light shines in and through me for others to see Your glory. I will serve and give to others my time and resources. I will be humble and thankful in all things, I will forgive, pray constantly and give all praise and glory to You, my LORD, my Savior, my God. In Jesus' name, I pray. Amen.

Many years ago Muriel and Floyd Sykes, two very dear friends and mentors, told me that one day I should write a book. Little did they know that writing a book was on my "bucket list." Often through the years, they reminded me of it and encouraged me to pursue it. In 2009 Muriel went home to live with Jesus, but Floyd and I still talked about this on several occasions. I will always be thankful to them for their love, support and encouragement. I've waited, prayed and talked to God about my dream of writing a book. For the last five years, I've written morning inspiration messages with God's help, and have shared them with a group of people via email. Now, I believe that God is telling me it is time to proceed and to publish a daily devotional book.

The title of this book is *Purple Wisdom*. The title came from God one day as I was walking and praying. I believe that God's royal color is purple and yes, I do love the color purple. The word purple is mentioned over 51 times in the Bible. It is associated with royalty, kings and Jesus. The wisdom aspect of this title comes from God's wisdom. It is His Wisdom that He shows us in the pages of His Word, the Bible. *Purple Wisdom*—God's daily messages to us to live life with Him as He is our King, Guide, Pilot, Heavenly Father, LORD and Savior.

Purple—God's color

Have you ever thought about color and how it affects our lives? When we see a particular color we get either relaxed or excited, feel alive or feel sad. We all have a favorite color and mine is PURPLE. I bet you didn't know that did you? Growing up I did not like purple and never could understand why my mom and sister did. In the color wheel it was not a color I would have chosen. At that time my favorite color was blue. I don't know why, but at the age of 40, PURPLE became my color. I absolutely wanted purple around me all the time because whenever I looked at it, I just got this overwhelming feeling of peace, tranquility and satisfaction. So now in the color wheel of life, purple is my passion. If I'm shopping and there is an item in different colors and one of them is purple—you got it, I will choose the purple one.

Throughout the Bible I notice that purple is considered the color of royalty. God chose the color purple for hangings in His tabernacle. In Proverbs 31, the woman of virtue will wear purple linen garments. In the Gospels, when Jesus was being led to be crucified, the soldiers put a royal purple robe on Him mocking His claim of being a king. At different times of the year, the altar in our church is dressed in purple. In Revelation, the twelfth wall of the city of The New Jerusalem is amethyst. On the color wheel the color purple means power, wisdom, leadership, royalty, truth, justice, and spirituality. My point is: I think purple is God's color, too. It warms my heart to think that God shared this beautiful color with us, and whenever I see it or wear it, I feel close to Him and I feel alive and enthusiastic for life. My favorite color is and will remain purple. Oh, by the way, purple is in rainbows, too, and a rainbow is a covenant between God and us.

Genesis 9:13-15: I have set my rainbow in the clouds, and it will be the sign of the covenant between Me and the earth. Whenever I bring clouds over the earth and the rainbow appears in the clouds, I will remember My covenant between Me and you and all living creatures of every kind.

Some examples of the color purple in the Bible:

Esther 8:15 [*The Triumph of the Jews*]
When Mordecai left the king's presence, he was wearing royal garments of blue and white, a large crown of gold and a **purple** robe of fine linen. And the city of Susa held a joyous celebration.

Proverbs 31:22—The wife of noble character
She makes coverings for her bed; she is clothed in fine linen and **purple**.

Mark 15:17 The soldiers were mocking Jesus and His Kingship.
They put a **purple** robe on him, then twisted together a crown of thorns and set it on him.

Revelation 21:20 The walls of the New Jerusalem
…the fifth onyx, the sixth ruby, the seventh chrysolite, the eighth beryl, the ninth topaz, the tenth turquoise, the eleventh jacinth, and the twelfth **amethyst.**

Wisdom
Wisdom is in God's lessons throughout the Bible. Wisdom means practical discernment; making wise decisions in difficult circumstances. Wisdom is not knowledge; wisdom is based on knowledge. Knowing God is the key to wisdom. When we choose God's way, He grants us wisdom. Wisdom is a basic attitude that affects every aspect of life. Trust in God—He will make you truly wise. For the LORD gives wisdom, and from His mouth come knowledge and understanding. True wisdom is God's and it is a gift to us by Him. It is only given to those who earnestly seek it. We gain wisdom through constant searching, growing, trusting and honoring Him.

***"Purple Wisdom"* comes from God and that is why purple is my favorite color and why I like to share these messages because they come from our LORD. It's all about Him and not about us. As we read these daily devotionals, let's think of God, His Son Jesus and the Holy Spirit. Maybe *"Purple Wisdom"* will live on in our hearts, and when we see the color purple, we will smile and look up to heaven and listen for God's whisper as He gives us a big Heavenly Hug and some wisdom... and maybe, we will see a rainbow.**

May our days be blessed, and I hope whenever we see the color purple, we will think of our LORD, His Kingdom and all that He has promised us in His Word. He is our King and He is royalty. Jesus obeyed His Father and left His kingdom to come to earth in human form as a baby to grow into a man. He is God but He is also man. He lived 33 sinless years and then died on a cross in the most deplorable way to take away our sins and for our salvation. The good news is He rose from the dead and now sits at the Right Hand of God, interceding for us, and He sent the Holy Spirit as our Counselor to live in us and remind us of His words and who He is so we are not left alone. Wow!!! What an awesome God we have. Thank You, Jesus, for all that You have done for us. Amen.

Oh, by the way, if you're looking for something purple, come see me because to me it's the color that makes any day a good day. Have a "purple" day full of love, life and passion.

I would like to thank Tim, my husband, for being my best friend and partner in life. I want to thank him for his inspiration, patience, encouragement and understanding as I worked on creating this book. I would like to thank our children and grandchildren for inspiring me as well. I want to thank my friends, Linda and Judy for their time, dedication, encouragement and proofing skills and Lara for helping me to get this book published. I want to thank the Lake Placid Lassies (Lisa, Diane, Kathy, and Debbie), because without you and our first trip to LP, the morning messages and this book would not have come to fruition. I also want to thank Diane for the photo of Mirror Lake as it was perfect for this book cover. I want to thank my friends, Jeanette, Floyd and Muriel, for seeing the potential in my writings and me and for encouraging me to pursue this dream. Most of all, I want to thank God for helping me every single morning to find ideas, Bible verses, quotes and thoughts to write about that might help others to know Him and His love and to find encouragement and comfort. God gets all the credit and glory as I am His humble servant and vessel. My goal in writing the morning messages and subsequently the book is that they might help others to know God. If one person comes to faith in Jesus after reading these then I've accomplished my mission of sharing God's story. I thank God for every one of these people and you.

In His Love and God Bless,
Char

January 1
Happy New Year!!!

Psalm 136:1
Give thanks to the LORD, for He is good. His love endures forever.

As each year winds down, I begin to search for words to focus on during the upcoming year. I search scripture and pray about those words. I look for them in things I read, cards I see, in nature and in conversations with people. The most important part of the search is my time spent in the Word and with Jesus. My former words have been Gratitude, Joy, Prayer, Grace, and Hope. Throughout this daily devotional, I will focus on all of these words because they have had such an impact on my daily life. As I focus on certain words, I've learned that I can pray anytime and anyplace, and it does not have to be long. In researching *"Gratitude,"* I've realized how important it is to be thankful each day. Gratitude leads to joy and joy assures peace and peace assures joy. *"Joy"* is Jesus, Others, You. Joy is powerful. When we put Jesus first in our lives we will be a blessing to others and that is where we will get our joy. *"Prayer"* is a conversation between me and God. It is the best kind of communication and because of prayer I believe my life is better. *"Grace"* is God's unconditional love and unmerited favor and what we are all in desperate need of but something that is often hard for us to grasp and understand. Grace is Jesus Christ. God reminds us that He is our *"Hope."* He is with us and guides us. God is sure and certain. God is who He says He is and He will do what He says He will do. True faith believes Him and that He will fulfill His promises, even though we may not see those promises being fulfilled any time soon. God is our hope for today, tomorrow and forever. Jesus is the true hope of the world and brings everlasting peace.

As we begin the New Year today, let's find words that have meaning and focus on them. We can pray about them and look them up in Scripture. We will see where God is leading us through the pages of His Word. We will be surprised what we will learn about ourselves and about our LORD and Savior. Happy New Year as we begin a new journey each day together.

"We will open the book. Its pages are blank. We are going to put words on them ourselves. The book is called Opportunity and its first chapter is New Year's Day." (Edith Lovejoy Pierce)

"Just a closer walk with Thee, Grant it Jesus, is my plea, Daily walking close to Thee, Let it be, dear Lord, let it be." (Author unknown)

January 2
An Attitude of Gratitude

1 Thessalonians 5:18
Give thanks with a grateful heart.

An attitude of gratitude is a blessing. What a mantra and what a way to begin and end each day. When we are thankful, we have enough and we appreciate all that we have. When we are thankful for what we have, we look at everything around us with a different perspective. A friend of mine once told me that he sends a thank you note each day to someone showing appreciation for them or for something they've done. I've tried this and it has amazing effects. When we look around us at all that we can be thankful for our attitude becomes joyful. We all have struggles. If we can step outside of them for just a moment and thank God for them, we know that we will become stronger. We might even learn a life lesson. Often as we count our blessings and appreciate them, we will see them multiplied. Let's begin today with an attitude of gratitude. We can write down three things that we are thankful for and begin today on a positive step. Dear LORD, today I am thankful for ...

"No matter what the situation is . . . close your eyes and think of all the things you could be grateful for in your life right now." (Deepak Chopra)

"Gratitude is one of the sweet shortcuts to finding peace of mind and happiness inside. No matter what is going on outside of us, there's always something we could be grateful for." (Author unknown)

January 3
Begin with Gratitude

1 Chronicles 16:8
Give thanks to the LORD, call on His name; make known among the nations what He has done.

Giving thanks seems so easy but by doing so it changes our lives. When we take a moment to say thank you to our God for all His blessings, we feel joy and peace. Our circumstances may remain the same but we can always find something to be grateful for each day. What changes is our attitude toward the situation. There are four elements of true thanksgiving: 1) remembering what God has done; 2) telling others about it; 3) showing God's glory to others; and 4) offering gifts of self, time and resources. If we are truly thankful, our lives will show it. By thanking God for all that He brings into our lives, we will find that we won't take His blessings for granted. This reminds me of that TV commercial, "What's in your wallet?" When I picture opening my wallet I see my blessings flying out like purple butterflies….we have a lot to be thankful for….

"As we express our gratitude, we must never forget that the highest appreciation is not to utter words, but to live by them." (John F. Kennedy)

"There are only two ways to live your life. One is as though nothing is a miracle. The other is as though everything is a miracle." (Albert Einstein)

January 4
Wake with Gratitude

Psalm 100
Shout for joy to the LORD, all the earth. Worship the LORD with gladness; come before Him with joyful songs. Know that the LORD is God. It is He who made us, and we are His; we are His people, the sheep of His pasture. Enter His gates with thanksgiving and His courts with praise; give thanks to Him and praise His name. For the LORD is good and His love endures forever; His faithfulness continues through all generations.

We can start each day with a grateful heart. A beautiful day begins with a beautiful mindset. When we wake up we should take a second to think about what a privilege it is to simply be alive. The moment we start acting like life is a blessing, we can be assured it will start to feel like one. Joyfully and willingly, we enter into God's presence and we worship Him with thanksgiving and praise. When we wake with gratitude and are thankful for every day, we will be blessed beyond measure. We can be thankful that something good is going to happen to us when we begin each day with a grateful heart.

Happy Moments, Praise God.
Difficult Moments, Seek God.
Quiet Moments, Worship God.
Painful Moments, Trust God.
Every Moment, Thank God. (Author unknown)

"I have held many things in my hands, and I have lost them all; but whatever I have placed in God's hands, that, I still possess." (Corrie ten Boom)

"Gratitude can transform common days into thanksgivings, turn routine jobs into joy, and change ordinary opportunities into blessings." (William A. Ward)

January 5
Inhale Love, Exhale Gratitude

Philippians 1:3
I thank my God every time I remember you.

We inhale the love of God and exhale gratitude that He loves us so much that He sent His Son to change our lives forever. God let His Son willingly die on a cross for us and our sins. He loves us so much that He sent the Holy Spirit to be with us always and for that we exhale our gratitude. There are people that God brings into our lives who leave footprints on our hearts and for that we are grateful. They stay in our hearts, lives and memories forever. We inhale love from them and we exhale gratitude for them.

"I'm thankful for nights that turned into mornings, friends that turned into family and dreams that turned into reality." (Author unknown)

"Be thankful for what we have today. Strengthen ourselves from within by learning how to be thankful for what we already have." (Author unknown)

"Piglet noticed that even though he had a very small heart, it could hold a rather large amount of gratitude." (A.A. Milne, Winnie the Pooh)

January 6
No Joy without Gratitude

Psalm 107:1
Give Thanks to the Lord, for He is good; His love endures forever.

1 Corinthians 15:57
But thanks be to God! He gives us the victory through our Lord Jesus Christ.

There is joy in gratitude. When we thank our LORD every day and give a part of ourselves to Him and honor Him, bubbles of joy will rise up in us because we have hope in Jesus. He defeated death and we have hope of eternal life with Him. No matter our circumstances or situations, we can continually thank Him for our blessings. There is always something to thank Him for no matter how small. We can focus on His promises such as in Hebrews 8:12, "For I will forgive their wickedness and will remember their sins no more." We can be thankful that God forgives our sins and that He has a "poor" memory. We can bask in the joy of gratitude each day. As we thank our LORD every morning and night, we will have abundant blessings and the love of God will be overflowing in our hearts and homes.

"Praying you are
Blessed in a way that brings God's presence closer than you have ever known it...
Blessed in a way that assures you of the plans He has for your life...
Blessed in a way that fills your heart with a thousand "thank-yous" for all that His hand will bring your way." (From DaySpring)

"Gratitude is a catalyst to all Christlike attributes. A thankful heart is the parent of all virtues." (Dieter F. Uchtedorf)

"Gratitude opens the door to...the power, the wisdom, the creativity of the universe." (Deepak Chopra)

January 7
A Daily Dose of Gratitude

Ephesians 1:3-6
Praise be to the God and Father of our Lord Jesus Christ, who has blessed us in the heavenly realms with every spiritual blessing in Christ. For He chose us in Him before creation of the world to be holy and blameless in His sight. In love He predestined us to be adopted as His sons through Jesus Christ, in accordance with His pleasure and will—to the praise of His glorious grace, which He has freely given us in the One He loves.

We have a lot to be thankful for every day and most importantly, a God who loves us so much that despite our sins, He gave us His Son. In Christ, we have all the benefits of knowing God. Knowing God means that we are chosen for salvation, we are adopted as His children, we are forgiven, and the gifts of the Spirit are ours. We have the hope of living with Jesus forever. Our blessings are eternal and not earthly. Our salvation totally depends on God. God chose us, and when we belong to Him through Jesus Christ, God looks at us as if we had never sinned. All we can do is express our thanks for His wonderful love. As we give thanks this day and every day, we should remember to give thanks to our LORD for His constant love and the blessings of His Son, Jesus Christ.

"I am a little pencil in the hand of a writing God who is sending a love letter to the world." (Mother Teresa)

"Let gratitude be the pillow upon which you kneel to say your nightly prayer. And let faith be the bridge you build to overcome evil and welcome good." (Maya Angelou)

January 8
Show Gratitude

Psalm 118:28-29
You are my God, and I will give You thanks; You are my God, and I will exalt You. Give thanks to the Lord, for He is good; His love endures forever.

Each day we have opportunities to show gratitude. We can thank our spouses and/or children for their love or for doing something for us. We can thank another person for their courtesy, help and customer service. It doesn't have to be something big, but when we smile and say "thank you" or send a note of thanks, it can go a long way to show someone appreciation for doing a good job or for being kind. Showing appreciation for friends and family, thankfulness for special gifts and everyday blessings and gratitude to our God for His unyielding love and His greatest gift, Jesus, will make our days better. Being grateful, saying thank you and spreading kindness will make us more joyful and will show others that we are grateful to have them in our lives. Sometimes, it can be forgetting a wrong by remembering a kindness. Our prayers of gratitude to our LORD as we remember our blessings will help us to live happier lives. By being grateful, our faith in our LORD will grow stronger, our love for our LORD will grow deeper and our fellowship with our LORD will grow sweeter! LORD, we know that You hear our prayers and that You also hear how grateful we are for all of our blessings.

"In daily life we must see that it is not happiness that makes us grateful, but gratefulness that makes us happy." (Brother David Steindl-Rast)

"Remember that detours are opportunities to experience new things." (Author unknown)

January 9
Faith, Hope, Love

1 Corinthians 13:13
And now these things remain: faith, hope and love. But the greatest of these is love.

Faith is the foundation and content of God's message. Hope is the attitude and focus and love is the action. When faith, hope and love are in line, we are free to love completely because we understand how God loves. Webster's describes *love* as "a deep and tender feeling of affection for or attachment or devotion to a person or persons, a feeling of brotherhood and goodwill toward people." Love is more important than all the other spiritual gifts because if we have love we will have those other gifts, too. Love makes our actions and gifts useful. Although people have different gifts, love is available to everyone. God's love is directed through us outward toward others. It is utterly unselfish. Thus the more we become like Christ, the more love we will show to others. Love is the greatest of all human qualities, and it is an attribute of God Himself. We can trust our Heavenly Father to walk us through all the days ahead as we share Jesus with those we meet. We must remember God loves and if we ever wonder or doubt, we can look to the cross.

"Gratitude is a shortcut which speedily leads to love." (Theophile Gautier)

"Love is the true means by which the world is enjoyed: our Love to others and others' Love to us." (Thomas Traherne)

January 10
Love

1 John 4:8-12
Whoever does not love does not know God, because God is love. This is how God showed His love among us: He sent His one and only Son into the world that we might live through Him. This is love, not that we loved God, but that He loved us and sent His Son as an atoning sacrifice for our sins. Dear friends, since God so loved us, we also ought to love one another. No one has ever seen God; but if we love one another, God lives in us and His love is made complete in us.

We are sinful so God had to seek a solution to the problem of sin. In the Old Testament, He tried many ways to help us see our sinful lives. He loves us so much, and He is absolute goodness, and the only solution was to send His Son to save us. We don't actually see God, but Jesus is the complete expression of God in human form, and He has revealed God to us. When we love one another, the invisible God reveals Himself to others through us, and His love is made complete. When God sees that we are ready to love others, He will bring people to us to love, and He will give us the strength and power to love.

"We can only learn to love by loving." (Iris Murdoch)

"Where there is great love there are always miracles." (Will Cather)

January 11
Take Time for Gratitude

Ephesians 5:19-20
Speak to one another with psalms, hymns and spiritual songs. Sing and make music in your heart to the Lord, always giving thanks to God the Father for everything, in the name of our Lord Jesus Christ.

As we take time to be grateful, we learn to celebrate our blessings and all that God has brought into our lives. An attitude of gratitude shows a lot about the character of a person. When we have an attitude of gratitude, it keeps God first, knowing that He is the source of every blessing we receive. Gratitude is never about feeling entitled. It's an attitude that says, "I know I don't deserve God's goodness, but I am sure grateful for it." Gratitude is choosing to be present in today. Gratitude is looking at each blessing, one at a time, and thinking about it, letting it soak in and acknowledging it as the day progresses, being more thankful again and again. Each blessing is a reminder to us to sit, be still and be grateful, trusting God to do the good works He has planned for our life. We can savor gratitude and savor the One who blesses us. We should take time today for gratitude. We must meditate on God's goodness and be thankful for all of our blessings. My heart sighs when I say the word gratitude.

"God's understanding of your need is much greater than your ability to express it." (Ray Lessin, DaySpring)

"Faith is having a positive attitude about what you can do and not worrying at all about what you can't do." (Author unknown)

January 12
Friendship

Proverbs 17:17 A friend loves at all times, and a brother is born for adversity.

Revelation 3:20 Jesus says, "Here I am! I stand at the door and knock. If anyone hears my voice and opens the door, I will come in and eat with him, and he with me."

A friend has your best interests at heart and may have to give you unpleasant advice at times, but you know it's for your own good. Two friends who bring their ideas together can help each other become sharper. Proverbs 27:17 says, "As iron sharpens iron, so one man sharpens another."

Friendship is a wonderful gift that God gives us to face our days with laughter, encouragement, hugs, joy, good counsel and sadness. Friendship is an anchor in the harbor of life to face the joys and storms that definitely will come and to celebrate the peace and calm afterwards. Jesus is our best friend. When He knocks at the door of our hearts and we let Him into our lives, we will never, ever be alone. He is our Rock and our strength. He wants to enter, so let Him in because when we do, our lives will never be the same. He will give us lasting fulfillment that exceeds worldly pleasures. Those pleasures will come and go and be destroyed but Jesus lasts forever. We can be thankful for Jesus being in our lives and for friends who are sisters and brothers in Christ.

"When I count my blessings, I count you twice." (Irish Proverb)

"A true friend is someone who thinks that you are a good egg even though he knows you are slightly cracked." (Bernard Meltzer)

January 13
I Thank God for You

Luke 6:32-35
If you love those who love you, what credit is that to you? Even 'sinners' love those who love them. And if you do good to those who are good to you, what credit is that to you? Even 'sinners' do that. And if you lend to those from whom you expect repayment, what credit is that to you? Even 'sinners' lend to 'sinners,' expecting to be repaid in full. But love your enemies, do good to them, and lend to them without expecting to get anything back. Then your reward will be great, and you will be sons of the Most High, because He is kind to the ungrateful and wicked. Be merciful, just as your Father is merciful.

Sometimes during the course of a day, we come in contact with someone who is rude and unpleasant. Our innate desire is to react and respond in the same way—to give back like we got. The stress of today affects many people's lives in ways that are unkind and make them difficult, rude and unpleasant. We have an advantage because we know the Word of God and have Him in our lives to help us, comfort us and keep us from falling into the same stressful traps. Jesus tells us that if we are kind to someone who would treat us unkindly (an enemy, so to speak), then we are doing well. People are everywhere and we will have contact with those who are not nice, but a little kindness on our part can lift them up and change a situation. We can watch their facial expressions change when we say, "thank you" or "I'm grateful for you today." Everyone wants to be complimented on a job well done. A smile, a 'thank you' and 'I'm praying for you today' will go a long way to mend a situation or give someone a much-appreciated boost. We bless them when we are kind to them and pray for them. Jesus gives us the grace to be kind to everyone—no matter how they act toward us. We can put His love into action. We should forgive as He forgives us and treat others generously, graciously and with compassion.

"I've always tried to meet people with respect, the way I wanted to be treated. I've always had the mentality that I never wanted to embarrass my parents. That fear is still there." (Derek Jeter, Yankee Great)

"When you are good to others, you are best to yourself." (Benjamin Franklin)

January 14
Faith

Matthew 17:20:
He replied, "Because you have so little faith. I tell you the truth, if you have faith as small as a mustard seed, you can say to this mountain, 'Move from here to there' and it will move. Nothing will be impossible for you."

Mustard seeds are extremely tiny. Faith, as small as a mustard seed, is very powerful when it is in God. It is not how much faith we have but who or what our faith is in. When we have faith in God and know He is with us, seemingly impossible things can occur. We will find answers to our biggest problems as we work for Him. Our God is an awesome God. He will see us through today and all the days ahead. He encourages us to have greater faith in Him and not our own abilities. Faith in Jesus makes a new us. "We can do all things through Christ who strengthens us." (Philippians 4:13)

"Faith is the conviction that God knows more than we do about this life and He will get us through it." (Max Lucado)

"Never be afraid to trust an unknown future to a known God." (Corrie ten Boom)

January 15
A Good Servant

Matthew 25:23
His LORD said to him, "Well done good and faithful servant; you have been faithful over a few things. I will make you ruler over many things. Enter into the joy of your LORD."

Today we said goodbye to an old friend—*our vacuum cleaner*. It bit the dust today and had to be replaced. On our way home from the store with a new one, my husband said, "We can't complain. It served us well for over 15 years." Instantly a thought came to me, "Well done good and faithful servant." Then it struck me that isn't it exactly what I want to hear my LORD say to me when I die to this life and meet Him in Heaven? I didn't have to do anything to my "mechanical" servant like feeding it or clothing it. What I had to do was try not to run it into the walls or furniture, change a bag every now and then when it was full, and not suck up anything bigger than a pea lying on the floor. Other than that I just turned it on and away we went. On the other hand, our God provides for us daily. He gives us "our daily bread." What He asks from us is to be His light in a dark world, love others as He loves us, share what He has given us and serve others for Him. My wish for us is that one day we will hear our LORD say the wonderful words above from Matthew 25:23. Oh, the color of my new vacuum servant is—PURPLE... hard to believe they even make purple vacuum cleaners. We did not buy it for the color, but, oh my, I certainly will not mind using it. It's the royal color of purple....God's color. I'm feeling blessed to use it.

"We deny our talents and abilities because to acknowledge or confess them would commit us to use them." (Zig Ziglar)

"All we need to make us really happy is something to be enthusiastic about." (Charles Kingsley)

January 16
Open Doors

Jeremiah 29:11
"For I know the plans I have for you," declares the LORD, "plans to prosper you and not to harm you, plans to give you hope and a future. Then you will call upon me and come and pray to me, and I will listen to you. You will seek me and find me when you seek me with all your heart."

Yesterday I was praying when God placed in my heart a thought about "an open door." We often hear "God will not close a door without opening a window" or "when one door closes look for the next one to open." Our decision becomes whether we should trust Him enough to walk through that open door or window. Anytime we face situations where we are disappointed because a chapter in our lives closes, we must look for that open door, be willing to trust Him enough and lean on Him totally in order to walk through it. Sometimes, it's not as easy as it sounds. We struggle, we don't like change, we're unsure of the future, we have responsibilities, we're not risk takers and it's not the plan we had in mind. The bottom line is we must keep our total focus on God because He does have a plan for our lives. My prayer for all of us today is that we trust our LORD totally and lean on Him. I pray that we know that we know that we know—He loves us. When that door swings wide open, we need to look to Him and ask Him to walk through it with us. He will. Let's have a good day walking with Jesus.

"Progress involves risks. You can't steal second base and keep your foot on first." (Frederick B. Wilcox)

"A wise man will make more opportunities than he finds." (Francis Bacon)

January 17
Our Personal Counselor

John 14:16-18
Jesus said: "And I will ask the Father, and He will give you another Counselor to be with you forever—The Spirit of truth. The world cannot accept Him, because it neither sees Him nor knows Him. But you know Him, for He lives with you and will be in you. I will not leave you as orphans; I will come to you."

The Holy Spirit is Jesus' spiritual presence in the lives of all His believers. God gave us the gift of the Holy Spirit at Pentecost. He lives in us to help us live as God wants and to help us live through all of our life experiences as we work to build Christ's church. The Holy Spirit gives us a whole new way to look at life as He teaches and reminds us of the words of Jesus. To have the Holy Spirit living in us is to have Jesus Himself. The Holy Spirit is called the Counselor—*the Spirit of God Himself.* Our personal Counselor tells us the truth of Jesus and His work provides us with a deep and lasting peace. The Holy Spirit will comfort and guide us. The peace of God can and will live in our hearts if we are open to Him and accept Jesus as our LORD and Savior. The Holy Spirit is the Spirit of truth, the Spirit of God and our wonderful Counselor. Because of the Holy Spirit living in us, we can have the *"mind of Christ."*

"We don't have to know the future to have faith in God; we have to have faith in God to be secure about the future." (NIV Bible)

"Guidance from the Scriptures may not be as flashy as an infomercial, but it's tried and true. Christ reminds us to observe His example, obey His commands, walk in the way He leads us, and learn how to discover the abundant life He offers." (Pamela Kennedy)

January 18
Wisdom in Gratitude

Philippians 4:4-7
Rejoice in the LORD always. I will say it again: Rejoice! Let your gentleness be evident to all. The LORD is near. Do not be anxious about anything, but in everything, by prayer and petition, with thanksgiving, present your requests to God. And the peace of God, which transcends all understanding, will guard your hearts and your minds in Christ Jesus.

The definition of *gratitude* is "a feeling of thankful appreciation for favors or benefits received; thankfulness." Thanking those around us for the deeds they do and thanking our LORD for His many blessings brings wisdom to us. As we take time for gratitude, we find that a certain peace and joy fills our hearts. When we show our gratitude to another, we give them joy and our joy in turn is multiplied. When we are living in gratitude, we get to experience God's Presence. Ultimate joy comes from Christ living in us. True peace and joy comes from knowing God is in control. We can rejoice in the LORD today and experience His Presence living in us. We should thank Him for this new day and the peace and joy that only He can give. That is wisdom in gratitude.

"Eternity is where true love exists." (Author unknown)

"If you can't be thankful for what you receive, be thankful for what you escape." (Wanda Brunstetter)

January 19
Gratitude in the Trenches

Psalm 75:1
We give thanks to You, O God, we give thanks, for Your Name is near; men tell of Your wonderful deeds.

Father, we are grateful that Jesus came so that we might have abundant life. Father, we are thankful for the promises and instruction that we read and study in the Bible. Today, we choose to live a thankful life simply because You instruct us to in Your Word. We will act in obedience, and we believe that Your Word teaches us the best way to live. LORD, when times are tough and we have no joy, help us to remember that You have promised we can enjoy our lives. When we are in the trenches, thank You for the joy, peace, and security we find in You. Amen

"Blessings come in disguise. And challenges can be a blessing." (Author unknown)

"If you want to feel rich, just count all the things you have that money cannot buy." (Author unknown)

January 20
Joy in Gratitude

Psalm 16:9
Therefore my heart is glad and my tongue rejoices; my body also will rest secure ...

Psalm 16:11
You have made known to me the path of life; You will fill me with joy in Your presence, with eternal pleasures at Your right hand.

There is joy in gratitude. Joy is everlasting and we can feel joy in spite of our deepest troubles. Happiness is fleeting and depends on feelings and outward circumstances. Joy is lasting because it is based on God's presence within us. As we seek God each day and thank Him, we see Him in the little things, and no matter what we are experiencing, there is hope, joy and contentment. As we seek God's will and thank Him for what He has already provided, we communicate with Him and this allows Him to counsel us and give us His wisdom. When we are constantly thinking about the LORD and His plan for the way He wants us to live, we will gain insights that will help us make right decisions. As we understand the future He has for us, we will experience joy. We must not base our lives on circumstances but on God. There is joy in gratitude and we should live in gratitude every day.

"Joy is a product of attitude and thought. It comes from you, not to you." (Author unknown)

"A truly happy person is one who can enjoy the scenery on a detour and be thankful for a new adventure." (Author unknown)

January 21
Gratitude in His Presence

Psalm 150:6
Let everything that has breath praise the LORD. Praise the LORD.

Gratitude is a royal road to draw near to God. A thankful heart has plenty of room for God. When we thank God, we affirm that He is God from whom all blessings flow. Focusing our thoughts on Him moves us to praise Him. The more we know Him, the more we can appreciate what He does for us every day. When we realize how we benefit from knowing God, we can fully express our thanks to Him and when we do, we develop spontaneity in our life and prayers. Let's fill up the moments of our lives with praise and thanksgiving to the One who provides for all of us and let's live in the intimacy of His Presence.

"Praise God from whom all blessings flow.
Praise Him all creatures here below.
Praise Him above ye Heavenly Host:
Praise Him, Father, Son and Holy Ghost." (Hymn, Thomas Ken)

"Now isn't then. Now is the beginning." (Chris Evert)

"Have you had a kindness shown? Pass it on. . . .Let it travel down the years, let it wipe another's tears, till in heaven the deed appears. Pass it on." (Henry Burton)

January 22
Approach God with Gratitude

Deuteronomy 33:27
The eternal God is your refuge, and underneath are the everlasting arms.

1 Chronicles 16:8
Give thanks to the LORD, call on His name; make known among the nations what He has done.

Every day we have an opportunity to approach God with gratitude. Praise and thanksgiving should be a regular part of our daily routine and not just reserved for celebrations. When we praise and thank God continually, we find that we won't take His blessings for granted. When we approach Him with a thankful heart, especially after a particularly tough time, we thank Him for not forsaking us. Our true refuge is the eternal God who always holds out His everlasting arms to catch us. If we are truly thankful, our lives will show it.

There are four elements of true thanksgiving:
—remembering what God has done;
—telling others about it;
—showing God's glory to others; and
—offering gifts of self, time and resources.

"For each new morning with its light, for rest and shelter of the night, for health and food, for love and friends, for everything Thy goodness sends. Father in heaven, we thank thee." (Ralph Waldo Emerson)

"We're concerned with how things turn out; God is more concerned with how we turn out." (Philip Yancey)

January 23
A Grateful Heart

Psalm 92:1-2
It is good to give praise to the LORD and make music to Your name, O Most High, To proclaim Your love in the morning and Your faithfulness every night.

Let's be thankful and faithful every day. When we begin our days in gratitude, we will notice that our attitude toward life and others will change. We will become more positive, gracious, loving and humble. Heavenly Father, please help us face each day with grace and appreciation for the blessings of Your love, and, as we lay our heads down on our pillows at night, help us remember to thank You for a day complete in You.

"A bad attitude is like a flat tire. You can't go anywhere until you change it. Happiness comes when we stop complaining about the troubles we have, and say thanks to God for the troubles we don't have." (Author unknown)

"People tend to think of happiness as a stroke of luck, something that will descend like fine weather if you're fortunate. But happiness is the result of personal effort. You fight for it, strive for it, insist upon it, and sometimes even travel around the world looking for it. You have to participate relentlessly." (Elizabeth George)

January 24
Wisdom and Discernment

Proverbs 2:1-12
My son, if you accept my words and store up my commands within you, turning your ear to wisdom and applying your heart to understanding, and if you call out for insight and cry aloud for understanding, and if you look for it as for silver and search for it as for hidden treasure, then you will understand the fear of the LORD and find the knowledge of God. For the LORD gives wisdom, and from His mouth come knowledge and understanding. He holds victory in store for the upright, He is a shield to those whose walk is blameless, for He guards the course of the just and protects the way of His faithful ones. Then you will understand what is right and just and fair—every good path. For wisdom will enter your heart, and knowledge will be pleasant to your soul. Discretion will protect you, and understanding will guard you. Wisdom will save you from the ways of wicked men . . .

Isaiah 55:8-9
"For My thoughts are not your thoughts, nor are your ways My ways," says the LORD. "For as the heavens are higher than the earth, so are My ways higher than your ways, and My thoughts than your thoughts."

True wisdom is God's and it is a gift to us from Him. It is only given to those who earnestly seek it. God's knowledge and wisdom are far greater than man's. We will find His wisdom when we read the Bible, obey Him, and pray asking Him to show us His wisdom. We gain wisdom through constant searching, growing, trusting and honoring Him. The gift of wisdom helps us to make decisions pleasing to God. As we read God's Word, pray continually, admire His creation, and walk with Him daily, we must keep searching for His wisdom and discernment and live it out in our lives. Let's have a good day walking with Jesus and be thankful for our many blessings.

"The doors of wisdom are never shut." (Benjamin Franklin)

"The true wisdom is to be always seasonable, and to change with a good grace in changing circumstances." (Robert Louis Stevenson)

January 25
Thank You....

Colossians 3:15
Let the peace of Christ rule in your hearts, since as members of one body you were called to peace. And be thankful.

Colossians 3:17
And whatever you do, whether in word or deed, do it all in the name of the LORD Jesus, giving thanks to God the Father through Him.

As Christians, we need to acknowledge that God is good and bring honor to Him in every aspect and activity of daily living. He gives us all things and He creates all things. We should always be thankful for the things God gives us because we are His creations. We should never forget that and remember that we represent Him. Life is a prize and we should be grateful for every second and enjoy it. Gratitude is like a muscle; it can be exercised and conditioned and it will perform better. We can become people with attitudes of gratitude as we practice, practice, practice it each day. As we practice and grow in our gratitude walk, we will realize that spiritual blessings come wrapped in trials. The one thing of which we can be certain is that our LORD is with us every day and in everything. God is with us in the everyday circumstances of life and we should thank Him!

"Reflect upon your present blessings—of which every man has many—not on your past misfortunes, of which all men have some." (Charles Dickens)

"Dear old world', she murmured, 'you are very lovely, and I am glad to be alive in you." (L.M. Montgomery, Anne of Green Gables)

January 26
Today is a Very Good Day

Psalm 118:24
This is the day the LORD has made, let us rejoice and be glad in it.

We woke up today. It's a good day. Thank You, LORD. Today is a gift and the appropriate response is "Thank You." We need to respond as if today is our first and last day. We can look around and see the colors of God's creation in the sky and in our surroundings. Today is a blessed day. Let our blessings overflow in our hearts, eyes, smiles and our very presence. Thank You, LORD, for all that You do in our lives. Today is a gift and we can thank our LORD for it.

"O Infinite Father, I'm grateful to Thee
    For the moon and the stars and deep rolling sea;
    For beauties of nature, where e'er they may be...
    For the handclasp of friends, so firm and so true;
    For sunrise and sunset and glistening dew;
    The fleecy white clouds and the Heavens, so blue;
    For these wonderful gifts, dear Lord, I thank you!"
(Gertrude T. Buckingham, "My Song of Thanksgiving")

"As each day comes to us refreshed and anew, so does my gratitude renew itself daily. The breaking of the sun over the horizon is my grateful heart dawning upon a blessed world."(Terri Guillemets)

January 27
Friendship

Psalm 119:63
I am a companion of all who fear You, and of those who keep Your precepts.

John 15:4,5,7
Abide in Me, and I in you. As the branch cannot bear fruit of itself, unless it abides in the vine, neither can you, unless you abide in Me. I am the vine, you are the branches. He who abides in Me, and I in him, bears much fruit; for without Me you can do nothing. If you abide in Me, and My words abide in you, you will ask what you desire, and it shall be done for you.

One of my favorite hymns is *What a friend we have in Jesus*. As we walk with Jesus and go about our daily lives, remember to obey His commands and look to Him in every situation. We should take some quiet moments to listen for His whispers and know that we are never ever alone, for the King is always with us. He is our friend. He loves us so much that He was willing to leave Heaven to come here as a man and suffer unthinkable things for us. Through it all, He never lost sight of His purpose and kept His eyes on His Father and obeyed Him. Now He sits at the right hand of His Father and still intercedes for us. Jesus is our friend and is a good One to keep us company as He will certainly heal and improve us.

"Keep company with those who make you better." (English Proverb)

"When we're stuck and feeling afraid, God is there. Reach out in prayer, take His hand, and feel His power pulling you to safety." (Pamela Kennedy)

January 28
Whatever....

Psalm 96:1
Sing to the Lord a new song...

Titus 3:4-7
But when the kindness and love of God our Savior appeared, He saved us, not because of righteous things we had done, but because of His mercy. He saved us through the washing of rebirth and renewal by the Holy Spirit, whom He poured out on us generously through Jesus Christ our Savior, so that, having been justified by His grace, we might become heirs having the hope of eternal life.

We open our hearts, minds and lives to more of You, God, to whatever You have for us. We will focus on our strengths and not on our fears. *Whatever* sounds a bit sarcastic or can be a phrase to brush off situations that are unimportant or out of our control. Sometimes it is comforting to just say *whatever* and walk away because we are accepting the situation and realizing that it is out of our control. *Whatever* means that we are open to the plans God has for us. God knows what is best. He knows us, our hearts, and the future. Accepting His path is an important part of our relationship with Him. Thanking and praising Him daily is our response back to Him for His continued blessings. Sharing with others what He has done in our lives is another way we give Him the glory. LORD, we thank You for all the blessings in our lives and the vision with which to recognize them. Every day, we thank You for coming into our world and into our hearts. Thank You for *whatever* comes our way so that we will eventually see You and Your Hand at work. Amen

"Discipleship is where God invites us to join the family business." (Peter Meier)

"One of my favorite quotes: "Patriotism is not short, frenzied outbursts of emotion, but the tranquil and steady dedication of a lifetime." (Adlai Stevenson)

January 29
God's Help

Psalm 119:105
Your Word is a lamp to my feet and a light for my path.

Psalm 121:1-2
I lift up my eyes to the hills—where does my help come from? My help comes from the LORD, the Maker of heaven and earth.

We have so very much to be thankful for and as we look around us, we can thank our LORD for His Hand in everything we do, see and say. He guides us, leads us on His paths, takes us by the hand and gives us assurance and hope.

"Thank You for the dark of night
Thank You for the moon so bright.
Thank You for the stars in sight
Thank You for dawn's early light.
Thank You for the gift of day and night
Thank You for holding us so tight.
Thank You for teaching us to do what's right
Thank You for Your love and delight." (Author unknown)

"My grandfather once told me that there were two kinds of people: those who do the work and those who take the credit. He told me to try to be in the first group; there was much less competition." (Indira Gandhi)

"Start by doing what's necessary, then what's possible, and suddenly you are doing the impossible." (St. Francis of Assisi)

January 30
Changes

Hebrews 13:8 ... Jesus Christ is the same yesterday and today and forever. He is the ultimate leader. In a changing world we can trust our unchanging LORD.

Colossians 3:1-2 Since you have been raised with Christ, set your hearts on things above, where Christ is seated at the right hand of God. Set your mind on things above, not on earthly things.

What is the status of the New Year's resolutions or goals we made on January 1? Have we made any changes in our lives or have we gone on as before? We have good intentions. We know what we want to happen, but life has a way of interrupting us. We get caught up in lives and our resolutions and goals get put aside. There is one thing that never changes and that is Jesus Christ. Jesus is the source of wisdom, knowledge and truth. Everything we need is in Him. We must live in union with Him as He is visible and has reconciled us with an invisible God. Let's go back to our resolutions and goal lists for the New Year. Goals are good to have and help us to achieve new heights but let's not get discouraged if we haven't started them or even looked at them since January 1. We still have time to begin. Let's remain rooted in Christ, drawing strength from Him because He is the source of knowledge, truth and power for the Christian life. Our resolutions and goal lists will be here tomorrow and the day after and the day after that. We need to change our thinking and look to Jesus for help to make the changes needed to reach our goals.

"LORD, grant me the Serenity to accept the things I cannot change, the Courage to change the things I can and the Wisdom to know the difference. Amen." (AAA prayer)

"The highest point of achievement yesterday is the starting point of today." (Author unknown)

January 31
Power Outages

Exodus 15:6-7 Your right hand, O LORD, was majestic in power. Your right hand, O LORD, shattered the enemy. In the greatness of Your majesty You threw down those who opposed You.

Hebrews: 4:12 The word of God is living and powerful, and sharper than any two-edged sword, and of joints and marrow, and is a discerner of the thoughts and intents of the heart.

We've all experienced electrical power outages. We are used to a daily routine and then when we wake up to no power, no heat, no coffee, no TV, no phone….our day is quite disrupted before we even put our feet on the floor. Not so with the power of God as His power never goes out. We find His power in His Word. We see His power in all of creation. He created the world in a majestic display of power and purpose. We see His power in the birth, life, death and resurrection of Jesus. We see His power in answered prayer and in the Holy Spirit that He sent to dwell in us so that we are never, ever alone. God is always with us. He is powerful and He is the Almighty—*the Alpha and Omega.* He is an awesome God and He is all knowing. He is our Heavenly Father who loves us so very much. So when darkness of any kind assails us, we must remember there is One whose power never goes out and He is there for all of us to plug into. Maybe in the quiet moments of "no electrical power," we can close our eyes and spend some quiet time with Him and listen for His whispers. We can be encouraged and have HOPE because our God has a plan. When the power comes back on, we should read His Word and be comforted. We can talk to Him and be thankful for all He has done for us. With our LORD, we can have a powerful day.

"Stay within whispering distance. If you stray, you won't hear His voice." (Author unkown)

"Do not pray for tasks equal to your powers; pray for powers equal to your tasks." (Phillips Brooks)

February 1
Our Choice

Psalm 103:21
Praise the LORD, all His heavenly hosts, you His servants who do His will.

Philippians 2:14
"Do all things without grumbling and faultfinding and complaining..."

We all have a choice; either we can complain and grumble or we can maintain an attitude of gratitude. When we begin our day being grateful for our blessings, we will gradually develop and nurture a thankful attitude. Will it be easy—probably not. Will it be worthwhile—absolutely. Grumbling and complaining opens the door for Satan to cause us trouble, but thankfulness opens the door for God to bless us. An attitude of gratitude—it's our choice.

"There is no such thing as gratitude unexpressed. If it is unexpressed, it is plain, old-fashioned ingratitude." (Robert Brault)

"Gratitude is the memory of the heart." (Jean Baptiste Massieu)

February 2
Walk Ourselves Strong

Isaiah 41:10
So do not fear, for I am with you; do not be dismayed, for I am your God. I will strengthen you and help you; I will uphold you with my righteous right hand.

Walking is one of the best ways to get to a healthier us. Just 30 minutes a day can lead to losing weight and developing more flexibility. There are articles about people who have walked all their lives and live to be in their 90s and 100s. I love to walk and when I walk alone, I'm not really alone because I talk to God and pray. There was a time when I didn't want to walk alone and I prayed about it. God nudged me to go out and just begin. I pictured Jesus walking beside me and reaching out His right hand to me, encouraging me to keep going. I researched the Bible for many verses on the *right hand of God* and would memorize them as I walked. I am so thankful to my loving God who shows Himself to me on these journeys. Jesus walked everywhere and even today He is walking with us everywhere we go. We are never alone. Let's "walk ourselves strong" with our LORD and Savior Jesus Christ and we will be healthier, physically and spiritually. It will be good for our bodies and souls.

"Every day as we walk through life we are reaching toward God and recognizing His touch. It is called—growing up." (Author unknown)

"Lord, give me an open heart to find You everywhere, to glimpse the heaven enfolded in a bud, and to experience eternity in the smallest act of love." (Mother Teresa)

February 3
The Great Teacher

Psalm 89:14
Blessed are those who have learned to acclaim You, who walk in the light of Your presence, O LORD.

Proverbs 4:12
As I go forward step-by-step, the way will be opened up to me.

Jesus is the Great Teacher. Everywhere He went He taught about God and His purpose. Everywhere He goes with us today, He is teaching us, too. When God brings us to something He promises to walk us through it. There are lessons for us in every situation. We need to look for them. Many times the lesson is to be quiet and listen for His whispers or it may be that it is to surrender to Him whatever challenges we face. I have learned that whenever I release a situation to Him, I feel such peace and it turns out just as He has planned. It may not be as I want but I've learned that He has the better plan. He knows what is best and by our surrendering and letting go, we believe and trust Him to handle everything—*all the details.* For many of us, this is hard because we want to be in control. When we became adults, we gained the freedom to make our own decisions, and to control of our own destinies. We either didn't know or we forgot that this is not the case because God is the One in control. In Scripture, He tells us that. Let's take a walk with Jesus today, either a physical walk if it's not too cold or maybe an indoor walk through the Scriptures. He's waiting to teach us and we must be ready to listen. We'll be glad that we did because He is the Great Teacher. God loves us and cares for us and if we are unsure, we should take look at the cross because His love is there for all to see.

"Often when the answer is no, there's a better yes waiting down the road." (Author unknown)

"Do you know what hurts so very much? It's love. Love is the strongest force in the world, and when it is blocked that means pain. There are two things we can do when this happens. We can kill that love so that it stops hurting. But then of course part of us dies, too. Or we can ask God to open up another route for that love to travel." (Corrie ten Boom)

February 4
God's Life Insurance

Psalm 31:15
My times are in Your Hand. Into Your hands I commit my spirit; redeem me, O LORD, the God of truth.

We can trust God beyond any measure. In Luke 23:46 Jesus said the same words above as He was dying on the cross. He had complete trust in His Father. In Acts 7:59 Stephen was being stoned to death and he also said these same words. Stephen knew that he would be passing over into the presence of the LORD. God took care of him on earth and now He would take care of him in heaven. We have the same life insurance policy that is good not only for this life, but also for the life to come! We need not make any premium payments to have this policy because Jesus paid it all, the full price, for all of us who believe that He died for our sins on Calvary's cross! As a result, we truly are in good hands. The ONE who has those hands is our loving God. We are safe and secure in His Hands! He will never disappoint us. We can be certain because His Hands have nail marks in them! We can commit ourselves completely to God. He loves us and has the best life insurance. With His policy, we are alive in Him and will live with Him in eternity.

"The certainty of our faith lies in the dependability of God." (Thrivent Financial)

"Our God is an awesome God." (Author unknown)

February 5
Our Mission

Micah 6:8
He has showed you, O man, what is good. And what does the LORD require of you? To act justly and to love mercy and to walk humbly with your God.

Acts 20: 18-21 Paul talking to the Elders of the Ephesus church:
When they arrived he said to them: "You know how I lived the whole time I was with you, from the first day I came into the province of Asia. I served the LORD with great humility and with tears, although I was severely tested by the plots of the Jews. You know that I have not hesitated to preach anything that would be helpful to you but have taught you publicly and from house to house. I have declared both to Jews and Greeks that they must turn to God in repentance and have faith in our LORD Jesus."

In Micah, God has made His wishes clear: He wants us to be just, merciful and to walk humbly with Him. In the verses from Acts, Paul is telling us to share the message of salvation with others. He instructs us to tell them to turn away from sin and turn to Christ by faith. We should always be ready to tell others what good things God has done for us. His blessings far outweigh life's difficulties. Life is worth nothing unless we use it for God's good and glory. Our most important mission is to tell others about Christ. We must walk humbly with our God and share all that He has done in our lives with others in order to bring them to Him.

"Let a man set his heart only on doing the will of God and he is instantly set free! No one can hinder him. It is only when we introduce our own will into our relations to God that we get into trouble. When we weave into the pattern of our lives threads of our own desires we instantly become subject to hindrances from the outside." (A. W. Tozer)

"True surrender is not simply surrender of our external life but surrender of our will—and once that is done, surrender is complete. And after surrender, your entire life should be characterized by an eagerness to maintain unbroken fellowship and oneness with God." (Oswald Chambers)

February 6
A Powerful Shield

Ephesians 6:16
In addition to all this, take up the shield of faith, with which you can extinguish all the flaming arrows of the evil one.

We can be thankful that our God has given us a powerful shield—*the shield of faith* which is His Word and His defense system. His shield provides protection and we can say out loud, *"God, I trust You in every situation."* Just as Jesus fought Satan those forty days in the wilderness by saying, *"It is written,"* we can do the same by quoting Scripture as we fight Satan at every turn. We can lift up God's Word as a powerful shield and can be confident that it is effective against everything the enemy tries to do in our lives. Our faith is based on God's Word and His promises. He promises to "never leave us nor forsake us." (Hebrews 13:5). We can take up God's shield of faith and trust Him in everything. It won't do us any good for our shield to lie on the ground next to us. Let's raise our shields of faith by having Scripture ready to shout at Satan when he tries to detour us on our journey with our LORD.

"Life loves to be taken by the lapel and told: I'm with you kid, let's go."
(Maya Angelou)

"The more one does and sees and feels, the more one is able to do."
(Amelia Earhart)

February 7
God's Present

Psalm 118:29
O give thanks unto the LORD; for He is good: His mercy endureth for ever.

There is nothing we can do about yesterday and all the days before that. They are over and there is no redo. Today is a gift from God and that is why it is called the "present." We only have today and what we do today will either be the victory for our tomorrow or maybe the regret. We don't know what tomorrow will hold or if we'll even have a tomorrow because Jesus may call us home today. So there is no sense in worrying about tomorrow as we must live for today and let tomorrow take care of itself. Today is all we have and our goal should be to share Jesus with someone. Share Him with all those we meet because maybe a smile, hug, laugh, understanding heart, verse in scripture that we've memorized, note written with that person in mind or a prayer for someone will make a difference. We should tell someone about the love of God and what Jesus has done for us on the cross, and do it all in the name of Jesus. By doing so, our day will be a success no matter what happens. We can rejoice and have a glorious day. No matter how our day unfolds, we must remember that Jesus is with us and give God thanks for the gift of today; it's a "present."

"Trust the past to God's mercy, the present to God's love and the future to God's providence." (St. Augustine)

"Yesterday is the past and gone. Today is the present and now. Tomorrow is the future and not here yet." (Author unknown)

February 8
A Heart of Thankfulness

Philippians 2:14
Do everything without complaining or arguing...

Have you ever noticed that once we begin to complain about something that a breeding ground develops for more and more of it, and the problem often gets bigger and bigger, creating other problems? The way around this is to have a heart of thankfulness each day. We can avoid the breeding ground of greater problems by having a continual lifestyle of thanksgiving. We can thwart Satan's plans by counteracting the complaining and arguing with a heart full of thanksgiving. We can be thankful for everything that God is doing in and through our lives. We can be thankful for the people in our lives and look for the goodness in them. Each day we should find a reason to be thankful and when we do, our LORD's light will shine in and through us for all to see Him. We can choose to be thankful for everything the LORD has done for us. Let's choose to have a heart of thankfulness and be ready for life-changing experiences.

"I pray that you all put your shoes way under the bed at night so that you gotta get on your knees in the morning to find them. And while you're down there thank God for grace and mercy and understanding." (Denzel Washington)

"Faith does not come from striving; it comes from surrender." (Author unknown)

February 9
Daily Thankfulness

Lamentations 3:22-23
Because of the LORD's great love we are not consumed, for His compassions never fail. They are new every morning; great is Your faithfulness.

We can be grateful every day because of our Lord's great love for us. His mercies are new every morning and He promises us forgiveness. Our God is faithful and promises restoration and blessings. Trusting in God's faithfulness day-by-day makes us confident in His great promises for the future. Our daily thankfulness humbles us and honors Him.

"Gratitude is heaven itself. To speak gratitude is courteous and pleasant, to enact gratitude is generous and noble, but to live gratitude is to touch heaven." (Author unknown)

"What can we make of the inexpressible joy of children? It is a kind of gratitude." (Annie Dillard)

February 10
His Will

Mark 14:36
"Abba, Father," He said, "everything is possible for You. Take this cup from Me. Yet not what I will, but what You will."

Anything worthwhile or worth having will cost something. Our commitment to God will cost us something, but in the end we will gain eternal life with Him and it will be worthwhile. The Bible promises that those who search for Him with all of their hearts will find Him. Are our hearts soft enough to see Jesus in a sunset? Will we feel His love in the kiss of the wind on our faces? Are the doors of our hearts open to Him? Do we see Him in the middle of a crisis in the most minuscule way? Has He aligned a cross for us out of rubber bands on the floor by our desk or out of marshmallows in our hot chocolate? The point—where are our hearts focused? *LORD Jesus, we want to see You wherever You choose to reveal Yourself. Give us open hearts to recognize You wherever You are in our day.* Sometimes it is not easy for us to trust but when we wait for Your will it is always for our good and Your glory. LORD Jesus, show us Your will for our days. Amen.

"The person who walks with God always gets to his destination!" (Author unknown)

"Stop focusing on how stressed you are and remember how blessed you are." (Author unknown)

In *Mere Christianity*, C. S. Lewis wrote, *"That is why the little decisions you and I make every day are of such infinite importance."*

February 11
Our Words Matter

Colossians 3:15-17
Let the peace of Christ rule in your hearts, since as members of one body you were called to peace. And be thankful. Let the word of Christ dwell in you richly as you teach and admonish one another with all wisdom, and as you sing psalms, hymns and spiritual songs with gratitude in your hearts to God. And whatever you do, whether in word or deed, do it all in the name of the Lord Jesus, giving thanks to God the Father through Him.

Our words matter—they encourage, inspire, and tell stories. We should always remember, whether few or many, our words matter! We must be thoughtful, kind and live in Christ's peace. Our words and actions should represent Christ at all times, bringing honor to Him in every aspect and activity of daily living. We should pray asking God what do with our lives and how can our words matter to help others. *Our words do matter because love matters.*

"Always be kinder than necessary." (Author unknown)

"You must do the thing you think you cannot do." (Eleanor Roosevelt)

February 12
Extraordinary Attitude

John 10:10
Jesus said, "I have come that they may have life, and have it to the full."

An extraordinary attitude can turn an ordinary day into an amazing adventure. We can take charge of our attitudes and create our own joy. We can control what we do and not depend on others to make us happy or joyful. Jesus is our Source of Joy. He gives life. He has given us this new day, and it is our choice whether or not we are going to enjoy it. The life He gives is abundantly rich and full. Life in Christ is lived on a higher plane because of His overflowing forgiveness, love and guidance. Let's have an extraordinary attitude as we begin today's amazing adventure. Let's find joy in every day as we spend it with our LORD, Jesus Christ. LORD, thank You that You have given us this new day to enjoy and that You are our Source of Life and Joy. With You, today is our greatest adventure. Amen.

"I am not afraid of storms for I am learning how to sail my ship." (Louisa May Alcott)

"I destroy my enemies when I make them my friends." (Abraham Lincoln)

February 13
Promises, Promises

Psalm 62:5
Find rest, O my soul, in God alone; my hope comes from Him.

In the Bible, God's Word, there are many, many promises from Him. These promises are ours and we can take them to heart and be assured that our LORD is with us. God is our dwelling place, our fortress. When we dwell in Him, we are perfectly safe and secure in Him. God is always present in the "temple of our heart...His home." We can meet Him there and once we do, we will find that it is a place of deep satisfaction, where every longing will be met. We have hope in Him and we can sing for joy knowing that He is dwelling in us. God gave us His Holy Spirit to be with us always so that we will never be away from Him. Promises, promises...they are ours because of the One who loves us forever and provides for us. He dwells in us and in our souls. We can rest and find hope in Him. Promises, promises—they are ours from our loving God.

"Always be in a state of expectancy, and see that you leave room for God to come in as He likes." (Oswald Chambers)

"Amazing things will happen. Rise above the little things and choose your own path." (Author unknown)

February 14
Be God's Valentine

John 3:16 True Love
"For God so loVed the world,
    That He gAve
        His onLy
            BegottEn
                SoN
                    That whosoever
    Believeth In Him
      Should Not perish,
    But have Everlasting life."

Romans 5:5
God has poured out His love into our hearts.

The true Source of love is God. We are His children. He kindles a flame in each of our hearts and we, in turn, who are warmed by His love, love others. He loves others through us. His love is perfect and immeasurable. His love quiets fears and gives us confidence. God's love reaches out and draws others in. God sets the pattern of true love, the basis for all love relationships. When we love someone dearly, we are willing to give freely to the point of self-sacrifice. We should remember to reach out and help someone by sharing love and time. When we do this we are sharing God's love. God, we remember that You are the lover of our souls on Valentine's Day and every day. With You, Valentine's Day is every day. You send us gifts by way of Your beautiful creations. Yes, even the cold and snow are from You and, despite the inconvenience, the snow is beautiful. Let's be God's Valentine today and every day. Happy Valentine's Day!

"Get on your knees and thank God you're still on your feet." (Author unknown)

"Open your hearts to the love God instills . . . God loves you tenderly. What He gives you is not to be kept under lock and key, but to be shared." (Mother Teresa)

February 15
Be of Good Cheer

Matthew 14:24-27
But the ship was now in the midst of the sea, tossed with waves: for the wind was contrary. And in the fourth watch of the night Jesus went unto them, walking on the sea. And when the disciples saw Him walking on the sea, they were troubled, saying, it is a spirit; and they cried out in fear. But straightway Jesus spake unto them, saying, Be of good cheer; it is I; be not afraid.

Daily we face many situations that are a normal part of life but then there are those that are tough and difficult. Because we love our family and friends, we tend to worry about them when they are away from us or are ill. We listen to the news and worry about what is going to happen to life as we know it. We may be wondering about our jobs, the economy, our safety and that of our family and what the future looks like for us. Our health or the health of a loved one may be compromised in some fashion. Whatever our concern or trouble—*Jesus knows.* He's right there with us. He's our lifeguard. We may not walk on water but He does. If we let Him, He will walk us through or carry us through every situation. We must keep our eyes on Jesus. If we continually focus on the circumstances or the waves around us, we will sink, but when we keep our eyes on Jesus and maintain our faith, He will get us through everything. We may have a few scars but so does the One who went to the Cross for us—*our Savior, our LORD, our Jesus.* Let's keep our eyes on the power of Jesus and not on our circumstances or inadequacies. He is the only One who can really help us. We can trust Him, go to Him and take His Hand; the water is fine. We have a lifeguard and He walks on water. We should go into the deep with Him and be of good cheer.

"Write it on your heart that every day is the best day of the year." (Ralph Waldo Emerson)

"Faith based on experience is not faith; faith based on God's revealed truth is the only faith there is." (Oswald Chambers)

February 16
God's Clay

Isaiah 64:8
O LORD, You are our Father. We are the clay, You are the potter; we are all the work of Your Hand.

2 Corinthians 4:6-7
For God, who said, "Let light shine out of darkness," made His light shine in our hearts to give us the light of the knowledge of the glory of God in the face of Christ. But we have this treasure in jars of clay to show that this all-surpassing power is from God and not from us.

We are God's clay. Every day we are on the wheel of life experiencing its ups and downs. We are clay in the hands of the Potter being molded, spun, wetted and squeezed, transformed. The object is to let Christ shine in and through us for all to see Him. It is not about us but about Him. Our bodies are the jars of clay and God's power dwells in us. We are weak and as He molds and shapes us, He uses us to spread His good news. He wants us to tell others what He has done in our lives. He is the Potter and we are His clay and we need to let Him mold, shape and transform us into who He wants us to be—*His image.*

"Keep still, and He will mold you to the right shape." (Martin Luther)

"Troubles are often the tools by which God fashions us for better things." (Henry Ward Beecher)

February 17
Jesus is Our Strength

Isaiah 40:29, 31
He giveth power to the faint; and to them that have no might He increaseth strength. But they that wait upon the LORD shall renew their strength; they shall mount up with wings as eagles; they shall run, and not be weary; and they shall walk and not faint.

During World War II these words were found carved on a wall in a concentration camp:
I believe in the sun, even though it doesn't shine,
I believe in love, even when it isn't shown,
I believe in God, even when He doesn't speak.

Just imagine the faith and strength that it took to believe in the LORD when this prisoner was in such dire times and horrible conditions. This person looked towards something unseen and still trusted. We may never be in such dire conditions, but we can hold onto God's promises no matter what we are experiencing. He is always with us. We must be strong in the LORD, lean on Him and have patience. He knows where we are and what we are going through. We can trust Him even when we cannot see Him. His love is the greatest love we'll ever know. We must believe in Him even when we cannot hear Him. He's with us. He dwells within us...He is our LORD and Savior, Jesus Christ.

"Be thankful for what we have; you'll end up having more." (Oprah Winfrey)

"The greater part of life is sunshine." (Thomas Jefferson)

February 18
Eternal Life

1 John 5:11-12
And this is the testimony: God has given us eternal life, and this life is in His Son. He who has the Son has life; he who does not have the Son of God does not have life.

Because of Jesus being raised from the dead, we've been given a brand-new life. Eternal life—what a gift and what a God we have! Because of Jesus and what He did on the Cross and the days following, we can live differently and faithfully. We know we have a place with Him in eternity. His resurrection power brings new life and His redemption power brings new hope. Eternal life is ours and it is guaranteed by our God. Eternal life is God's promise to us and it is given to us who believe through His Son. Thank You, God, for loving us so much that we have Jesus and will live forever with You. We know that we are unworthy but You still love us and show us mercy. LORD, You are our final and ultimate goal. Our joy is in You and You are all we need. Amen

"I have held many things in my hands and have lost them all; but whatever I have placed in God's hands, that I still possess." (Martin Luther)

"You are never too old to set another goal or to dream a new dream." (C.S. Lewis)

February 19
A Clean Heart

Psalm 51:10
"Create in me a pure heart, O God, and renew a steadfast spirit within me."

Only God can create a clean and pure heart in us. Because of Adam we are natural born sinners. It is hard to imagine a baby born as a sinner, but that is what the Bible tells us. Because of Jesus' death and resurrection, we have the means by which He washes us in His forgiving, cleansing love and we are forgiven. Through our baptism we become a member of God's family and forgiveness and mercy are ours. Each day we make choices and have desires that cause us to sin, but we have a God, who when we repent, will mercifully forgive us. We can ask God to cleanse us from within, opening our hearts and spirits for new thoughts and desires. Right conduct can come only from a clean heart and spirit. We should ask God to create a pure heart and right spirit within us and know that He will do so again and again.

"If you come to a fork in the road, take it!" (Yogi Berra)

"Nothing is worth more than this day." (Johann Wolfgang von Goethe)

February 20
Jesus is the Way, the Truth and the Life

John 14:6
Jesus saith unto him, "I am the way, the truth, and the life: no man cometh unto the Father, but by me."

Jesus is both God and man. Jesus is the path to God and eternal life. He has already prepared the way. He promises all of us who believe in Him that we will live with Him in eternity. The key is that we must believe in Him who is unseen to us. He didn't leave us alone because He left us the Holy Spirit who lives in us. The Holy Spirit guides and teaches us and all we have to do is listen and follow. Jesus is the "three in one." He is God, He is the Son and He is the Holy Spirit—*the Trinity*. He is the "Way," the "Truth" and the "Life." The Way is the path to the Father. The Truth is that Jesus is the reality to God's promises, and the Life is Jesus joining His Divine life to ours, both now and eternally.

"Character is not in the mind; it is in the will." (Fulton J. Sheen)

"Love is a language in which no words say everything. In order to hear it you must listen through your heart." (Susan E. Schwartz)

February 21
Thankful Trust

Nahum 1:7
The Lord is good, a refuge in times of trouble. He cares for those who trust in Him...

Zephaniah 3:17
The Lord your God is with you, He is mighty to save. He will take great delight in you, He will quiet you with His love, He will rejoice over you with singing.

Thankful trust is a new mindset. Imagine choosing to confess and meditate on trusting God completely and allowing Him to be with us every day while being thankful, not worrying and trusting Him for everything. How enjoyable our lives will be when we decide to pray about everything and worry about nothing as we fellowship with God. It will take a while, but, in due time, we will see the benefit of our relentless decisions to live a life of thankful trust. His mercy is a refuge and He will supply all of our needs according to His will. We will habitually look for the good and magnify it as we draw close to our Source, thanking God for each victory along the way. Father, we trust You completely; there is no need for us to worry—You can handle everything we are facing. Thank You that You are trustworthy and dependable and You are always on time. We will trust You. Now that is *Thankful Trust.*

"In the Kingdom of hope, there is no winter." (Author unknown)

"Faith is the centerpiece of a connected life. It allows us to live by the grace of invisible strands." (Terry Tempest Williams)

February 22
Thankful Peace

Proverbs 14:30
A heart at peace gives life to the body ...

John 14:27
Peace I leave with you; My peace I give you. I do not give to you as the world gives. Do not let your hearts be troubled and do not be afraid.

Thankful peace is when we are thankful for God's peace living in us, which is a deep and lasting peace. This peace is confident assurance that in any circumstance we have Christ's peace through the Holy Spirit, and we have no need to fear the present or the future. Thankful peace is God moving into our hearts and living in us to restrain conflict and stress and to offer comfort instead. Because we accept Jesus and love Him, He gives us "peace that passes all understanding" and we are thankful and thus, thankful peace abounds. We can go in peace and serve the Lord and be thankful.

"God does not give us everything we want, but He does fulfill His promises." (Dietrich Bonhoeffer)

"Keep adding, keep walking, keep advancing; do not stop, do not turn back, do not turn from the straight road." (St. Augustine)

February 23
Thanks for the Grace: God's Riches At Christ's Expense

Hebrews 12:15
See to it that no one misses the grace of God...

Galatians 2:20
I have been crucified with Christ and I no longer live, but Christ lives in me.

God is in the business of changing hearts—a spiritual heart transplant, if you will. "I will give you a new heart and put a new spirit within you." (Ezekiel 36:26) Thank You, LORD, for when grace happens, You enter into our hearts. Grace is everything Jesus. Our sins are forgiven once and for all. Our sins were crucified with Christ on the Cross. We are no longer condemned. We have been saved and are no longer alone for Christ lives in us. To be saved by grace is to be saved by Jesus Himself. When we've made a mess of our lives, grace is what we need. God loves, stoops, comes to the rescue and gives Himself generously in and through Jesus Christ. Thank You, LORD, for grace. You are our power for living and our hope for the future.

"God's grace—His unconditionally loving, unmerited favor which is truly much more than we deserve and greater than we imagine." (Max Lucado)

"Should anyone knock at my heart and say, "Who lives here? I should reply, "Not Martin Luther, but the Lord Jesus Christ." (Martin Luther)

February 24
Thanks for the Talk

John 16:24
Until now you have not asked for anything in My name. Ask and you will receive, and your joy will be complete.

Thank You, God, for the talk. Because of what Jesus did on the cross we can speak directly to God. It is a wonderful relationship because we don't have to go through anyone else to talk to God. We can go directly to the Source. As believers, we have a direct line to Him because Jesus has made us acceptable to God. We can pray anytime and anywhere to the One who hears us. We can talk to God in the car as we drive, at home as we do our chores, at work where we spend a good deal of our days or anywhere we are because God is there. We talk, He listens, and then when we listen, He often whispers in the quietness. There is joy in these talks with our Lord. Thanks for the talk, Father. You are a wonderful listener.

"I woke today with gratitude for those who share me in their lives. I am thankful for those who are part of my journey." (Millie Mestril)

"Your beliefs don't make you a better person, your actions do." (Zig Ziglar)

February 25
God Listens

Psalm 55:22
Cast your cares on the Lord and He will sustain you; He will never let the righteous fall.

Isaiah 60:1
Arise, shine, for your light has come, and the glory of the Lord rises upon you.

We have a God who wants us to cast our burdens and cares upon Him. Afterwards, He wants us to walk in peace by trusting Him to take care of all that is concerning us. Imagine we can talk to our God and He listens and promises to take care of all that is concerning us. He is in control and He will weave our lives into His plan. God is our light. He is the One true God and we can trust Him with everything. When we do, we will have peace. He will do the work, and once we surrender all our cares and burdens to Him, we can be assured that in His time and in His will, all will be done to His glory and our peace. LORD, thanks for listening.

"Take my moments and my days, let them flow in ceaseless prayer." (Frances Havergal)

"Use today as an opportunity to listen to God's voice. Obedience to the Lord's voice in your life is a must for victory in your spirit." (DaySpring)

February 26
Faith in Jesus Christ

Hebrews 11:1
Now faith is being sure of what we hope for and certain of what we do not see.

Hebrews 13:8
Jesus Christ is the same yesterday and today and forever.

Faith is sure and certain. Christ is our foundation and this foundation is secure and built on solid rock. He is who He says He is and He will do what He says He will do. True faith believes that God will fulfill His promises even though we don't see them materializing yet. God will never change and He can help us. He can change our hearts. We should lean on and trust Him. Christ is the same as He has always been and will be forever. We should choose faith and go to Him because He's waiting.

"Faith is the conviction that God knows more than we do about this life and He will get us through it." (Max Lucado)

"Life without Christ is a hopeless end. With Christ it's an endless hope." (Wanda E. Brunstetter)

February 27
Lent—Let's Eliminate Negative Thinking

John 15:16
It was not you who chose me, but I who chose you and appointed you to go and bear fruit—fruit that will last.

2 Corinthians 10:5 We capture every thought and make it obedient to Christ.

Lent is a journey. It is a display of God's great love for us and is a time for us to look at ourselves to see if we are really living out Christ's message. Lent draws us to the Cross to challenge and comfort us, and it is a special time of year that encourages us to change to be more like Jesus. It reminds us of great love and leads us to our Savior. The Cross is the place of God's great triumph, love's triumph. Lent can change us. It can change our negative thinking, our fears, our worries and all those thoughts and things that we struggle with every day. Lent can transform us as we walk with Jesus to the Cross and afterwards on Easter morning as we go to the empty tomb with His followers. We should go to the Cross, lay down all our negative thinking and walk into the loving embrace of the crucified and risen Christ. The love that is waiting there is amazing and will transform our lives.

"Show me the way, oh Lord
Help me to do your will
Make me a vessel for Your love
That You may always fill." (Author unknown)

"Today be thankful and remember how rich you are. Your family is priceless, your time is gold, and your health is wealth." (Zig Ziglar)

"What lies behind us and what lies before us are tiny matters compared to what lies within us." (Ralph Waldo Emerson)

February 28
God with Us

Genesis 21:22
God is with you in all that you do.

Jesus lives our lives with us. He dwells within us in the manger of our hearts. We must not let the "Inn" of our minds be too overcrowded with worldly things that leaves no room for Him. He only wants to dwell in our hearts and once He's there, He'll move in to the "Inn" of our being. He will speak to us in the dessert of our lives and in the times of prosperity. Let's open our hearts and let Him be our guide. Immanuel—God with us.

"Come as you are in our brokenness. We are mosaics. Jesus is the Master artist. He takes our brokenness and can make it into something beautiful." (Author unknown)

"We paint our walls and God paints our souls." (Author unknown)

March 1
We Thankfully Have Hope

Psalm 119:114
You are my refuge and my shield; I have put my hope in Your Word.

When we read God's Word, we are fed with His Love and hope. The spiritual nourishment that Jesus gives us lasts forever. All the virtues in the Bible end with love and because of God's love we have hope. We know that we are not alone and that we can take anything to Him in conversation and prayer. We can discuss everything with Him and we know that He hears us and that He will guide us. When we pray we can ask for His wisdom and discernment for every situation. We have hope for the future as we commit our days to our Lord. He will be with us when we succeed and when we fail. We will thank Him for all successes and seek His grace for all failures. We thankfully have hope because of our God's love and promises.

"*Capture every thought*—the minute they appear we go into action. *Selfishness, step back! Envy, get lost! Find another home, Anger…you aren't allowed on this turf!* Capturing thoughts is serious business! But, we can do it!" *(Max Lucado)*

"*Every day you write the ticket for the rest of your life, and the past only matters when you decide to include it.*" *(Author unknown)*

March 2
Thanks for the Help

Psalm 121: 1-2
I lift up my eyes to the hills where does my help come from? My help comes from the LORD, the Maker of heaven and earth.

As children of God, we can depend upon Him for help. We are assured of God's protection day and night because He has established a relationship with us. He gives us assurance of His strength, help and victory over sin and death. We should stop and think about all the ways God has helped us. He is there to meet all of our needs. He provides for us and that is our hope and assurance. LORD, thank You for Your help each and every day.

"Be happy and a reason will come along." (Robert Brault)

"One of the secrets of a happy life is continuous small treats." (Iris Murdoch)

March 3
Let There be Light

Genesis 1:3-4
And God said, "Let there be light," and there was light. God saw that the light was good, and He separated the light from the darkness. God called the light "day," and the darkness He called "night." And there was evening, and there was morning—the first day.

This time of year we begin to notice that our days are brighter. Daylight begins earlier in the morning and stays with us longer in the evenings. It is a good sign that spring is not far behind. The dark days of winter are slowly becoming brighter and it is good because it gives us hope. God created light and He named the light "day" and He called the darkness "night" and said it was good. He created everything for His own pleasure. Creation originated from God and was His—it wasn't happenstance. In all of creation His deepest desire was to fellowship with us and to have a relationship with us because God is love. As we go through Lent, we can thank God for the Light—the light of the universe that takes away the darkness of night and the Light of the world that is His Son, Jesus Christ who came to take away the darkness of sin in our lives. Jesus is the Light of the world. In John 8:12 Jesus said, "I am the light of the world. Whoever follows Me will never walk in darkness, but will have the light of life." Jesus brings the Light into our lives. He brings God's presence, protection and guidance to us. He brings hope. His Light shines brightly and it takes away the darkness. We should follow Jesus, the Light of the world.

"Love must be as much a light, as it is a flame." (Thoreau)

"The Bible will keep you from sin, or sin will keep you from the Bible." (D.L. Moody)

March 4
Comfort

Matthew 5:4
Blessed are those who mourn, for they will be comforted.

2 Corinthians 1:3-4
Praise be to the God and Father of our LORD Jesus Christ, the Father of compassion and the God of all comfort, who comforts us in all our troubles, so that we can comfort those in any trouble with the comfort we ourselves have received from God.

We've all suffered loss of some sort. We've experienced the loss of loved ones, friendships, relationships, jobs, pets, financial stability, our health, etc., etc. We've mourned and grieved. God mourned for His Son. Jesus mourned for Lazarus and grieved in the Garden of Gethsemane. Matthew 26:38, "...My soul is overwhelmed with sorrow..." and when He prayed to His Father in verse 39 ... "may this cup be taken from Me..." Our Heavenly Father and Jesus know the depths of mourning. As Christians and followers of Jesus, the Bible tells us that we *will* be comforted. Our troubles may not disappear anytime soon, but we will receive strength, encouragement and hope to deal with our loss and troubles. The more we suffer, the more comfort God gives us when we turn to Him. As we endure each loss and trial, they help us to reach out and comfort others who are also suffering from similar troubles. Christ suffers with us because we are united with Him. We can be assured that as children of a compassionate and loving Triune God, we will be comforted. It's a promise. We can be thankful for His love and promise to give us comfort.

"Be comforted in the fact that the ache in your heart and the confusion in your soul means that you are still alive, still human and still open to the beauty of the world." (Paul Harding)

"Follow hard after Him, and He will never fail you." (C.H. Spurgeon)

March 5
The Treasure

Matthew 13:44-46
The kingdom of heaven is like treasure hidden in a field, which a man found and covered up. Then in his joy he goes and sells all that he has and buys that field. Again, the kingdom of heaven is like a merchant in search of fine pearls, who, on finding one pearl of great value, went and sold all that he had and bought it.

LORD, thank You for the treasure of Jesus. We can all have this treasure because He is Your gift to us. The question is: Do we recognize Him? He is the hidden treasure in Baptism and Communion. Jesus shows us the treasure of complete obedience and faith in God. He was obedient all the way to the cross. The kingdom of God is more valuable than anything we have, and we must be willing to give up everything to obtain it. God knows us and forgives us our sins and He loves us beyond all measure. We can have the treasure of Jesus. He is ours. Are we willing to follow Him and give up everything for Him? The kingdom of God is God Himself. That is what we are to seek. Heaven is our reward for seeking the kingdom. What a treasure we have in Jesus.

"Faith does not come from striving; it comes from surrender." (Bill Johnson)

"I never knew God was all I needed till God was all I had." (Author unknown)

March 6
White as Snow

Isaiah 1:18
"Come now, let us reason together," says the LORD. "Though your sins are like scarlet, they shall be as white as snow; though they are red as crimson, they shall be like wool."

Psalm 51: 1-3, 7
Have mercy on me, O God, according to Your unfailing love; according to Your great compassion blot out my transgressions. Wash away all my iniquity and cleanse me from my sin. For I know my transgressions, and my sin is always before me. Cleanse me with hyssop, and I will be clean; wash me, and I will be whiter than snow.

Matthew 28:3
His appearance was like lightening, and His clothes were white as snow.

When snow covers the "dirty" ground, I think of the verse in Isaiah that our sins are forgiven and we will be as white as snow. Sin is in everyone's life; we can't escape it as we are all born in sin and are sinful people. But what we can do is trust our LORD to take away our sins. This is why Jesus Christ came—He took all of our sins upon Himself. He went to the cross for each of us. He will remove the stain of sin from our lives. No sin is too great to be forgiven. We can go to Him and lay down our sins on the altar at the foot of the cross. He's waiting. We will be washed in His love and forgiveness. Then we can go out and play in the snow as we rejoice that we have a LORD and Savior who loves us so much that He sends a little snow to remind us of Heaven. White as snow—that is what we will be in heaven with Jesus.

"One leak will sink a ship; and one sin will destroy a sinner." (John Bunyan)

"We are not sinners because we sin; we sin because we are sinners." (R.C. Sproul)

March 7
Our Heart's Story

Ecclesiastes 3:11
He has planted eternity in the human heart.

We are created in God's image and so we can never be completely satisfied with earthly pleasures and pursuits. We have a spiritual thirst, eternal value, and nothing but the eternal God can satisfy us. Because He is our Creator, He has built in us a restless yearning for the kind of perfect world that can only be found in His perfect rule. He has given us a glimpse of the perfection of His creation but it is only a glimpse. We can only trust Him as we do His work on earth. Our hearts know Him and the story that is written on our hearts comes from Him. That is why we yearn to be with Him and follow Him. We know that there is more to our story in Him.

"From the Heart of the universe come our beating hearts. From this Fellowship spring all of our longings for a friend, a family, a fellowship—for someplace to belong." (John Eldredge, the EPIC)

"We should live our lives as though Christ were coming this afternoon." (Jimmy Carter, thirty-ninth president of the United States)

March 8
Our Talents

Matthew 25:14-18
"Again, it will be like a man going on a journey, who called his servants and entrusted his property to them. To one he gave five talents of money, to another two talents, and to another one talent, each according to his ability. Then he went on his journey. The man who had received the five talents went at once and put his money to work and gained five more. So also, the one with the two talents gained two more. But the man who had received the one talent went off, dug a hole in the ground and hid his master's money."

Everything we have belongs to God and these are our talents. Our talents include our time, gifts, resources and anything God gives us according to our abilities. He wants us to use them in His kingdom to make a difference in the world. We are all given talents and we are managers or stewards of what God gives us. We are not owners and do not own anything. Our job is to use these blessings for His kingdom. He will use whatever we have to help His kingdom grow. Every little bit matters, so let's not bury our talents but use them wisely. It is not a matter of how much we have but how well we use what we are given. It is our responsibility to wisely use what God gives us.

"People spend their lives in the service of their passions instead of employing their passions in the service of their lives." (Sir Richard Steele)

"There is only one way to succeed at anything and that is to give everything." (Vince Lombardi)

March 9
Thanks to the LORD

Psalm 105: 1-4
Give thanks to the LORD, call on His name; make known among the nations what He has done. Sing to Him, sing praise to Him; tell of all His wonderful acts. Glory in His holy name; let the hearts of those who seek the LORD rejoice. Look to the LORD and His strength; seek His face always.

We should give thanks to the LORD as we search His Word and pray to Him and praise Him for all that He has done for us. We should share the Good News of Jesus with others. We must remember that when we feel far away from Him, God is always close by. The way to know God is to look at how He has helped His people throughout the Bible. He is a loving and forgiving God who is waiting for us to seek and find Him. We should live for Him and not everything else in our lives. We must pay attention to His story because He yearns to become part of our story.

"We mutter and sputter, we fume and we spurt. We mumble and grumble; our feelings get hurt. We can't understand things; our vision grown dim. When all that we need is a moment with Him." (Author unknown)

"No prayer is too big. No prayer is too small. Otherwise, we might not pray at all." (Author unknown)

March 10
God Enables us to Love

1 John 4:10
This is love: not that we loved God, but that he loved us and sent his Son as an atoning sacrifice for our sins.

1 John 4:16
….God is love.

The greatest love mankind will ever experience is God's eternal love. He gives us the greatest treasure in all creation: a heart. We have free will to choose to love Him and to love others. He is so awesome and wants us to choose Him. He won't force us to love Him. Even when we don't choose to love Him and we go about our own way, He still loves us enough to be right where we need Him to be—along side of us. We need to go to Him. We can love because God first loved us. We should tell God we love Him each and every day.

"The cold world needs warm-hearted Christians." (Anonymous)

"Love that reaches up is adoration. Love that reaches across is affection. Love that reaches down is grace." (Donald Grey Barnhouse)

March 11
We are Forgiven

Psalm 38:18
I confess my iniquity; I am troubled by my sin.

Luke 23:34
Jesus said, "Father, forgive them, for they do not know what they are doing."

We are sinners. Yes, it is a fact and every last one of us sins. The good news is that God is a gracious God and knows we will sin. He chooses to show mercy on us and forgive us. As we travel the road of Lent, we come face-to-face with the cross and what it means—death. Each year we take this journey with Jesus and are reminded of His sacrifice for our sins. We are reminded of what God did for us on that cross. We thank You, God, that it is not our death but the death of Jesus, Your Son, that took away the sin of the world. We are forgiven. God says, "I forgive you" when we confess our sins and lay them at the foot of the cross. God gave His only Son to save us. The cleansing blood of Jesus is on each of us and He saved us. We are innocent, we are forgiven and free. God forgives us and gives us a new life through His Son. As forgiven children of God, we know that at the end of our days on earth when we come face-to-face with God, He will only see His Son and not us or our sins. Thank You, LORD, for Your love and forgiveness.

"Even if you're on the right track, you'll get run over if you just sit there." (Will Rogers)

"Rejoice in the LORD, and your bones will flourish and your cheeks will glow. Joy is balm and healing, and if you will but rejoice, God will give power." (A. B. Simpson)

March 12
We can Forgive

Ephesians 4:32
Be kind and compassionate to one another, forgiving each other, just as in Christ God forgave you.

We are to love and forgive others because God loves and forgives us. God is for us and forgives us because of His great mercy. Having received forgiveness means that we can now pass it on to others and forgive them. Our lives should bring glory to Him. We act in love towards others just as God acted in love by sending His Son to die for our sins. With Him, we can forgive because He will give us His grace and strength to do so. "Forgive us our trespasses as we forgive those who trespass against us." (Matthew 6:12)

"Always pray to have eyes that see the best in people, a heart that forgives the worst, a mind that forgets the bad, and a soul that never loses faith in God." (GodFruits.com)

"Love never asks how much must I do, but how much can I do?" (Author unknown)

March 13
God's Footprints

Psalm 37:3-6
Trust in the LORD and do good; dwell in the land and enjoy safe pasture. Delight yourself in the LORD and He will give you the desires of your heart. Commit your way to the LORD; trust in Him and He will do this. He will make your righteousness shine like the dawn, the justice of your cause like the noonday sun.

We see Jesus' footprints throughout the Bible. In Him we have a guide and a path to follow. He is with us in everything we experience, and there are those times when we are blessed to have Him carry us. There are moments when we wonder, "Where are You, Jesus?" Later, we look back and see that He was right where He always is—with us, carrying, lifting, supporting, forgiving and loving us. Thank You, Jesus, for not leaving nor forsaking us. (Hebrews 13:5) Thank You for Your footprints throughout the Bible and on our hearts.

The Footprints Prayer
One night I had a dream... I dreamed I was walking along the beach with the LORD, and across the sky flashed scenes from my life. For each scene I noticed two sets of footprints in the sand; one belonged to me, and the other to the Lord. When the last scene of my life flashed before me, I looked back at the footprints in the sand. I noticed that many times along the path of my life, there was only one set of footprints. I also noticed that it happened at the very lowest and saddest times in my life. This really bothered me, and I questioned the LORD about it. "LORD, You said that once I decided to follow You, You would walk with me all the way; But I have noticed that during the most troublesome times in my life, there is only one set of footprints. I don't understand why in times when I needed you the most, you should leave me. The LORD replied, "My precious, precious child. I love you, and I would never, never leave you during your times of trial and suffering. When you saw only one set of footprints, it was then that I carried you." (Margaret Fishback Powers)

March 14
Godly Wisdom

Proverbs 1:7
The fear of the LORD is the beginning of knowledge, but fools despise wisdom and discipline.

Proverbs 2:6
For the LORD gives wisdom, and from His mouth come knowledge and understanding.

Wisdom and knowledge are different. Knowledge is plentiful and wisdom is scarce. Wisdom is applying facts (knowledge) to life. Wisdom is a basic attitude that affects every aspect of our lives. Wisdom is the mind of God revealed in us. Knowing and loving God is the key to wisdom. The book of Proverbs is considered a book of wisdom for everyday life that tells us how we can live in close relationship to God. Our faith in God should be the controlling principle for our understanding of the world, our attitudes and our actions. We should trust in God because He will make us truly wise. Our job is to listen for His wisdom. Wisdom is His gift to us, but we must earnestly seek it, and, as we do, He will guide us. God's wisdom is truly a blessing and a gift.

"All of life is an experiment. The more experiments you make the better." (Ralph Waldo Emerson)

"Don't go through life. Grow through life." (Author unknown)

March 15
Wisdom and Understanding

Proverbs 9:10
The fear of the LORD is the beginning of wisdom, and knowledge of the Holy One is understanding.

2 Peter 1:3
His divine power has given us everything we need for life and godliness through our knowledge of Him who called us by His own glory and goodness.

Wisdom begins with knowing God. He gives insight into living because He created life. To know God is not just to know the facts about Him, but to stand in awe (fear) of Him and have a relationship with Him. To be wise means getting to know God better and better. Wisdom means practical discernment. It begins with respect for God which leads to right living and results in increased ability to tell right from wrong. Our goals must be God-centered and not self-centered. We should read God's Word and ask Him to show us how to obey it and ask for His wisdom to guide our choices. We must not grope in the dark, hoping to stumble on the answers. Godly wisdom comes with understanding and peace, joy and eventually happiness.

"Where your pleasure is, there is your treasure; where your treasure, there your heart; where your heart, there your happiness."
(St. Augustine)

"Happiness is like Jam...You can't spread even a little without getting some on yourself." (Author unknown)

March 16
Feed My Sheep

John 21:17
Feed My sheep.

After Jesus died and rose again and had not yet ascended into heaven He asked Peter three times "Do you love Me?" Earlier Peter had denied Jesus three times. It is always amazing how Jesus takes one incident and brings it around to another to make His point or to show us a lesson which we can use in our lives and on our walk with Him. Jesus wants Peter's complete devotion and shows Peter what He wants Him to do. "Feed My sheep." Jesus is commissioning Peter to be faithful to Him and to the ministry He is calling Peter to do. Peter was a fisherman and became a fisherman of mankind. What is Jesus calling us to do? Often, we get over involved and we are doing so many different things instead of focusing on what He is asking us to do. When reading Scripture and in our quiet time with Him, He will often point us in the direction He wants us to go. We must be still and listen for His whispers. He has something for us all to do. Jesus wants our complete devotion and then He will lead us to Feed His Sheep. We know that God is in control so we can confidently follow Him.

"When in Doubt, Stand at the crossroads and look. Ask for the ancient paths. Ask where the good way is and Walk in it. You will find rest for your souls." (Akiane)

"If God sends us on stony paths, he provides strong shoes." (Corrie ten Boom)

March 17
St. Patrick's Day

Numbers 6:24-26
The LORD bless you and keep you. The LORD make His face to shine upon you and be gracious to you. The LORD lift up His countenance upon you and give you peace.

God go before you. God stand behind you. God watch above you. Always, God love you. Have a blessed St. Patrick's Day.

"May God give you...
For every storm, a rainbow,
For every tear, a smile,
For every care, a promise,
And a blessing in each trial.
For every problem life sends,
A faithful friend to share,
For every sigh, a sweet song,
And an answer for each prayer." (Irelandcalling.ie)

"These things I warmly wish for you, someone to love, some work to do, a bit o' sun, a bit o' cheer and a guardian angel always near." (Irish Proverb)

March 18
A Happy Heart

Psalm 44:8
We will give thanks to Your name forever.

Galatians 2:20
It is no longer I who live, but Christ who lives in me.

We can begin our days with a happy heart. We all face adversities and have troubles, but our attitudes determine how we maneuver through them. We can have a happy heart or we can be glum. We've all had those days when we just cannot get out of our own way. We want to go back to bed and cover our heads. Then there are those days when our hearts sing and we find happiness wherever we go despite what is going on in our lives. With God as our partner, we can begin each day with a happy heart. We can be thankful for all that we have and all those He has brought into our lives. We are truly blessed because we have a loving God who provides for us daily. We are His and He loves us and that alone should give us a happy heart. Whatever we face, we can be assured that we have a Pilot who is a leader. We have hope. We should remember that Easter follows Good Friday. Jesus was victorious and we will be, too. Thank You, LORD, that we can begin our days with You and have a happy heart.

"When life gives you lemons...make lemonade." (Author unknown)

"Never underestimate the power of a cozy warm cup of tea."
(Author unknown)

March 19
A Servant

John 13:3-5
Jesus knew that the Father had put all things under His power, and that He had come from God and was returning to God; so He got up from the meal, took off His outer clothing, and wrapped a towel around His waist. After that, He poured water into a basin and began to wash His disciples' feet, drying them with the towel that was wrapped around Him.

When Jesus washed the disciples' feet, He was being the model servant and showing His servant attitude to them. He was doing a job that in those days only the lowliest servant would do. Here our LORD and Savior, God in the flesh, was willing to serve, and, by doing so obeyed His Father. We, too, should strive to be a servant of God in our daily lives by doing the little things. Some of these things will certainly go unnoticed by others, but the point is as we willingly serve God and glorify Him in everything, He notices and He knows. So go ahead! We can serve our LORD in our own backyards by being kind to someone, smiling at someone in the grocery line, making a meal for an ill neighbor, sending a card to encourage someone, doing the little things in our daily lives to glorify our LORD. It will change our lives.

"Every act of love is a prayer." (Mother Teresa)

"God is not looking for more stars; He's looking for more servants." (Howard Hendricks)

March 20
His Hands

John 20:27-28
Then He said to Thomas, "Put your finger here; see My hands. Reach out your hand and put it into My side. Stop doubting and believe." Thomas said to Him, "My LORD and my God!"

A few years ago a sweet and special friend gave me a pencil drawing. It's a drawing of Jesus with a lamb nestled in His left arm. The lamb's head is resting on Jesus' shoulder. Jesus' face is bent towards the lamb, His eyes are closed and His head is resting on the lamb. Jesus has His left hand with a wound in it holding the lamb. When I first saw this drawing, tears came to my eyes because Jesus is our Shepherd and we are His lambs. Whenever we go to Him in prayer we are safely in His arms. The first quote below is one of my favorites and I keep it with me to recite and to remind me that He has us in every situation. Of course, Satan is going to do everything he can to take us away from Jesus because we are a threat to him but we know our LORD and Savior. No matter what, Jesus has us. He calmed the waters, healed the sick, fed the hungry, washed the feet of His disciples and so much more. His Hands did these things then and are still doing things today for all who believe in Him. Jesus' hands with the great wounds will lift us up, hold us close and comfort us. We can trust the Hands with the great wounds.

"When the enemy of your soul slaps you around and knocks you down and says, "Why don't you stay down this time?" The Hands with the great wounds reach down and lift you up, and the Lover of your soul whispers in your ear so only you can hear, "I got this." He defends the weak and heals the broken and knows there is infinitely more to your story." (Geoff Ludlow)

"Let no one ever come to you without leaving better and happier. Be the living expression of God's kindness: Kindness in your face, Kindness in your eyes, Kindness in your smile." (Mother Teresa)

March 21
Little Children

Jeremiah 17: 7-8
"But blessed is the man who trusts in the LORD, whose confidence is in Him. He will be like a tree planted by the water that sends out its roots by the stream. It does not fear when heat comes; its leaves are always green. It has no worries in a year of drought and never fails to bear fruit."

Mark 10:16
And He took the children in His arms, placed His hands on them and blessed them.

Spending time with little children is such a learning experience. They look at life so differently and with such awe. Everything to them is an adventure and full of discovery. There is nothing in this world like children's laughter. Their hugs and smiles will melt the roughest person's heart. Just as children want to feel secure and loved, all of us want the same thing. To feel secure, what all children need is a loving look and gentle touch from someone who cares. All they need and want is someone to love them. This is what we need, too. We are God's children. We have a God who loves us, and we should trust Him with a child's simplicity and receptivity. As we walk and talk with God, it is a learning experience full of discovery. Let's go to Him trusting Him as children trust the ones they love and feel secure with because there is no other who loves us more and promises to be with us forever. Jesus said in Mark 10:14 "Let the little children come to Me, and do not hinder them, for the kingdom of God belongs to such as these."

"You can't change the past, but you can ruin a perfectly good present by worrying about the future." (Author unknown)

"Eyes that look are common; eyes that see are rare." (J. Oswald Sanders)

March 22
Just as I Am

Matthew 15:6-7
Rejoice with Me; I have found my lost sheep. I tell you that in the same way there will be more rejoicing in heaven over one sinner who repents than over ninety-nine righteous persons who do not need to repent.

"Just as I am, without one plea But that Thy blood was shed for me And that Thou bidd'st me come to Thee, O Lamb of God, I come." (LSB 570:1) Amen

Jesus wants us just as we are and His love for us is so great that He looks for us. He knows we need Him even if we don't think so. He rejoices when one of us is found. He seeks the lost, the lonely, the unwanted and those considered beyond hope. He seeks us—sinners who come to Him for mercy. His love is so great that He searches for us like a shepherd searching for one lamb and when He finds us—He rejoices. Let's go to Him, just as we are and repent of our sins. We know and can be assured that He is waiting. He's the Lamb of God. He loves us and forgives us. We can go to Him, just as we are.

"A journey is a person in itself, no two are alike." (John Steinbeck)

"Why did you do all this for me?" he asked. "I don't deserve it. I've never done anything for you." "You have been my friend," replied Charlotte. "That in itself is a tremendous thing." (E.B. White, Charlotte's Web)

March 23
Tribulation

John 16:33
In the world you will have tribulation. But take heart; I have overcome the world.

Colossians 3:2
Set your minds on things that are above.

Every day we will face tribulation and adversity. Just because we are Christians and believers of Jesus Christ does not mean that we will be immune. When we are dealing with trials and tribulations, other people are watching us to see how we react. In order to be a light in a dark world, we need to prove we are who we say we are by reacting in a Godly manner. Jesus said that we will have trouble, but promised that He will be with us in the trouble. He does not necessarily take us out of it but makes us stronger as we walk through it. We must rely on God daily, and when troubles come, we will be stronger for them and know that He has us in the palms of His hands. As we face the challenges of daily living, the Lord will guide us in thought, word and deed. He will supply us with the strength we need to make wise decisions and to walk through whatever adversity comes our way. He will be our light to a dark world and give us the peace and comfort that only He can give. We lay it all on the altar for Him to handle. We are His vessels.

"If there ever comes a day where we can't be together, keep me in your heart. I'll stay there forever." (Winnie the Pooh)

"Worship is no longer worship when it reflects the culture around us more than the Christ within us." (A.W. Tozer)

March 24
Peace

Joshua 24:15
...choose today whom you will serve...But as for me and my household, we will serve the LORD.

Philippians 4:6
Do not be anxious about anything, but in everything, by prayer and petition, with thanksgiving present your requests to God. And the peace of God, which transcends all understanding, will guard your hearts and your minds in Christ Jesus.

Serving the LORD will bring about a certain peace in our hearts. Letting God be in control and letting His Spirit control us will help take away some of the indecision about how we should live. We have a covenant with Him, and He promises to never leave us nor forsake us. Let His peace fill us and give us the strength to go forward. With our LORD and Savior by our side, we can do all things.

"Peace be to this house and to all who dwell in it. Peace be to them that enter and to them that depart." (Author unknown)

"Your peace is more important than driving yourself crazy trying to understand why something happened the way it did. Let it go." (Author unknown)

March 25
The LORD's Prayer

Matthew 6:9-13
Our Father, who art in heaven,
hallowed be Thy name.
Thy Kingdom come,
Thy will be done,
on earth as it is in heaven.
Give us this day our daily bread.
And forgive us our trespasses,
As we forgive those who trespass against us.
And lead us not into temptation,
But deliver us from evil.
For Thine is the kingdom, the power,
and the glory, for ever and ever. Amen

"*The LORD's Prayer may be committed to memory quickly, but it is slowly learnt by heart.*" *(Frederick Denison Maurice)*

"*To pray is to sit openhanded before God.*" *(Peter G. Van Breemen)*

March 26
Quietness

Psalm 46:10-11
Be still and know that I am God: I will be exalted among the heathen, I will be exalted in the earth. The LORD of hosts is with us; the God of Jacob is our refuge.

Why is God quiet sometimes? Why doesn't He answer our prayers as quickly as we want Him to or answer them at all? Only He knows the answer to these questions and will reveal them to us in His time. I wonder if He is quiet at times so that we will come closer to Him in prayer and read His Word. God was quiet when Jesus was on the cross. Maybe we need to quiet our lives and just spend time with Him. Maybe once we are quiet He will whisper His answer or then again, maybe not. Maybe He wants us to quiet our hearts, thoughts, cares, worries and fears. Maybe He wants us to rely on Him for all things and "Be still and know that I am God…" He has us and we need to lean on Him. Let's quiet our hearts today and rest in the arms of Jesus because He's got us. "Jesus."

"You may not understand today or tomorrow, but eventually God will reveal why you went through everything you did." (Author unknown)

"Morning is God's way of saying one more time, go make a difference, touch a heart, encourage a mind, inspire a soul and enjoy the day." (Author unknown)

March 27
Prayer

Psalm 88:2
Let my prayer come before thee: incline thine ear unto my cry.

Romans 8:26
The Spirit helps us in our weakness. We do not know what we ought to pray for, but the Spirit Himself intercedes for us with groans that words cannot express.

Prayer is that private moment between God and us when we take a breath and talk to the One who loves us beyond all measure. Sometimes it is the most important moment of our whole day whether we are giving thanks, petitioning for troubles and/or giving our LORD praise. Sometimes that moment is when we talk to God to tell Him that we love Him. No matter what we talk to Him about, we can be assured that He is listening. These moments with God are precious, simple and intimate. We should go to Him in prayer. We can take a moment here and there out of our day to talk to the One who loves us, listens to us and will answer us when the time is right. We must keep it simple and pray and talk to our Heavenly Father—He's waiting.

"A single grateful thought toward heaven is the most complete prayer." (Gotthold Ephraim Lessing)

"Feeling gratitude and not expressing it is like wrapping a present and not giving it." (William A. Ward)

March 28
Jesus Died for Us

Romans 5:8
God demonstrates His own love toward us, in that while we were still sinners, Christ died for us.

Jesus died for us! Jesus died for us because we needed a Savior. Sermons will be preached throughout the world during this time of year that proclaim this precious truth, *"Jesus died for us."* The Gospel proclaims that God not only loved the world, but He loved us; that God not only sent His Son to die for the sins of the world, but He sent His Son to die for our sins. Jesus died and rose for us. Does this not say it all? Jesus died and rose for us! If we only knew this one truth, it would be sufficient. If we only had this loaf of spiritual bread to eat, it would satisfy our hunger. If we only had this living water to drink, it would quench our spiritual thirst. Jesus died and rose for us. This is the taproot from which the tree of life grows. This is the headwater from which the healing river flows. This is the pen from which the great doctrines of faith are written—justification, sanctification, redemption, salvation—Jesus died and rose for us. Jesus died and rose for us. This is our true hope, our eternal hope, our blessed hope. Does God love us? Yes...*Jesus died and rose for us.* Does God care about us? Yes...*Jesus died and rose for us.* Does God forgive us, save us, receive us, and call us His own? Yes...*Jesus died and rose for us.* (Roy Lessin, Meet Me in the Meadow, DaySpring)

The New
I came with my struggles and found Your peace,
I came with my bondage and found Your release.
I came with my burdens and found Your care.
I came with my loneliness and found You there,
I came with my weakness and found You strong,
I came with my heaviness and found Your song.
I came with my questions and found You true,
I came with my tattered ways and found the new. (DaySpring)

March 29
The Cross

John 8:31-32
Then Jesus said to those Jews who believed Him, "If you abide in My word, you are My disciples indeed. And you shall know the truth, and the truth shall make you free."

The deceiver tells me I am good enough.
The Cross tells me I am a sinner.
The deceiver tells me there are many ways to heaven.
The Cross tells me there is no other way for me to be saved.
The deceiver tells me to keep following what feels good.
The Cross tells me I am lost.
The deceiver tells me I am innocent.
The Cross tells me I am guilty.
The deceiver tells me I can save myself.
The Cross tells me I need a Savior.
The deceiver tells me Christ's work is incomplete.
The Cross tells me it is finished.
The deceiver tells me I am condemned.
The Cross tells me I am justified.
The deceiver tells me I cannot be made clean.
The Cross tells me the blood of Jesus cleanses me from all sin.
The deceiver tells me I must work for my salvation.
The Cross tells me it is by grace alone.
The deceiver tells me my life will never change.
The Cross tells me all things will be made new.
The deceiver tells me to be true to myself.
The Cross tells me that I am not my own.
The deceiver tells me I can do as I please.
The Cross tells me I have been bought with a price.
The deceiver tells me God is against me.
The Cross tells me God is for me.
The deceiver tells me I owe a debt I cannot pay.
The Cross tells me He paid the debt He did not owe!! (Roy Lessin, Meet Me in the Meadow)

March 30
Disappointment

Nehemiah 8:10
Do not be grieved, for the joy of the LORD is your strength.

Often when we face disappointment and frustration, we must step back and look at the reason for it. Is there a lesson in it for us? Is God trying to teach us something or bring us up to a higher level? Do we trust Him to lead us through and are we joyfully praising Him? Sometimes as we get caught up in the situation, we forget to lean on Him and ask for His help. We must remember that His love will never go away and He will give us the strength we need to face each and every challenge.

"Faith is having a positive attitude about what you can do and not worrying at all about what you can't do." (Author unknown)

"Life always offers you a second chance. It's called tomorrow." (Author unknown)

March 31
God Is Rich In Love

Psalm 145:8
The LORD is gracious and compassionate, slow to anger and rich in love.

Think about the people we love most in our lives. Can we imagine that our God loves us even more than that? He has given us illustrations that the church is His bride and He is the groom. We must remember that the love we feel for our loved ones, which can shake us to our very core, is the same love that brings us closer to the love of our LORD. He shows us a glimpse of His love as He gives us our earthly family to love and cherish. He loves us so much more and we should love Him back. He is the greatest love we will ever have and He's waiting to hear us tell Him that we love Him. He loved us so much that He gave us His Son to carry our sins to the cross. In the end Jesus said, "It is finished." We are free, salvation is won, and there is no greater love than that. God is rich in love because God is love.

"There is no pit so deep, that God's love is not deeper still." (Corrie ten Boom)

"To love at all is to be vulnerable." (C.S. Lewis)

April 1
The Donkey

Zechariah 9:9
Behold, your king is coming to you humble and mounted on a donkey.

Imagine that Jesus Christ, King of the Jews, rode into Jerusalem on a lowly donkey. What an honor for the donkey. How humble our Jesus was to make such a simple statement by choosing to ride in on a donkey. He is the greatest King ever and He chose a simple mode of transportation. He leaned down with humility and chose a simple way to reach His people. However, at that time, the people did not realize the type of king He was or that He was coming to Jerusalem to face His death. He knew how His journey would end and He did it anyway. The people did not realize that this King would rule in eternity and would be the greatest King ever but Jesus knew. The donkey had the humble honor of carrying our LORD. Jesus, in His humility, did not run from His mission. He persevered with courage. He knew the end of the story. It was such a great honor for the donkey and for us to know such a King and LORD who would forever change our lives. As the hymn says, *"Ride on, ride on in majesty! In lowly pomp ride on to die."*

"Each day comes bearing its own gifts. Untie the ribbons." (Ruth Ann Schabacker)

"Many things will catch your eye, but only a few will catch your heart...pursue those." (Author unknown)

April 2
To-do Lists

Proverbs 3:6
….in all your ways acknowledge Him and He will make your paths straight.

We lead very busy lives. Each day we get up with a "to-do" list filled with all that we want to accomplish in the day. Sometimes this list is so long we wonder if we will ever mark off anything listed, and many times we don't. Starting our day with the LORD and giving Him reign over our lives will help us to fulfill all that He has purposed for us each day. When we talk to Him throughout the day, He listens, calms our hearts and gives us the peace that we need to keep checking things off the "to do" list. He helps us accept that we may not have a completed list by the end of the day. He'll throw some surprises in there and may tell us to just rest and leave the list for tomorrow. Above all, He would rather we spend time with Him in thought, word and prayer. Once we acknowledge Him in all that we do, He will guide us and help us to simply live with the purpose of leaning on Him and trusting Him to show us His way all day long. We can enjoy our day and lean on the LORD because He's got us and has a great day planned for us.

"Success is the maximum utilization of the ability that you have."
(Zig Ziglar)

"If God maintains sun and planets in bright and ordered beauty, He can keep us." (F.B. Meyer)

April 3
It is Finished

John 19:30
When Jesus had received the sour wine, He said, "It is finished," and He bowed His head and gave up His spirit.

The sign placed above the cross read: *Jesus of Nazareth, The King of the Jews.* Christ died for our sins. He took our place on a cross so that we would not have to suffer the punishment we deserve. He was our substitute. His Father sent Him here for this purpose. He was a substitutionary atonement for the sins of the world, for our sins. Jesus said He was the final sacrifice for all sins. He paid the price in full and now we can go freely and directly to God. As we go about our day, we should remember what He did for us and why. Every sin ever committed by us was taken by Jesus to that cross and nailed there. Those nails or spikes were driven into His wrists and feet and they represent our sins. The pain and agony that He suffered was for every one of us and He did it because He loves us so much. Do you see the heart on the cross? Keep looking—it's there. It's Jesus' heart for us. Our sins are forgiven because every sin has been accounted for and God's plan of salvation has been completed. There is nothing we can do to earn our salvation. It has been done for us by Jesus, the only perfect man in God's perfect plan.

"The purpose of the cross is to repair the irreparable." (Erwin Lutzer)

"Jesus took our hell so that we might take His heaven." (Author unknown)

April 4
The In-Between Day

Isaiah 53:5
But He was pierced for our transgressions, He was crushed for our iniquities; the punishment that brought us peace was upon Him, and by His wounds we are healed.

1Peter 3:19
By which also He went and preached unto the spirits in prison;

Holy Saturday is considered the *in-between day*. This is the day after the crucifixion and the day before the resurrection. We are still reeling from what Jesus did for us on the cross. The sight of His beaten and naked body, the crown of thorns upon His head, the droplets of blood, the sound of the spikes/nails being driven into His hands and feet, the dark sky, the roar of thunder, His last words, the overwhelming sense that we should have been on that cross and the light of the world being stricken from us. For Jesus, Holy Saturday was the day that He faced Satan in hell and declared victory. Life over death was won on the cross. Jesus is the bridge between life and death. He is our Savior. Our sins are forgiven. Tomorrow is Easter, His resurrection day, and we proclaim His victory and we rejoice! But on Holy Saturday, we wait, we remember, we reflect as the darkness of the crucifixion hangs over us. There's a hush over mankind as we wait, wait, wait….and we have the hope of tomorrow.

Yes, yesterday was Good Friday, today is Holy Saturday—the bridge, the in-between as Jesus declares victory in hell. He has done it for us. We will remember and wait for the joy of the morning—Jesus is our LORD and Savior. Our Messiah suffered the unbearable for us resulting in forgiveness for all mankind. We will enjoy Holy Saturday, the in-between day and let the quietness fill us as we reflect on all that Jesus did for us.

"Would you know what makes heaven heaven? It is communion with God. And would you know what makes hell hell? It is to be forsaken of God." (Anonymous)

"There are only two kinds of people in the end: those who say to God, "Thy will be done," and those to whom God says in the end, "Thy will be done." (C.S. Lewis)

April 5
The Stone Rolled Away Day

John 3:16
"For God so loved the world that He gave His one and only Son, that whoever believes in Him shall not perish but have eternal life."

John 20:8
John saw the grave clothes looking like an empty cocoon from which Jesus emerged, he believed that Jesus had risen.

John 20:29 (Jesus talking to the disciples after He rose.)
…. Because you have seen Me, you have believed; blessed are those who have not seen and yet believe.

He is alive! He is risen! He is risen indeed! Easter… it is what perfect love looks like! God's greatest gift is Jesus! Rejoice! Alleluia! Jesus Christ is risen today! Because we believe in Jesus and His promises, we will live with Him forever in eternity. Death is not the end—there is life after death.

The Jellybean Prayer (Author unknown)
Red is for the blood He gave.
Green is for the grass He made.
Yellow is for the sun so bright.
Orange is for the edge of night.
Black is for the sins that were made.
White is for the grace He gave.
Purple is for the hour of sorrow.
Pink is for the new tomorrow.
Give a bag of jellybeans. Colorful and sweet.
Tell them it's a Prayer. It's a Promise.
It's an Easter treat!

Happy Stone Rolled Away Day! Jesus Christ is risen today! He is risen indeed! Alleluia!! What a death He died; What a life He lives! What a love He gives! What a King He is! Alleluia!!!!

April 6
The Day After

John 20:31
But these are written that you may believe that Jesus is the Christ, the Son of God, and that by believing you may have life in His name.

Each year as we go through Holy week from Palm Sunday to Easter Sunday, we experience so much of what Christ went through to fulfill the promises made in the Bible. Each year we are changed a little bit more by what happened on the cross. We begin to look at the cross differently, and we read the Bible with a deeper perspective and yearning. We know the end of the story. We know that Jesus is victorious over death, and because He is victorious, we will be victorious. The stone is rolled away—the grave is empty. The grave clothes are folded. He is alive! He is risen! We have hope! There is life after death. We who believe in Him will live in Eternity with Him forever! When we take our last breath on earth, our next breath will be with Jesus. Imagine that!!! Plus, He didn't leave us alone. He gave us the Holy Spirit who lives in us helping us to face each and every day. We have a direct line to God with the Holy Spirit in us and with Jesus sitting at the right hand of God. We can enjoy the day after with all the hope and love that flows from the cross. Jesus did it for us. He is alive and well! He is risen! He is risen indeed! Alleluia!

"Jesus is the Savior, but He is even more than that! He is more than a Forgiver of our sins. He is even more than our Provider of eternal life. He is our Redeemer! He is the One who is ready to recover and restore what the power of sin and death has taken from us." (Jack Hayford)

"Waiting to come to the LORD when you get your life cleaned up is like waiting to go to the ER when you stop bleeding. He doesn't love some future version of you; He loves us in our mess. God loves you just the way you are…but He loves you too much to leave you that way!" (Author unknown)

April 7
HOPE

Galatians 2:20
"I have been crucified with Christ; it is no longer I who live, but Christ who lives in me..."

After going through Lent, Holy week and Easter, the word hope should mean even more to us than ever before. We have hope because of what our LORD did on the cross. Once we surrender to Him and give Him all of our sins, He forgives us and that gives us hope. We were crucified with Him, our sins were crucified on the cross and we were raised with Him. We are forgiven and we will be remembered in paradise. We have HOPE because we believe and trust Jesus Christ. We can go to Him, give Him our sins and know that He remembers them no more. We should spend time with Jesus. We can have HOPE because the God of hope raised Jesus Christ from the grave and He lives. Because He lives, we live, too. We have HOPE in the God of Glory.

"You will find it necessary to let things go, simply for the reason that they are too heavy." (Corrie ten Boom)

H-heavenly
O-opportunities
P-presented
E-everywhere
(Lori Kolb-Speer)

H-heavenly
O-omnipotent
P-powerful
E-everlasting Savior
(Thelma Wells)

April 8
Spring Brings Hope

2 Corinthians 1:10
He delivered us from such a deadly peril, and He will deliver us. On Him we have set our hope that He will deliver us again.

I think God put spring directly after winter for a reason. Spring is a season of hope. After a long, snowy, cold winter in comes spring with its newness and rebirth. The snow melts and the ground turns green. The trees bud and flowers begin to peek out of the ground to color our lives. The sun shines longer and brighter. Some winters are very cold and snowy and even though the calendar says it is spring, we only see glimpses. There are patches of ground beginning to turn green and some flowers pop through. Although the forecast may be for a coating of snow, we have hope that it will melt quickly and not last. That is just like Easter. Everything was dark and dreary, sad and forlorn and then Christ was resurrected on Easter morn and all became bright and new. We rejoice because that is our hope. We experience darkness in our lives and we wonder if we will see the light again and how long will we have to stay in the dark. Then we look to the cross and to Jesus. Jesus is the light and hope of the world. He will help us walk through the valley of the shadow of death. He will lead and guide us to everlasting life. Spring brings Easter, spring brings hope. We can rejoice! Christ is risen! He is risen indeed! Happy Easter! Happy Spring!

"Some days all I do is watch the sky." (Author unknown)

"Learn from yesterday. Live for today. Hope for tomorrow." (Albert Einstein)

April 9
Never Alone

John 16:32
"...you will leave me all alone. Yet I am not alone, for My Father is with Me."

During holy week we walked to the cross with Jesus, realizing that amidst the pain and suffering, the beatings, and total isolation He must have felt, He kept His focus on God. He knew His mission and purpose was to love us and bring us salvation. Jesus had spiritual fortitude. The Glory of God did something that no one else could do. Everywhere He went, He walked in love for others. Whatever He did, He did in love for others. Everything He did was done in love for the Glory of God...the doing and the giving. When we look at the cross, we see God's Glory and feel His love. We can share His love with others. We can do it in our everyday lives in our own backyards. We can be kind, share our blessings and reach out to others who are hurting. We can ask Jesus to show us a need and how to fulfill it. We can pray and know that whatever He brings into our lives, He will show us how to accomplish it. All we need to do is believe and trust Him. Our mission is to walk daily with Him and lean on Him. We are not alone.

"It is not how much we do, but how much love we put in the doing. It is not how much we give, but how much love we put in the giving." (Mother Theresa)

"Just slipping quietly into the presence of God can be so exotic and fresh that it delights us enormously." (Author unknown)

April 10
Jesus Forgave

Luke 23:34
Jesus said, "Father, forgive them, for they do not know what they are doing."

1 Peter 2:24
He Himself bore our sins in His body on the tree, so that we might die to sins and live for righteousness; by His wounds you have been healed. For you were like sheep going astray, but now you have returned to the Shepherd and Overseer of your souls.

After the scourging, beatings, condemning and suffering, Jesus still loved and forgave all for what had been done to Him. Yes, we played a part in what happened to Him. He did it for us and for our salvation. Because we are forgiven and loved by our Lord, we can forgive and love others.

"The first to apologize is the bravest. The first to forgive is the strongest. The first to forget is the happiest." (Author unknown)

"Treat people the way you want to be treated. Talk to people the way you want to be talked to. Respect is earned, not given." (Author unknown)

April 11
Rainbows

God made a promise in Genesis 9:12-13
And God said, "This is the sign of the covenant I am making between Me and you and every living creature with you, a covenant for all generations to come: I have set my rainbow in the clouds, and it will be the sign of the covenant between Me and earth.

Some days can be sunny, then cloudy and at times be warm and then very cool and rainy. The sky is amazing with clouds of different colors, shapes and sizes. At one point the sky can be divided. On one side it will be sunny with a bright blue sky and white puffy clouds and on the other side it can be overcast and gray; directly in the middle, the sky can be a deep steel blue gray with storm clouds and sheets of rain. Two thoughts come to mind. The first one is that into every life a little rain must fall and "where is my umbrella?" None of us have the perfect life. Things go awry, we sin and things happen. The other thought is, "When one door shuts, God opens another door or a window."

We welcome the rain at times because it opens up the earth and gives it a much-needed drink. A rainy Saturday or Sunday gives us a chance to rest, relax, read a book or spend some time with our family. In life, the rain of problems falls upon us, but in all things, God is there waiting for us to trust Him to see us through. At times when all things seem dark and overpowering, there is that ray of sunshine or hope that He is in control. He has us in the palm of His Hand and will show us the way out and walk us through the valley. In every life a little rain must fall, but look for the rainbow. A rainbow is a sign that God will keep His promises and His faithfulness to His Word. No matter what we experience on a day-to-day basis, God is there with a rainbow. We should look to Him for help, hope and life. "I'm singing in the rain, I'm singing in the rain. What a glorious feeling I'm happy again."

"Try to be a rainbow in somebody's cloud." (Maya Angelou)

"And when it rains on your parade, look up rather than down. Without the rain, there would be no rainbow." (Gilbert K. Chesterton)

April 12
True Friendship

Ecclesiastes 4:9-10
Two are better than one; because they have a good reward for their labor. For if they fall, the one will lift the other.

After spending time with some phenomenal friends, it confirms for me just how blessed we are to have a God who created us and brings friends into our lives to enjoy. We are blessed to be surrounded by friends who share their faith and are able to laugh, talk, walk and pray with us. These experiences are most enjoyable and filled with encouragement, love and blessings. God is an awesome God. Thank You, LORD, for Your love and guidance and for all the people You bring into our lives to enhance us and who help make us the people You wish us to be.

"Friendship is precious, not only in the shade, but in the sunshine of life." (Thomas Jefferson)

"Your friendship blesses me in our days of joy and laughter and in times of trouble or sadness. You dive headfirst into my heart. Thank you for being my friend!" (Author unknown)

April 13
Our Security

1 John 5:20
We know also that the Son of God has come and has given us understanding, so that we may know Him who is true. And we are in Him who is true—even in His Son Jesus Christ. He is the true God and eternal life.

We all have those "mountain top" experiences where we feel wonderful, fit for anything, secure, life-is-good moments and then we must come down to reality. Often we let the feelings we had on the "mountain top" go, and we can't remember them. That makes the everyday things we face all that much harder or does it? I think Easter is that type of experience. We work up to the crescendo of Easter through Holy week, and then on Easter morn, we go through the glorious celebration of Christ's resurrection. We're full of joy and celebration and thankful for all that God did for us, but then Monday comes and the week after and the week after that. As we get farther away from Easter, do we see "the Light of the world?" The Good News is: we do. We know that we are secure in Christ. We know that He is the Light of the world, He is the "Bread of life," and we are forgiven. We know that by His wounds we are healed. The truth is our relationship with Christ is secure. No matter what we face today, we have a loving God who promises to never leave us nor forsake us. Thank You, Jesus, for Easter.

"Can't we seek aid for our sour attitudes? Of course we can. Jesus can change our hearts! He wants us to have a heart like His!" (Author unknown)

"Remember that the God of the mountain top is also the God of our today." (Author unknown)

April 14
God's Help

Psalm 121:1-2
I lift up my eyes to the hills—where does my help come from? My help comes from the LORD, the maker of heaven and earth.

The Maker of heaven and earth helps us. That's it. He created everything and He sent His Son to live as a man for a short time on earth. Jesus was crucified for our sins. When we repent of our sins and ask for forgiveness, we are forgiven. We have a lot to be thankful for because we have a God who loves us and whose sinless Son took all of our sins to the cross so that we can live eternally with Him. Our sins are washed away by His blood and we are made white as snow. We are forgiven. God is there for us in our good times and in our times of trouble. We must look to Him and be thankful for all that we have and ask His help for whatever we are facing at the moment. Jesus is there in the midst of whatever we are facing. We should thank Him for what He has done and for what He will do for us. He is an awesome God and we have so much to be thankful for—we woke up today and we got up this morning…. that's a start. We can thank Him for the day that lies ahead and for His bringing about the answers to what we are facing. We must celebrate Jesus for His leadership, guidance, promises and help.

"God is the sunshine that warms us, the rain that melts the frost and waters the young plants. The presence of God is a climate of strong and bracing love, always there." (Author unknown)

"To live will be an awfully big adventure." (J.M. Barrie, Peter Pan)

April 15
Get Ready

Exodus 3:4
When the LORD saw that he had gone over to look, God called to him from within the bush, "Moses! Moses!" and Moses said, "Here I am!"

1 Samuel 3:10
The LORD came and stood there, calling as at the other times, "Samuel! Samuel!" Then Samuel said, "Speak, for your servant is listening."

We must get ready for when God visits us today. He will visit us and we won't even realize it because we are too busy. We must be ready in thought and spirit for when He calls us to do something. It doesn't even have to be a large task—it could be a menial task that we should do to the best of our ability. He could be calling us to listen to someone. We should slow down to give that person a few minutes of our time and maybe some of Jesus' love. We need to be ready at any moment to share Jesus by listening, doing or praying. When our relationship is right with God, and we know where we are in Him, we are in readiness to be God's tool no matter the task, large or small. It's not our choice; it's His and we must be ready for our Captain to give us our marching orders. We must be ready now and wait for God's visit. We should not try to get ready after He visits as it takes too long, and we may miss a wonderful opportunity. We must be ready and be on fire for God and look for His surprise visit today! Are we ready? You betcha because we are on fire for Jesus!!!

"Unless you try to do something beyond what you have already mastered, you will never grow." (Author unknown)

"Wherever you go ... go there with all your heart." (Author unknown)

April 16
Listen Up

Psalm 46:10
Be still and know that I am God.

Each day we are given twenty-four hours: 1,440 minutes or 86,400 seconds. There must be time somewhere in there to listen for God. We talk to Him but do we take some quiet time to listen for Him? He does want to talk to us and often we are so busy telling Him what we need that we are not listening to Him for the answer. He is the great I AM and He knows us. We should take some time today to be still and quiet to focus on Him and let Him whisper to our hearts. His whispers are nudges of peace that guide us in the direction He wants us to go. He could be telling us, "*I love you.*" Let's be still and know that He is God. We can turn off the radio of life and tune into the God of the universe. He's on the Great I AM channel….

"I know God will not give me anything I can't handle. I just wish He didn't trust me so much." (Mother Teresa)

"Looking unto Jesus is at the same time a looking away from everything else." (Erich Sauer)

April 17
Because He Lives

John 14:19
...Because I live, you will live. On that day you will realize that I am in My Father, and you are in Me, and I am in you.

God knows all and He has chosen not to tell us what lies ahead. All that He asks is that we obey and trust Him. *He will not leave us nor forsake us. (Hebrews 13:5)* He will live in us so we need not fear what tomorrow will bring. *"Because He lives, we can face tomorrow. Because He lives, all fear is gone." (Gaither Hymn)* We need to believe Him, have faith in Him, and trust Him to be our security for the future. We need not worry about tomorrow; rather, we need to live for today in the loving presence of our LORD.

"Live realistically. Give generously. Adapt willingly. Trust fearlessly. Rejoice daily." (Charles Swindoll)

"Let my soul take refuge...beneath the shadow of Your wings: let my heart, this sea of restless waves, find peace in You, O God." (Augustine)

April 18
Basking in the Warmth of Jesus

Hebrews 11:1
Now faith is being sure of what we hope for and certain of what we do not see.

Weather is always unpredictable. One day it's in the 90s and the next it's in the 30s. One day we're wearing shorts and short sleeves and the next we're in turtle necks, sweatshirts and ear muffs. One day there is an unbelievable amount of rain and the next there is two feet or more of snow. One day it is calm and beautiful and the next tremendous tornadoes tear up entire towns in three minutes or less. Go figure. Aren't we that way with God, too? As long as everything is going along great and our way, we're believers trusting Him. When something goes wrong or we face an uncertain future, then we become angry and turn away from Him. Yes, we're as bad as the weather. The question now becomes that when our circumstances change, are we going to be faithful to our LORD? God is waiting for our answer. We can depend on our LORD through all things, good and bad. He is there and will not leave us. It's sure and certain, that God is who He says He is because He keeps His promises. When everything else goes awry, God never does. No matter what the weather is, we can bask in the warmth of Jesus. That's a promise.

"You are braver than you believe, stronger than you seem, and smarter than you think." (Author unknown)

"Faith is not about everything turning out okay. Faith is about being okay no matter how things turn out." (Annetta Powell)

April 19
Ever-Present Helper

Romans 8:34
Who is he that condemns? Christ Jesus, who died—more than that, who was raised to life—is at the right hand of God and is also interceding for us.

Jesus Christ gave His life for us and the gift of salvation is ours. He will not hold back anything we need to live for Him. Jesus is in heaven at the right hand of God interceding for us. He is the mediator between God and us and is always available to hear our prayers. He faced temptations but He did not give in to them. He can sympathize with us as He knows the temptations that we face daily. WOW!!! Jesus is our advocate and ever-present helper. It doesn't get any better than that. When God sees us, He sees His Son and we are forgiven.

"Every time I thought I was being rejected from something good, I was actually being re-directed to something better." (Author unknown)

"The book to read is not the one that thinks for you, but the one that makes you think." (Harper Lee)

April 20
Life is Like a Casserole

Isaiah 46:10
God affirms, "My counsel shall stand, and I will accomplish all My purpose."

When we think of casseroles, we think of leftovers or many ingredients thrown together to create a delicious meal. When we are grouped together with other people in life, we are often teamed up with those who have different agendas, personalities, lifestyles, beliefs, etc. In order for us to get something done, it takes a lot of love, patience and perseverance. Throughout the process, we must keep our eye on the goal and our focus on God. Easy, no. We put together a casserole by mixing and adding tasteful spices and ingredients. The ingredients in God's casserole of life are praying, communicating and reading His Word. When we mix together these components, it will help us to get along with others creating God's casserole that will be tastefully delightful. *Bon Appétit!*

"To make a difference in someone's life you don't have to be wise, rich, or beautiful. YOU JUST HAVE TO BE THERE WHEN THEY NEED YOU." (Steve Aitchinson)

"Faith is seeing light with your heart when all your eyes see is darkness." (Author unknown)

April 21
Hi Ho, Hi Ho, Off To Work We Go

Colossians 4:23-24
Whatever you do, work at it with all your heart, as working for the LORD, not for men, since you know that you will receive an inheritance from the LORD as a reward. It is the LORD Christ you are serving.

Whatever work we do, we need to do it for the LORD. We need an attitude of worship and service to God, whether it is school work, home work, working at a job, housework, or anything that needs to be done after we open our eyes for the day. Whatever we do, we should first seek the LORD, pray about the task, and then thank Him for the opportunity to serve Him. Imagine what our lives would be like if we did everything as an act of worship to our LORD. Imagine the freedom from drudgery and boredom. What an example to others if we are able to go through our days with smiles on our faces and singing praises to our LORD, doing what needs to be done without complaint or resentment. This is discipleship to its fullest. Imagine the amount of work we will get done with this attitude because God will be glorified as others watch Jesus at work in us. Hi ho, hi ho, off to work we go. Hi ho, hi ho, hi hoooooooo. We should enjoy each day, and, whatever we are doing, do it for the LORD. Let's praise the LORD and worship Him in all we do.

"True willpower and courage are not on the battlefield, but in everyday conquests over our inertia, laziness and boredom." (D.L. Moody)

"Success is the maximum utilization of the ability that you have." (Zig Ziglar)

April 22
Pouring Out Our Hearts

Psalm 62:8
Trust in Him at all times, O people; pour out your hearts to Him, for God is our refuge.

I've heard two versions of the song *"The Prayer"*- one sung by Josh Groban with Celine Dion and the other with Josh Groban and Charlotte Church. Both are beautiful, and they make me think about prayer and how more often than not we don't pray enough. God wants to hear from us throughout our day. He wants us to take everything to Him. Every time we turn a situation over to Him, He works it out for His Glory and our best. We also may learn something that He is trying to teach us. We must remember the power of God is with us. We just need to tap into it and love, trust and believe in Him. We can pour out our hearts to God in prayer and He listens.

Here are some of the words to the song, *"The Prayer."*
I pray You'll be our eyes
And watch us where we go
And help us to be wise
In times when we don't know
Let this be our prayer.
When we lose our way
Lead us to a place
Guide us with Your Grace
To a place where we'll be safe.
I pray we'll find Your light
And hold it in our hearts
When stars go out each night
Let this be our prayer.
When shadows fill our day
Lead us to a place
Guide us with Your Grace
Give us faith so we'll be safe.
We ask that life be kind
And watch us from above
We hope each soul will find
Another soul to love
Let this be our prayer.
Just like every child
Needs to find a place
Guide us with Your Grace
Give us faith so we'll be safe.

April 23
Let the "Son" Shine

Matthew 5:14
"You are the light of the world. A city on a hill cannot be hidden. Neither do people light a lamp and put it under a bowl. Instead they put it on its stand, and it gives light to everyone in the house. In the same way, let your light shine before men, that they may see your good deeds and praise your Father in heaven.

2 Corinthians 4:6
For God, who said, "Let light shine out of darkness," made His light shine in our hearts to give us the light of the knowledge of the glory of God in the face of Christ.

Whatever we do, let's do it for the LORD. Let's have a heart for Jesus and let the "Son" shine in and through us. When we go forth with the LORD and share Him with others, we are sharing His heart and love. He will shine in us, our smiles, our eyes and in our very actions. Let the "Son" shine in all we do and say today and always. He is the Light of the world. Let's go out there and shine for the "Son," our LORD. Those who bring "Son" shine to the lives of others will bask in it themselves.

"It doesn't take a huge spotlight to draw attention to how great our God is. All it takes is for one committed person to so let His light shine before men, that a world lost in darkness welcomes the light." (Author unknown)

"Into all our lives, in many simple, familiar…ways, God infuses this element of joy from the surprises of life, which unexpectedly brighten our days, and fill our eyes with light." (Samuel Longfellow)

April 24
Getting to Know Him

Matthew 11:25-26
At that time Jesus said, "I praise You, Father, Lord of heaven and earth, because You have hidden these things from the wise and learned, and revealed them to little children. Yes, Father, for this was Your good pleasure.

We need childlike faith to get to know God. It is not difficult, and it means we need to be humbly open to receive the truth of God's Word. God knows the answers and reveals them to us in His own time when He knows we are able to understand and accept His message. Our role in this relationship with Him is to trust and to "know" Him. That means to communicate with Him continually and read His Word. The answers are in the Bible. It always amazes me how we can read the same verse at different times and God will give us different meanings. No matter how old we are, we can have a child-like faith because we are children of God. He wants to teach us and wants us to know Him. We must get to know God and talk to Him. He's waiting and He's the best listener.

"Our faith is what connects our weakness to God's power." (Author unknown)

"Prayer: The world's greatest wireless connection." (Author unknown)

April 25
Caterpillars to Butterflies

2 Corinthians 5:21
God made Him who had no sin to be sin for us, so that in Him we might become the righteousness of God.

We are born as caterpillars and are sinful. We are in the cocoon of life, and, as we learn more about Jesus, we begin to stretch and want to break out. Once we accept Jesus as our LORD and Savior, we become butterflies and then a metamorphosis takes place. We are forgiven and we have everlasting righteousness. We trade our sin for His righteousness. In His Love, we change. Being "born again" is always a hard concept. We know of God, but we don't truly know Him intimately and the depth of His love much less let Him be in control of our lives. We need to surrender everything to Him. As we read His Word, we see that He loves us so very much. He is bigger than anything we face and we realize that *"we are the righteousness of God through Jesus Christ." (2 Corinthians 5:21)* Yes, we are not perfect and we still sin. The difference is that we know we can go to our Father and ask for His forgiveness. Just like that, we are forgiven and He promises that He will remember our sins no more. There may still be consequences, but, because of Jesus and the cross, we are assured of forgiveness. God loves us and in His love, we are changed from caterpillars to butterflies.

"Life itself is a gift." (Author unknown)

"The greater part of life is sunshine." (Thomas Jefferson)

April 26
I Am a Christian.
"Jesus loves me this I know, for the Bible tells me so." (Christian Hymn)

Christians - By Maya Angelou
When I say... "I am a Christian"
I'm not shouting "I'm clean livin' "
I'm whispering "I was lost,
Now I'm found and forgiven."

When I say... "I am a Christian"
I don't speak of this with pride.
I'm confessing that I stumble
and need Christ to be my guide.

When I say... "I am a Christian"
I'm not trying to be strong.
I'm professing that I'm weak
And need His strength to carry on.

When I say... "I am a Christian"
I'm not bragging of success.
I'm admitting I have failed
And need God to clean my mess.

When I say... "I am a Christian"
I'm not claiming to be perfect,
My flaws are far too visible
But, God believes I am worth it.

When I say... "I am a Christian"
I still feel the sting of pain.
I have my share of heartaches
So I call upon His name.

When I say... "I am a Christian"
I'm not holier than thou,
I'm just a simple sinner
Who received God's good grace, somehow!

Share this with somebody who already has this understanding as reinforcement. But more importantly, share this with those who do not have a clear understanding of what it means to be a Christian so that the myth that Christians think they are "perfect" or "better than others" can be dispelled.

April 27
Jesus Here

Psalm 19:14
May the words of my mouth and the meditation of my heart be pleasing in Your sight, O LORD, my Rock and my Redeemer.

My Mom always said, "Think before you speak." I carry that thought with me all the time and at times I forget it until it's too late. When we focus on everything and everyone around us and not on Jesus, we say and do things that are not what Jesus would have us do, think or say. When we say the above verse over and over to ourselves, we tend to listen more and think before we speak. It is a good way to spend our day. Let's live each day as if Jesus is physically beside us, hearing and seeing everything we do. Let's listen more than we speak because it's amazing what we will hear and learn about others and ourselves and, most importantly, about Jesus. We must remember, "Think before you speak."

"God walks with us. He scoops us up in His arms or simply sits with us in silent strength until we cannot avoid the awesome recognition that yes, even now, He is there." (Gloria Gaither)

"One of the best ways to demonstrate God's love is to listen to people." (Bruce Larsen)

April 28
Why Me? Why Not You?

Psalm 61:1-4
Hear my cry, O God; listen to my prayer. From the ends of the earth I call to You, I call as my heart grows faint; lead me to the Rock that is higher than I. For You have been my refuge, a strong tower against the foe. I long to dwell in Your tent forever and take refuge in the shelter of Your wings.

John 16:33
"I have told you these things, so that in Me you may have peace. In this world you will have trouble. But take heart! I have overcome the world."

Why me, LORD? Why not you? God never promised that because we are Christians we will never experience trials or tribulations. What He did promise is that whatever we experience, we will not be alone. God says, *"My Grace is sufficient for you."* Mercy, comfort and peace come through Jesus Christ. God gives us the ability to bear all things. We must stay faithful even under pressure. Our trials will produce perseverance and it is a time of learning. How can we ever know the depth of our character if we don't know how we react under pressure? Can we still be kind to others under pressure? Our characters are produced when we go through the valleys of troubles and we press our way through with God. God is there in the trenches with us and will help us to grow and learn. We know that all things work together for the good to those that love the LORD and are called according to His purpose. Whatever trials and tribulations we are experiencing, we need to wait on the LORD with trust and confidence because He has brought us through before. We know that what we are experiencing will end one day and we will be victorious. We know that our God will bring us through anything and we have faith in Him. His "will" will be done and one day God will answer the "whys" of our hearts. He promises to "never leave us nor forsake us." *(Hebrews 13:5)*

"Your worst day with Jesus will still be better than your best day was without Him." (Joyce Meyer)

"Don't give up; look up!" (Thrivent Financial)

April 29
Praise ye the LORD

Psalm 24:1
The earth is the LORD's, and everything in it, the world and all who live in it; For He founded it upon the seas and established it upon the waters.

Psalm 66:1-4
Shout with joy to God, all the earth! Sing the glory of His name; make His praise glorious! Say to God, "How awesome are Your deeds! So great is Your power that Your enemies cringe before You. All the earth bows down to You; They sing praise to You, they sing praise to Your Name."

Good Morning by Char Gaylord
The birds are singing
The sky is clearing
The sun is rising
The day is beginning.
Praise ye the LORD.
The earth is waking
The grass is growing
The flowers are blooming
Spring is rejoicing.
Praise ye the LORD.
Temperatures are rising.
It is a good morning
His love is unfailing
Spring is singing.
Praise ye the LORD.
Amen.

April 30
People Whisperer

John 15:26
"When the Counselor comes, whom I will send to you from the Father, the Spirit of truth who goes out from the Father, he will testify about me."

Romans 8:9
You, however, are controlled not by the sinful nature but by the Spirit, if the Spirit of God lives in you. And if anyone does not have the Spirit of Christ, he does not belong to Christ.

We have dog whisperers, horse whisperers and a people whisperer. Yes, indeed, we have a people whisperer. It is the Holy Spirit. When Jesus rose to be with His Father, God sent the Holy Spirit to live in all believers to remind us of God, Jesus and Heaven. Through the Holy Spirit, Jesus is spiritually present with us. God sent the Holy Spirit to guide, comfort and remind us of Jesus' words and truth. When we accept and receive Jesus as our LORD and Savior, we receive the Holy Spirit. The Holy Spirit helps us to become more like Jesus and helps us to have a personal relationship with Him. Jesus calls the Holy Spirit the Counselor and Spirit of Truth. Counselor conveys the helping, encouraging and strengthening work of the Spirit, and Spirit of Truth reminds us of the teaching and illuminating work of the Spirit. We are Christians because we have trusted Christ and acknowledged Him as our LORD, and the Holy Spirit lives in us. The Holy Spirit is God's promise or guarantee of eternal life for those who believe in Him. The Spirit is in us now by faith, and, by faith, we are certain to live with Christ forever. We must listen for the people whisperer. He will guide us in each prayer, each conversation and through each problem. He will empower us to serve our LORD and Savior, Jesus Christ, every moment of every day. The Holy Spirit is our people whisperer.

"Those who put everything in God's hand will eventually see God's hand in everything." (Author unknown)

"Solitude leads to enlightenment." (Greg Olsen)

May 1
God Is Faithful

1 Corinthians 1:9
God, who has called you into fellowship with His Son Jesus Christ our LORD, is faithful.

God is worthy of our trust and devotion. He is faithful all the time. We are His and He will lead us where He wants us to go. When we are afraid, lonely, sad, confused, happy, or celebrating life and blessings, we have a God who is faithful. In all things, He will work for our good because we love and trust Him. No matter what the day holds for us, we can have peace. We are His forever and when all else fails, God is faithful.

"The first and fundamental law of nature is to seek out peace and follow it." (Thomas Hobbes)

"Darkness cannot drive out darkness: only light can do that. Hate cannot drive out hate: only love can do that." (Martin Luther King, Jr.)

May 2
Doing the Laundry

Matthew 23:26
First wash the inside of the cup, and then the outside will become clean, too.

1 John 1:8-9
"If we claim to be without sin, we deceive ourselves and the truth is not in us. If we confess our sins, He is faithful and just and will forgive us our sins and purify us from all unrighteousness."

I love to do laundry. There is something gratifying about putting dirty clothes into the washing machine with soap and water, and then pushing a button. Within half an hour, poof—it comes out clean. That is easy enough for our clothing, but what about coming clean with Jesus? Jesus is waiting to wash away our stains of sin. Our part is to go to Him, confess our sins and ask for His forgiveness. Some stains are deeper than others, but He is the great "stain remover." He takes us and every one of our sins and washes us in His blood so that one day we will be whiter than snow. God's GRACE has come to us. We can step into the presence of Jesus. We should go to Him, and tell Him what is troubling us. We can trust Him to keep it all with Him as He is the great "secret keeper." Once He forgives, He promises to never, ever remember our sins again. WOW! That's my kind of doing laundry—to have those stains of sin removed forever. Will we sin again? Of course, that is our nature but we have the great "stain remover" and Washer who will cleanse us of our sins by forgiving us and drawing us closer to Him. By His blood on the cross, Jesus washes and removes all of our sins every day. There is nothing He will not forgive. It's time to do the laundry. Let's go get clean by the blood of Jesus.

"Courage does not always roar. Sometimes courage is the quiet voice at the end of the day saying I will try again tomorrow." (Author unknown)

"God puts each fresh morning, each new chance of life, into our hands as a gift to see what we will do with it." (Author unknown)

May 3
GRACE Stoops

John 8:6-8
But Jesus bent down and started to write on the ground with His finger. When they kept on questioning Him, He straightened up and said to them, "If any one of you is without sin, let him be the first to throw a stone at her." Again He stooped down and wrote on the ground.

Ephesians 2:4-5
But because of His great love for us, God, who is rich in mercy, made us alive in Christ even when we were dead in transgressions—it is by grace you have been saved.

Did we know that Jesus stoops? He does. He stoops low and lies on the ground to reach us. No matter how low we feel or how deep down we hurt, He is there. Jesus stoops. Jesus doesn't condemn us. Our own hearts condemn us because Satan is constantly attacking us with feelings and thoughts of guilt, shame, worthlessness and reminders of our failures. Satan is a liar and his accusations are not true. God knows everything about us, every detail. He created us and we have a unique purpose. God is in the mix with us. He doesn't leave us on our own to deal with a negative, accusing Satan. NO, He has risen. He has risen from the gates of hell, defying death, and now sits at the Right Hand of God, His Father and our Father, as our Priest. He intercedes for us with God. No more earthly condemnations. He rises to our defense. Jesus is our advocate and defender. He is the best defense attorney in the universe, pleading our cases before God. Jesus is the Judge's Son!! We are saved by GRACE—a GRACE that stoops to us in the lowest areas of our lives with forgiveness, love and compassion.

"Grace is God loving, God stooping, God coming to the rescue, God giving Himself generously in and through Jesus Christ." (John Stott)

"How great a God is He who gives God!" (Augustine)

May 4
We are a "Building" for Christ

2 Peter 1:5-8
For this very reason, make every effort to add to your faith goodness; and to goodness, knowledge; and to knowledge, self-control; and to self-control, perseverance; and to perseverance, godliness; and to godliness, brotherly kindness; and to brotherly kindness, love. For if you possess these qualities in increasing measure, they will keep you from being ineffective and unproductive in your knowledge of our LORD Jesus Christ.

We are a building. We are a building for Christ to dwell in, and we must keep growing in Him each and every day. We do that by reading His Word and learning about Him so that we can resemble Jesus and love and serve others. Our faith must result in action, growth in Christian character and the practice of moral discipline. We must be diligent about our Christian growth in order to be the best we can be in Christ and for Christ. It requires our discipline and obedience to Him. God empowers and enables us, but He also gives us the responsibility to learn and to grow. He wants to instill His character in us. Our "building" must be built on the solid rock foundation of Christ so that we will be the disciples He wants us to be.

"Knowledge is knowing what to say. Wisdom is knowing when to say it." (Author unknown)

"Train your mind and heart to see the good in everything. There is always something to be grateful for." (Simple Reminders)

May 5
Right, Left or Centered

Isaiah 30:21
Whether you turn to the right or to the left, your ears will hear a voice behind you, saying, "This is the way; walk in it."

God will correct us when we get off His path. The question then becomes are we willing to follow Him when we hear His voice of correction? We must remember, He always acts out of love for us, and He is walking with us on our life's journey. Are we following God or following the way of the world? Wherever we are, we need to stop, look at our decisions, and ask for His guidance, wisdom and discernment. We must patiently wait for His answer as we trust Him and pray for His love, grace, mercy, and peace to surround us. At the same time, we need to stay in His Word and keep His promises close to our hearts. We can believe and trust the One who, out of His great love for us, sent His Son to the cross for our salvation. We must not go willy-nilly on our way, following the idol of the day. It is our choice. What will it be—right, left or better yet, staying centered on the One who loves us beyond our imagination.

"Life has many different chapters; one bad chapter doesn't mean it is the end of the book." (Zig Ziglar)

"Strength doesn't come from what you can do. It comes from overcoming the things you once thought you couldn't." (Rikki Rogers)

May 6
"I Lift Things up; I Put Them Down."

1 Thessalonians 5:16
Be joyful always; pray continually; give thanks in all circumstances, for this is God's will for you in Christ Jesus.

A couple of years ago, there was a Planet Fitness commercial with a weight lifter repeating over and over in his best Arnold Schwarzenegger rendition, "I lift things up; I put them down." It gave us a good laugh. In our prayer life, we continually "lift up" our prayers to our Heavenly Father as we take everything to Him. We praise and thank Him for all of our blessings. We take our troubles and cares to God and when we do, we lay them down on the altar at the foot of the cross, supposedly never to pick them up again. Oh, we want to pick them up—our "crosses to bear" and often we do, but that is not what God wants. He wants us to come to Him to share what's in our hearts and then trust Him to handle our circumstances. We must give everything over to Him. As we "lift things up," we must remember to put them down and LEAVE them at the foot of the cross. God's will is the best for us and He can handle everything. We should step back and let Him.

"Progress involves risks. You can't steal second base and keep your foot on first." (Frederick B. Wilcox)

"Perfection exists not in doing extraordinary things but in doing ordinary things extraordinarily well." (Angelique Arnauld)

May 7
To Forgive

Micah 6:8
"What does the LORD require of you? To act justly and to love mercy and to walk humbly with your God."

Micah 7:18
"Who is a God like You, who pardons sin and forgives the transgression of the remnant of his inheritance? You do not stay angry forever but delight to show mercy. You will again have compassion on us; you will tread our sins underfoot and hurl all our iniquities into the depths of the sea."

The other day I was asked to give my definition of what it means to forgive. It was a question that took me by surprise, but one that I've thought about a lot throughout my lifetime. Webster's defines the word *forgive* as "to give up resentment against or the desire to punish; stop being angry with; pardon. To give up all claim to punish or exact penalty for (an offense); overlook; to cancel or remit."

As children of God, we cannot go through life without forgiving others, because unforgiveness will devour and eventually destroy us. God forgives us and remembers our sins no more, and, because He forgives us, He expects us to forgive others. It doesn't mean that whatever happened will not have consequences for the person(s) involved, but it does mean that we can let go and move on in order to heal and grow. We can't keep stirring the pot of resentment and anger as this will eventually destroy us, our relationships with others and maybe with God. Often, we are angry at God for circumstances out of our control. We need to talk to Him and pray about our anger and ask for His forgiveness. Forgiving doesn't take away from the situation, but it acknowledges our desire to let God handle the problem and allows us to have peace. It may take awhile but, in the end, we will not be eaten up with anger, disappointment, resentment or destruction of other beautiful relationships that He has put in our lives. We should forgive as God forgives us and be free of the bitterness. By the blood of Jesus, we are forgiven all of our sins, so how can we not obey our LORD and forgive others.

"What a lesson I learned, forgiveness, forgiveness, forgiveness again." (Dr. Wayne W. Dyer)

"Even as the angry vengeful thoughts boiled through me, I saw the sin of them. Jesus Christ had died for this man; was I going to ask for more? LORD Jesus, I prayed, forgive me and help me to forgive him....Jesus, I cannot forgive him. Give me your forgiveness....And so I discovered that it is not on our forgiveness any more than on our goodness that the world's healing hinges, but on His. When He tells us to love our enemies, He gives along with the command, the love itself." (Corrie ten Boom)

May 8
To Forget

Isaiah 43:25
"I, even I, am He who blots out your transgressions, for My own sake, and remembers your sins no more."

Hebrews 8:12
"For I will forgive their wickedness and will remember their sins no more."

Hebrews 10:17
"Their sins and lawless acts I will remember no more."

Forgiving is often a lot easier than forgetting. People have often said, "I can forgive but I will never forget." As Christians we read God's Word and learn that He forgives and forgets our sins. God forgives completely and remembers our sins no more so that there is no need to confess our past sins repeatedly. We can be confident that the sins we confess and renounce are forgiven and forgotten instantly. Through Grace, Jesus, by His blood, forgives us our sins and brings us into a loving relationship with God. Because God forgives our sins and remembers them no more, He requires us to also forgive and forget. He doesn't want us to keep dwelling on an offense or hurtful situation. As we contemplate forgiveness, we also should be contemplating the forgetting of offenses committed by us and others. It may take years to forgive and more years to forget, but God is waiting to help us at every opportunity. God is waiting to heal us of the burdens of not forgiving and forgetting. Jesus forgave those who put Him to death. In Luke 23:34, Jesus said, "Father, forgive them, for they do not know what they are doing." God is gracious and He will forgive us and give us a new life through His Son. Once we are able to forgive and forget, we will have a peace that we have never experienced.

"Forgiveness is an act of the will, and the will can function regardless of the temperature of the heart." (Corrie ten Boom)

"Courage does not always roar. Sometimes courage is the quiet voice at the end of the day saying I will try again tomorrow." (Author unknown)

May 9
Our Hope

Psalm 100:5
For the LORD is good and His love endures forever; His faithfulness continues through all generations.

We can face anything when we have total confidence in our God and trust Him in all areas of our lives. Do not lose sight of God. He wants all of us and He knows the areas of our lives that we have not yet surrendered to Him. We must go deep and look in at ourselves and the areas that we still want to control. We must surrender them to Him and ask Him to take control. He will because He is the SOURCE of everything. In prayer we can go to God. We can ask Him anything especially to help us handle things. God will use many different avenues to answer our prayers. He may whisper directly to us or He may use another person or even nature. He may direct us to a certain verse or verses in Scripture to answer our prayer. We must wait on Him, be open to His direction, keep looking for Him all around us and then obey Him. We'll know when it is God because we'll have peace or a certain confidence. When we put Him first and trust our very lives and those we love to Him, we will live a life of peace, hope and most certainly love. God will reveal Himself to us in the most amazing ways. He is the God of all hope, love and peace. He gave His all for us when He sent His Son, Jesus, to save us so let's give Him our all and trust His love.

"Do not look to your hope, but to Christ, the SOURCE of your hope." (Charles H. Spurgeon)

"Faith is the centerpiece of a connected life. It allows us to live by the grace of invisible strands." (Terry Tempest Williams)

May 10
A Mother's Love

Proverbs 31:25-26
She is clothed with strength and dignity; she can laugh at the days to come. She speaks with wisdom, and faithful instruction is on her tongue.

A mother is that very special person God has given to us to be His hands on earth. A mother's love for her family and others is a blessing that goes on and on! It is not always an easy job and it can be messy. However, the job of being a mom is one that has meaning and purpose. A mom loves, teaches, laughs and cries, but she wouldn't have it any other way because deep down, hidden under all the mess, is something beautiful. It's called love and joy. When a mother looks into the faces of children, she sees God's love. These children do not have to be her own as a woman can be a mother to other children. Biologically, not all women are mothers, but they can be a mother to others in such a way that children will know the love of God. Women are members of unique clubs called Womanhood and Motherhood. Women can share the love and joy that God has given them with a child of any age today and every day.

"For a season, a woman is a mother in her home. For all of her life, she's a mother in her heart." (Holley Gerth)

"To the world, we are a mother. To our family, we are the world." (Author unknown)

"When God thought of mother, He must have laughed with satisfaction…so rich, so deep, so divine, so full of soul, power, and beauty was the conception." (Henry Ward Beecher)

May 11
Joy for Every Day

Ecclesiastes 8:15
So I commend the enjoyment of life, because nothing is better for a man under the sun than to eat and drink and be glad. Then joy will accompany him in his work all the days of the life God has given him under the sun."

We can have joy every day because each day God gives us what we need. There is a daily measure of work, food and pleasure, *"Thy daily bread,"* if you will. Our job is to learn to accept and enjoy what He has given to us and to be thankful for each day as we continue to do His work. Every morning is new and we are refreshed, stronger and ready to tackle what comes our way. We need to trust Him knowing that He is in control. No matter what the future holds, we have a loving God who will guide us through the quagmires of each day. We must not let what we don't know about the future destroy the joy God wants to give us today. We can be joyful and content each day of our journey with Him.

"God is like oxygen, you can't see Him but you can't live without Him." (Wanda West)

"Don't wait for things to get better. Life will always be complicated. Learn to be happy right now, otherwise you'll run out of time. (Author unknown)

May 12
Our LORD Can Do Anything

Luke 1:37
For nothing is impossible with God.

2 Corinthians 12:9
But He said to me, "My grace is sufficient for you, for My power is made perfect in weakness."

When we are weak, He is strong. When we are tired and don't feel like we can take another step, God carries us and continues on with His plan. In our weaknesses, He can do His best work. He can fill us with His power and then we will be stronger than ever before—"For nothing is impossible with God."

"Some people grumble that roses have thorns; I'm grateful that thorns have roses."
(Alphonse Karr)

"Those who contemplate the beauty of the earth find reserves of strength that will endure as long as life lasts." (Rachel Carson)

May 13
Now We See Him....Now We Don't

Acts 1:6-11
So when they met together, they asked Him, "LORD, are You at this time going to restore the kingdom of Israel? He said to them: "It is not for you to know the times or dates the Father has set by His own authority. But you will receive power when the Holy Spirit comes on you; and you will be my witnesses in Jerusalem, and in all Judea and Samaria, and to the ends of the earth." After He said this, He was taken up before their very eyes, and a cloud hid Him from their sight.

Ascension Day, the day that Christians celebrate Jesus Christ's ascension into heaven to sit at the right hand of God the Father, occurs 40 days after Easter. It is the day Jesus blessed the disciples and then disappeared into a cloud. Just like that, poof—He was gone. Now we see Him...now we don't. The good news is that He didn't leave them or us alone because, just as Jesus promised, He sent the Holy Spirit to live in us. Jesus may not be here physically but He is here spiritually. Jesus sits at God's right hand where He has authority over heaven and earth, but the Holy Spirit is Jesus living in us to love, guide and comfort. Jesus' ascension into heaven tells us that there is something more after this life. It gives us hope of eternal life and the glorious promise of God's love, power and strength. He didn't leave us to our own devices. He's right here with us because the Holy Spirit is the third part of the Trinity—God the Father, Jesus the Son and the Holy Spirit, the Counselor and Guide. Jesus dwells in us through the Holy Spirit. We can talk to Him at any time because, as baptized children of God, we believe in His life, resurrection and ascension into heaven and the Holy Trinity. The disciples were witnesses to God's great power and to the promises of Jesus. We, too, can be witnesses for Jesus as we share the Good News with all those we meet. Now we see Jesus as we get to know Him better.

"Life is about finding the joy and purpose and meaning in all the chaos." (Author unknown)

"Remember that at every single moment of your life, you have the choice to either be a host to God or a hostage to your ego." (Dr. Wayne W. Dyer)

May 14
Seeds of Faith

Matthew 13:31-32
He told them another parable: "The kingdom of heaven is like a mustard seed, which a man took and planted in his field. Though it is the smallest of all your seeds, yet when it grows, it is the largest of garden plants and becomes a tree, so that the birds of the air come and perch in its branches."

Spring is a time of growth and new beginnings. The ground turns green, the trees bud, and we plant flowers, patiently waiting for them to bloom into flourishing arrays of color. Spring is a season of hope. The seeds of faith we plant are like that, too. We read the Word, pray, worship and sing praises to God. We live our lives with God at the center, constantly listening for His guidance. We are planting seeds of faith when we teach and share the Word of God with others and when they see our faith working in us. It can be a facial expression, a request for prayer, a Bible verse we quote or a simple "please" and "thank you." We plant seeds wherever we go and with whatever we do. God, through the Holy Spirit, uses our words and actions to lead others to Him. It is not us but Him shining through us that grow these seeds. The mustard seed is the smallest of seeds and can produce a great harvest, just as our seeds of faith, although small, can produce great results impacting those around us. The ground is fertile, so we should plant some seed and wait for the flourishing bouquets of color to bloom. It is amazing what our God can do with a little seed, and we may never know the impact that we have on others, but God knows because we do it for Him.

"At some point in life the world's beauty becomes enough. You don't need to photograph, paint or even remember it. It is enough." (Toni Morrison)

"The littlest birds sing the prettiest songs." (The Be Good Tanyas)

May 15
Open and Shut Doors...

Revelation 3:7-8
.... "What He opens no one can shut, and what he shuts no one can open. I know your deeds. See, I have placed before you an open door that no one can shut. I know you have little strength, yet you have kept My Word and have not denied My name."

There are times that we are waiting patiently for God to show us what He wants us to do for Him. Oftentimes, we think we have an answer and, then, at the very last minute, we get a nudge or something happens to change our plan or thoughts. The virtual door shuts and it shuts tightly. Disappointment or relief washes over us like an early morning shower. What we must remember is that God has a plan for our lives. He will open doors that will most benefit and glorify Him, and when He does, we have a decision to make as to whether or not we are going to walk through. At other times, God will close a door. In fact, He may actually slam it shut. Now what? Do we push through it because we want it so badly and then realize we have made a very big mistake because we are not going with His help and blessing? We must pray and wait and wait and pray. Anytime God has something for us to do, no matter how difficult, if He has opened the door and we walk through, He will be with us. He will help us to achieve whatever He has planned as long as we glorify Him and work to build His kingdom. If the door shuts, then we must pray and rely on Him to guide us wherever He wants us to go. We should look for those open and shut doors. We must ask God for His guidance and discernment and then trust Him. If it is His will, we'll have peace even if it changes our lives and circumstances. He will provide for us when we obey Him and follow His commands. He is an awesome God.

"People were designed for accomplishment, engineered for success, and endowed with the seeds of greatness." (Zig Ziglar)

"Direct the total energy of your powers so that you may achieve everything your election as a child of God provides; rise every time to whatever occasion may come your way. We are here to submit to His will so that He may work through us what He wants. Once we realize this, He will make us broken bread and poured-out wine with which to feed and nourish others." (Oswald Chambers)

May 16
Forgiveness

Luke 6:37
Do not judge, and you will not be judged. Do not condemn, and you will not be condemned. Forgive, and you will be forgiven.

Colossians 3:13
Bear with each other and forgive whatever grievances you may have against one another. Forgive as the LORD forgave you.

We have all faced those days when someone has treated us in an unkind or harsh manner. For some reason, we walk away feeling that stabbing pain of hurt, rejection or loneliness. Our initial reaction may be to lash out at them and often we do. Then we feel the guilt that comes from knowing that our Father in Heaven would not want us to react in such a manner. He forgives us and He has commanded us to forgive others. So as we face these situations, we must remember His love for us and His forgiveness of our sins. Of course, it is hard to forgive someone. Then again, how many times do we ask our Lord for His forgiveness? We should forgive others, let go and find the amazing peace that only God can give.

"He that cannot forgive others breaks the bridge over which he must pass himself; for every man has need to be forgiven." (Thomas Fuller)

"After a good dinner, one can forgive anybody, even one's own relations." (Oscar Wilde)

May 17
Children of God

1 John 3:1
How great is the love the Father has lavished on us, that we should be called children of God!

1John 2:28
And now, dear children, continue in Him, so that when He appears we may be confident and unashamed before Him at His coming.

As children of God who read the Word, we learn about Him and how much He loves us. There are four points we should always remember: 1) we are all children of God and He loves us very much; 2) we should always abide in Him because God is a safe place for us; 3) we should stay connected to God through worship, Bible study and our Christian community; and 4) we need to cling to the cross and the forgiveness God gave us through Jesus. He is not expecting perfection from us, but He wants to be the center of our lives and wants us to put our faith in Him. We can continue to grow in our faith and learn who we are in Jesus as we continue on our journey with our loving Heavenly Father.

"Out of clutter, find simplicity." (Author unknown)

"I bring you the gift of these four words: I believe in you." (Author unknown)

May 18
We Belong to God

John 17:25-26
"Righteous Father, though the world does not know You, I know You, and they know that You have sent Me. I have made You known to them, and will continue to make You known in order that the love You have for Me may be in them and that I myself may be in them."

Wherever we go and whatever we do, we belong to God. Jesus prayed for us before He went to the cross to die for us and our sins. He came here with a mission and He completed it. We are His. It is the most amazing thing to know that Jesus prayed for us before we were even born. He prayed for unity with Him, protection and holiness for us. What confidence that gives us to know that our LORD was thinking of us as He was facing the unthinkable. He was with His Father before He came here and was separated from Him for a time. He suffered the most from that separation, but He loved His Father and obeyed Him and in turn, loved us too. Thank You, Jesus, for Your love and sacrifice. We are Yours.

"We could never learn to be brave and patient, if there were only joy in the world." (Helen Keller)

"Works of love are always works of joy. We don't need to look for happiness: if we have love for others we'll be given it. It is the gift of God." (Mother Teresa)

May 19
Our Father

Matthew 6: 9
…"Our Father in heaven, hallowed be Your name,"

God, our Father in heaven, loves us. He hears our prayers and listens to us whenever we call. He is never too busy. He doesn't play video games, watch television, or get involved in activities that take His attention away from us. He is always there. He is personal and loving as well as majestic and holy. The word "hallowed" means to honor or make sacred, santify. We need to be respectful of God, honor and praise Him every day, and use His name in ways that would honor Him. Our Father in heaven forgives us and takes us back when we turn away from Him and sin. He welcomes us back with open arms no matter what we've done. He is the most wonderful, loving and gracious Father. We can go to Him with anything; we are His children. Our Father is always here for us and loves us unconditionally. No matter what we do or where we go, He is there listening and always has time for us.

"One evening a little girl was taking a walk with her father. Looking up at the stars she exclaimed, "Daddy, if the wrong side of heaven is so beautiful, what must the right side be like!" (Author unknown)

"God loves you. Hammer the truth into your heart and mind every day. It will make a difference." (Billy Graham)

May 20
One with the Father

John 17:21
"...that all of them may be one, Father, just as You are in Me and I am in You. May they also be in Us so that the world may believe that You have sent Me."

God's purpose or plan for us is to be one with Him and to have a relationship with Him. Above all else, He wants us to seek His kingdom and to put Him first. We get caught up in the everyday business of life and forget to think about God and His promises to take care of us. Often we worry so much about our lives, our families and our situations that we forget the One who knows all and can take care of everything. Jesus prayed that we would be one with Him and His Father. He knew that is what God wanted, too. God will work on us until we are one with Him. Jesus prayed to Him about us and for us. We should be thankful that God loves us so much that He wants us to be one with Him.

"More than anybody, better than anybody, that's how God loves you. Feel His love." (Author unknown)

"Where there is great love there are always miracles." (Willa Cather)

May 21
Know God—Know peace
No God—No peace

Philippians 4:6-7
Do not be anxious about anything, but in everything, by prayer and petition, with thanksgiving, present your requests to God. And the peace of God, which transcends all understanding, will guard your hearts and your minds in Christ Jesus.

"Know God—Know peace. No God—No peace." We've probably all seen this saying at one time or another and how true it is!! Knowing God and that He loves us and is with us in all situations gives us a certain peace. Without Him, there is no peace. No matter what we are facing, when we talk to Him, pray to Him and surrender all to Him, a peace fills us. A deep-seeded peace that is comforting and assuring. This peace will give us the assurance that we will get through every situation with Him by our side, no matter the outcome. This is an assurance that all of us need. Knowing God is to know peace. Worry less—pray more. True peace is to know that our loving God is in control and we are His children. He will take care of us and the peace that we have is a "peace that passes all understanding."

"God's help is near and always available, but it is only given to those who seek it." (Max Lucado)

"Look up and receive the quiet contentment of the LORD Jesus. Reflecting His peace is proof that you are right with God, because you are exhibiting the freedom to turn your mind to Him. When a person confers with Jesus Christ, the confusion stops, because there is no confusion in Him." (Oswald Chambers)

May 22
Shut the Door

Psalm 46:10
"Be still, and know that I am God;"

Matthew 6:8 Jesus said:
"But when you pray, go into your room, close the door and pray to your Father, who is unseen. Then your Father, who sees what is done in secret, will reward you. And when you pray, do not keep on babbling like pagans, for they think they will be heard because of their many words. Do not be like them, for your Father knows what you need before you ask him."

Private communication with God is the essence of prayer. There is a time and a place for public prayer, but private prayer when God is the only audience is where we can be honest, sincere and pour out our hearts to Him. Prayer takes effort. It shouldn't be but it often is because we need to slow down and stop our minds from working overtime. We need to "shut the door" on all those things that keep wandering in whenever we get into a quiet state to pray. Going into our room and shutting the door can mean freeing our minds from any interruption of idle and wandering thoughts. Deliberate praying takes discipline and conscious effort. We should have a "secret place" where we go to meet God and have a conversation with Him. God is with us all the time. He knows us and He loves it when we talk to Him all day long. The "secret place" is inside us where we focus on Him and talk to Him knowing that He is there and He's listening. God is right in the middle of all we are going through and waiting for us to lean on Him and tell Him what we are feeling. When we "shut the door" we are being still before God in a time and a place where we turn off our emotions, focus on Him and remember Him. We can't doubt a God who is with us every moment of our lives. We should "shut the door" on all that is going on around us and talk to the One who is on the inside of us, waiting. His footprint will be forever on our hearts and on all we do. We can "shut the door" and have a nice moment with the One who loves us beyond imagination. We must take time to be still and know Him because He knows us and all that we need. We can "shut the door" because our Father is waiting.

"Let prayer be the key of the morning and the bolt of the evening." (Matthew Henry)

"A prayerless Christian is a powerless Christian." (Billy Graham)

May 23
Nourishment

Matthew 4:5
Jesus answered, "It is written: 'Man does not live on bread alone, but on every word that comes from the mouth of God.'

A church goer wrote a letter to the editor of a newspaper and complained that it made no sense to go to church every Sunday. "I've gone for 30 years now," he wrote, "and in that time I have heard something like 3,000 sermons, but for the life of me, I can't remember a single one of them so I think I'm wasting my time and the priests are wasting theirs by giving sermons at all." This started a real controversy in the "Letters to the Editor" column. Much to the delight of the editor, it went on for weeks until someone wrote this clincher: "I've been married for 30 years now. In that time my wife has cooked some 32,000 meals. But, for the life of me, I cannot recall the entire menu for a single one of those meals. But I do know this... They all nourished me and gave me the strength I needed to do my work. If my wife had not given me these meals, I would be physically dead today. Likewise, if I had not gone to church for nourishment, I would be spiritually dead today!" When you are DOWN to nothing....God is UP to something! Faith sees the invisible, believes the incredible and receives the impossible! We can thank God for our physical AND our spiritual nourishment!

"Nourishment: If you're spiritually alive, you're going to love this! If you're spiritually dead, you won't want to read it. If you're spiritually curious, there is still hope!" (Author unknown)

"B. I. B. L. E. BIBLE simply means: Basic Instructions Before Leaving Earth! Did you know that ...When you carry "the Bible" Satan has a headache; When you open it, he collapses; When he sees you reading it he loses his strength, AND When you stand on the Word of God, Satan can't hurt you! When you are about to share God's Word with others, the devil will discourage you!" (Author unknown)

May 24
The Holy Spirit

Acts 1:5
For John baptized with water, but in a few days you will be baptized with the Holy Spirit.

Pentecost is when the Holy Spirit descended some 2,000 years ago after Jesus ascended to heaven to sit at the right hand of God. In Joel 2:28-29 it says, "And afterward, I will pour out my Spirit on all the people. Your sons and daughters will prophesy, your old men will dream dreams and your young men will see visions. Even on my servants, both men and women, I will pour out my Spirit in those days." This is about a God who is available to every believer. It is about seeing God as active or visible in the world now that Jesus has ascended into heaven and the Holy Spirit has arrived.

The Holy Spirit lives in all who believe in Jesus and what He did on the cross and His resurrection. The Holy Spirit was sent after Jesus ascended to heaven to live in our hearts. God's kingdom remains in all believers through the presence of the Holy Spirit—*God with us and in us.* AWESOME!! We're not alone. The Holy Spirit will comfort, guide, teach, love and be with us. The Holy Spirit works in us to help us become like Christ. We receive the Holy Spirit when we receive Jesus. Pentecost is a time for us to discover that we, along with other Christians, can take the Good News of God's vision to others so that they will know and believe in Him.

"The Holy Spirit is God the evangelist." (J.I. Packer)

"Though every believer has the Holy Spirit, the Holy Spirit does not have every believer." (A.W. Tozer)

May 25
The LORD is Our Strength

Exodus 15:2
The LORD is my strength and my song; He has become my salvation. He is my God, and I will praise Him, my father's God, and I will exalt Him.

Psalm 118:14
The LORD is my strength and my song; He has become my salvation.

As we turn on the morning news, we see the reports of devastation. Our hearts wring with the pain, suffering and grieving with what others are going through. It is beyond most of our imaginations. We think we know but we don't unless we've lived through similar situations. We are bystanders and we wonder what we can do to help. As ambassadors for Christ, we are to be about His business representing Him to a lost world. Jesus said in Luke 22:27, "I am among you as the one who serves." His ultimate act of service was giving His life as a ransom for many. (Matthew 20:28). We can serve others by praying. We may not know what people need but God does. We can ask Him to bring help and comfort. We can give of our talents and treasures by giving to trustworthy organizations that are on the ground in the midst of the devastation. We can also help our neighbor. Give them a ride if they need it. A smile and a kind word will go a long way to help someone face the day. As children of God, we are called to come alongside someone who is struggling. To walk with the LORD is to walk with someone else. Our greatest treasure is to share Jesus with others and His message of salvation. We share His love when we help others and serve others as He served us. In the midst of devastation and grief, there is hope in the LORD. "The LORD is my strength and my song; He has become my salvation." We can go in peace and serve the LORD.

"Like water from a cool spring, generosity refreshes both the giver and the receiver." (Thrivent Financial)

"Take life day by day, and be grateful for the little things. Don't get stressed over what you can't control." (Author unknown)

May 26
Details, Details, Details

He collects every tear in a bottle. (Psalm 56:8)
He numbers every hair on our heads. (Luke 12:7)
He knows every hurt in our hearts. (Psalm 34:18)

God cares about every detail of our lives. He knows all that we are experiencing. Even in our deepest sorrows—God cares! He understands us—He even knows the number of hairs on our heads. When we feel discouraged and are sure that no one understands, we must remember that God knows every problem and sees every tear. He loves us, He cares for us and He will make sure not one detail is overlooked. God promises to be close to the brokenhearted. He promises to be our Source of power, courage and wisdom, helping us through our problems and daily lives. No matter how insignificant something may seem to us, God cares because we belong to Him. He cares right down to the last detail. Our LORD knows we need His help and He is by our sides.

"God cares about every detail." (Author unknown)

"The choice is up to you. It can be, "Good morning God!" or "Good God, morning." (Dr. Wayne W. Dyer)

May 27
Remembering

Psalm 116:15
Precious in the sight of the LORD is the death of His saints.

God stays close to us even in death. Believers (saints) are precious and valuable to God.
Every day we should remember and be thankful for all those who have made the ultimate sacrifice for our freedoms. We should ask our LORD to bless those service men and women who have died in the line of duty for our country. We also ask Him to bless their families who are left behind and who must go on without them. May we never, forget them and may we help those left behind. We should forever be thankful for these very brave souls, for America and our freedoms. We should ask the Lord to always keep His Hand on us, watch over and guide us. We should thank our LORD for our blessings of freedom and life. No matter what happens we are the LORD's. He has us in His Hands and we will be redeemed. God bless America and all those who serve and protect us each and every day.

"We know not what the future holds, but we do know who holds the future." (Willie J. Ray)

"Above all the grace and the gifts that Christ gives to His beloved is that of overcoming self." (St. Francis of Assisi)

May 28
Assurance

John 14:6 Jesus answered, "I am the Way and the Truth and the Life."

Hebrews 10:22
...let us draw near to God with a sincere heart in full assurance of faith, having our hearts sprinkled to cleanse us from a guilty conscience and having our bodies washed with pure water.

Webster's Dictionary says *assurance* "means sureness; confidence; certainty; a promise; a guarantee." The Bible says "assurance" is characterized by full conviction or confidence; made certain. We have the assurance that we can draw near to God without anything standing in the way. Jesus is the path and the only way to get to God. By uniting our lives with His, we are united with God. We have this assurance that God forgives us, loves us and accepts us for who we are. Blessed Assurance, Jesus is mine.

Blessed Assurance by Fanny Crosby
Blessed assurance, Jesus is mine;
Oh, what a foretaste of glory divine!
Heir of salvation, purchase of God,
Born of His Spirit, washed in His blood.

Refrain:
This is my story, this is my song,
Praising my Savior all the day long.
This is my story, this is my song,
Praising my Savior all the day long.

Perfect submission, perfect delight,
Visions of rapture now burst on my sight;
Angels descending, bring from above
Echoes of mercy, whispers of love.

Perfect submission, all is at rest,
I in my Savior am happy and blest;
Watching and waiting, looking above,
Filled with His goodness, lost in His love.

May 29
Thankful for Prayer

1 Thessalonians 5:17
Pray without ceasing

Prayer is an opportunity for us to walk through our day and every situation with the confidence that Jesus is by our side. Because we are able to talk to Him, praying is our lifeblood, and it is our certainty that somebody is watching over us. We can talk to God silently and continually in our hearts. We know that prayers are answered every time at the right time. The answers that God gives may not be what we are praying for but they are perfect for us. Let's have a prayerful attitude and keep praying because God is listening, and He will answer at just the right time. Being thankful for prayer is another way to praise our LORD for His wisdom, promises and His sense of humor.

"Great works are performed not by strength but by perseverance." (Samuel Johnson)

"A well-developed sense of humor is the pole that adds balance to your steps as you walk the tightrope of life." (William Arthur Ward)

May 30
Our Anchor

Romans 15:13
May the God of hope fill you with all joy and peace as you trust in Him, so that you may overflow with hope by the power of the Holy Spirit.

Hebrews 6:18-20
God did this so that, by two unchangeable things in which it is impossible for God to lie, we who have fled to take hold of the hope offered to us may be greatly encouraged. We have this hope as an anchor for the soul, firm and secure. It enters the inner sanctuary behind the curtain, where Jesus, who went before us, has entered on our behalf. He has become a high priest forever, in the order of Melchizedek.

The definition of *anchor* is "anything that gives or seems to give stability or security; to keep from drifting away." Jesus is our anchor. We can be secure in His promises because He is truth. He embodies all truth and He cannot lie. Just as a ship anchor holds firmly to the seabed, our hope is secure and immovable, anchored in God. Jesus Christ is our foundation, hope, creator, and path to eternal life. He is faithful and true. We can place our hope and very lives in His Hands because He has us and won't let go. When we honestly and sincerely ask Him to forgive us from our sins, He will do it. This alone should give us encouragement, assurance, confidence and HOPE. Let's grab hold of this unstoppable and immoveable anchor because Jesus is firm, secure and in control. We are anchored in God. We are accepted and loved by God.

"What counts is not necessarily the size of the dog in the fight—it's the size of the fight in the dog." (Dwight D. Eisenhower)

"If you do not hope, you will not find what is beyond your hopes." (St. Clement of Alexandria)

May 31
A Moment with Him

Romans 15:13
May the God of hope fill you with all joy and peace as you trust in Him, so that you may overflow with hope by the power of the Holy Spirit.

It only takes a moment to take everything to our LORD. He's waiting and He is always listening. "Jesus." That's the only word we need to say and, amazingly, a peace will come over us, a peace that surpasses all understanding. We should just keep saying "Jesus" over and over again. Jesus loves us; yes He does. We can spend a moment with Jesus. He knows us and wants our burdens. He took everything to the cross and bore everything for us. He knows what we are going through. We must trust and lean on Him. It only takes a moment, spend it with Him. We should walk with Jesus in all that we do.

"We mutter and sputter,
We fume and we spurt.
We mumble and grumble;
Our feelings get hurt.
We can't understand things;
Our vision grown dim.
When all that we need is
A moment with Him." (Author unknown)

"When we slow down, quiet the mind, and allow ourselves to feel hungry for something that we do not understand, we are dipping into the abundant well of spiritual longing." (Elizabeth Lesser)

June 1
The Tree of Life

Genesis 2:9
And the LORD God made all kinds of trees grow out of the ground—trees that were pleasing to the eye and good for food. In the middle of the garden were the tree of life and the tree of knowledge of good and evil.

Revelation 22:1-2
Then the angel showed me the river of the water of life, as clear as crystal, flowing from the throne of God and of the Lamb down the middle of the great street of the city. On each side of the river stood "The Tree of Life," bearing twelve crops of fruit, yielding its fruit every month. And the leaves of the tree are for the healing of the nations.

The cross is "The Tree of Life." The cross is where Jesus' suffering and death restored us to God and to life eternal. "The Tree of Life" is the love of God. Our sins are forgiven through the blood of Jesus on the cross and we have a secure future with God. Eternal life with God has been pictured as eating from the Tree of Life. The Tree of Life in Revelation is like the Tree of Life in Genesis. After Adam and Eve sinned in the Garden of Eden, they were forbidden to eat from the Tree of Life because they could not have eternal life as long as they were under sin's control. Because Jesus' blood sacrifice was to save us and not to eliminate sin, we are forgiven. We will be able to eat freely from the Tree of Life when sin's control over us is destroyed and our eternity with God is secure.

"God writes the Gospel not in the Bible alone, but also on trees, and in the flowers and clouds and stars." (Martin Luther)

"Take care of your life; and the LORD will take care of your death." (George Whitefield)

June 2
Our Purpose

Micah 6:8
He has showed you, O man, what is good. And what does the LORD require of you? To act justly and to love mercy and to walk humbly with your God.

We've all wondered, at one time or another, what is our purpose. Jesus came with a purpose. He came with a "cross purpose." He knew His purpose and did not vary from it. He knew why He came and that He was to suffer, die, be separated from His Father and rise again for us. He embraced His purpose and gloried in it. Jesus was an obedient Son. God gives us a purpose, too. He wants us to love others, be fair and just in our dealings with them, and to forgive and to walk humbly with Him. He gave us Jesus as an example of how He wants us to live. We can do this because we have been baptized in the Holy Spirit who lives in us. We can ask for God's help through prayer and the reading of the Word. If we whisper Jesus' name in loving trust, we become aware of His presence in our lives. The Holy Spirit will reveal the teachings of God to us and help us with our purpose. We will learn the nature of God and learn to live with His purpose for our lives. We will share what He has taught us and spread the Good News to others. We all have a purpose for our lives, God's purpose.

"Carry out a random act of kindness, with no expectation of reward, safe in the knowledge that one day someone might do the same for you." (Princess Diana)

"One day, your heart will stop beating, and none of your fears will matter. What will matter is how you lived." (Henri Junttila)

June 3
Jesus is the Light

John 8:12
When Jesus spoke again to the people, He said, "I am the light of the world. Whoever follows Me will never walk in darkness, but will have the light of life."

1 John 1:5
This is the message we have heard from Him and declare to you: God is light; in Him there is no darkness at all.

The days are getting longer as we approach June 21, the first day of summer and the longest day of the year. We now see longer periods of daylight. The light of day ends the darkness of night. Light represents what is good, pure, true, and holy. Darkness represents what is sinful and evil. Light exposes whatever exists in the darkness, the good and bad. In the dark, they look alike; in the light, they can be clearly distinguished. Whenever we go through a tough period in life, the light at the end of the tunnel of darkness always gives us hope. The light that Jesus brings into our lives when we are walking in darkness reminds us that Jesus Christ is the Creator of life, and we are not alone. When we follow Jesus, "the light of the world," we will have "the light of life." The darkness of evil never has or never will overcome or extinguish God's light. His life brings that Light to mankind. When we follow Jesus, the true Light, we can avoid walking blindly and falling into sin. He lights the path ahead of us so we can see how to live. Jesus brings us God's presence, protection and guidance.

"Some days you will be the light for others, and some days you will need some light from them. As long as there is light, there is hope, and there is a way. (Jennifer Gayle)

"Life has many different chapters; one bad chapter doesn't mean it's the end of the book." (Zig Ziglar)

June 4
Prayer and Praise

Psalm 146:1-2
Praise the LORD. Praise the LORD, O my soul. I will praise the LORD all my life; I will sing praise to my God as long as I live.

Prayer and praise seem to go hand-in-hand. Prayer and praise take our minds off our problems and put our focus on God. Praise causes us to think of our LORD, the cross upon which He died for us, and His character. Praise lifts our souls from earthly problems to heavenly bliss. Prayer and praise will lift us up from our burdens as we turn to our God for help. God's help is lasting and complete. When there is something bothering us, we should take it to God. We can pray and talk to Him about whatever is on our hearts. We should praise our LORD for all that He has done in our lives even though we don't yet know or understand His plans. Next, we can watch how our attitudes will turn into joy and smiles. We should praise God in prayer and song.

"In the words of a wise counselor.... can't live your life looking in a mirror—you have to look forward or you will crash!!" (Author unknown)

"God's gifts puts man's best dreams to shame." (Elizabeth Barrett Browning)

June 5
Worry, Worry, Worry

Matthew 6:34
Therefore, do not worry about tomorrow, for tomorrow will worry about itself. Each day has enough trouble of its own.

Worrying immobilizes us and Jesus tells us not to do it. Worrying will not add one more day to our lives. God gives us 24 hours in a day. In Matthew 6:11 it says, "Give us today our daily bread."—today, not tomorrow, not next week and not next month, just today. Give God first place in our lives. Give Him our today and let Him be the captain of our ship. If He can take care of the lilies of the field and the sparrows, He can take care of us, our families, our lives and all of our tomorrows. Let God be the head of our households and let Him sit on the thrones of our lives so that we live one day at a time. When Almighty God is in control, we can rest in Him and have a quiet peace. We must let God be the pilot of our lives and trust Him in the midst of all we face. God is the great *"I AM."* We should let go of yesterday and not worry about tomorrow but focus on today, the present. When we open our eyes each morning, we should surrender everything to Him and let Him control the day. We can give God first place and turn all our worries and cares over to Him. Worry, worry, worry—not today, because we are giving it all to our Heavenly Father.

"I'm an old man and I've known a great many troubles and most of them never happened." (Mark Twain)

"Prayer: The world's greatest wireless connection." (Author unknown)

June 6
Stand Firm on a Solid Foundation

Luke 6:47
I will show you what he is like who comes to Me and hears My words and puts them into practice. He is like a man building a house, who dug down deep and laid the foundation on rock. When a flood came, the torrent struck that house but could not shake it, because it was well built.

We can be assured that God will never leave us nor forsake us. (Hebrews 13:5) That is His promise. We can stand on that promise because it is rock solid. Obeying God is like building a house on a strong, solid foundation that stands firm when storms appear. When life is calm, our foundations don't seem to matter, but, in crises situations, our foundations are tested and we will be shaken to our core. We must make sure our lives are built on the solid foundation of knowing and trusting Jesus Christ. We are the righteousness of God through Jesus Christ. Because of what Jesus did on the cross, we were made righteous. Our sins are forgiven and we have a loving Father who promises that He will remember those sins no more. Alleluia!!! We have God's assurance that "The LORD is my helper; I will not fear." (Hebrews 13:6) We can be assured that, with the help of God, all things are possible. Whenever something shakes our foundations, we must trust God to meet our needs. "My hope is built on nothing less than Jesus' blood and righteousness."

"My hope is built on nothing less, Than Jesus' blood and righteousness; No merit of my own I claim But wholly lean on Jesus' name. On Christ, the solid rock, I stand; All other ground is sinking sand." (Lutheran Service Book, pp 575)

"Be sure to put your feet in the right place, then stand firm." (Abraham Lincoln)

June 7
Eternity in Our Hearts

Ecclesiastes 3:11
He has made everything beautiful in its time. He has also set eternity in the hearts of men; yet they cannot fathom what God has done from beginning to end.

God created us and He has given us eternity in our hearts. We know Him and have seen but a glimpse of eternity's beauty in His creation. We cannot even imagine how glorious all that awaits us in eternity. We have a longing to know Him and what He has prepared for us. He gives us little gifts of Himself so we can experience joy, love, peace, grace and mercy. They are nuggets of what lies ahead when we finally go home to be with Him. We can never be completely satisfied with the things of the earth and the pleasures we have here because somewhere deep inside we know that there is more. Eternity is more perfect than anything we know. God only gives us a glimpse because we cannot comprehend everything that is ahead—the perfection of His creation. As we trust God, we know in our hearts that eternity with Him is better than any day full of the greatest joy, love and peace that we experience in our lives.

"God's gifts put man's best dreams to shame." (Elizabeth Barrett Browning)

"The greatest happiness of life is the conviction that we are loved—loved for ourselves, or rather, loved in spite of ourselves." (Victor Hugo)

June 8
Hope for the Heart

Romans 12:12
Be joyful in hope, patient in affliction, faithful in prayer.

We will have the joy of hope, while we patiently wait for God's blessings. During this waiting period, we should be faithfully praying, living by His Word and trusting Him completely. God determines who we are and what we will become as we grow in our faith. Where have we placed our hope and faith? Are our hope and faith placed in our God, the creator of everything, or are they placed in the world and material things? We have hope in our hearts because we have a God who is faithful to us. Every time we look at the cross, hope is there. Our hope is secure because we have Christ. We need to be faithful to Him and trust Him with everything as we patiently wait for whatever He has planned for us.

"Hope is never ill when faith is well." (John Bunyan)

"The world hopes for the best; but the LORD offers the best hope." (John Wesley White)

June 9
Jesus—the Name Above All Names

John 16:23-24
In that day you will no longer ask Me anything. I tell you the truth, My Father will give you whatever you ask in My name. Until now you have not asked for anything in My name. Ask and you will receive, and your joy will be complete.

Acts 4:12
Salvation is found in no one else, for there is no other name under heaven given to men by which we must be saved.

Because of what Jesus did for us on the cross, we can speak personally and directly to God. This is not because of our own merit but because of Jesus, our High Priest. He has made us acceptable to God through His sacrifice, taking all of our sins upon Himself. He is our Savior—the only One to call on for salvation. Jesus is the only name to call on to have an eternal loving and living relationship with God. We can draw near to God personally. We can do this in the name of Jesus. All we have to do is say "Jesus" and we have God's attention. He wants to hear from us and He wants us to worship Him. There are many who take His name in vain and don't worship Him. It breaks His heart. When we come to Him, He's delighted and welcomes our talks and worship. Thank You, Jesus, for being our Savior and LORD.

"Jesus"—what a beautiful name.
"Jesus"—a name above all names.
"Jesus"—what a friend we have in Jesus. (Author unknown)

"Life without Christ is a hopeless end. With Christ it's an endless hope."
(Wanda E. Brunstetter)

June 10
Decisions, Decisions, Decisions

Psalm 119:125
I am your servant; give me discernment that I may understand Your statutes.

Psalm 121:1-2
I lift up my eyes to the hills—Where does my help come from?
My help comes from the LORD, the Maker of heaven and earth.

Psalm 139:3
You discern my going out and my lying down; You are familiar with all my ways.

Decisions are a part of our everyday lives. What do we do? Where do we go? Which way do we go—left or right, in or out, up or down? What color do we want? Where do we eat? What do we eat? Who to vote for? What is the best scenario and what is not? Is this the right decision for us? Decisions, decisions, decisions....how do we decide? Often we decide very quickly. Then there are those times we research a decision until we are more confused than ever. Finally, there are those times we just don't have a clue so we meditate on the Word of God and ask for His help, which is the ideal way to be making all decisions. What decisions are we facing today? Have we talked them over with the LORD? He knows what is best and He is waiting to listen and help. Whatever decisions we need to make, we should take them to the LORD in prayer and talk to Him as He knows everything about us and wants to help us. He's waiting. We can decide with His help.

"We are always in the forge, or on the anvil; by trials God is shaping us for higher things." (Henry Ward Beecher)

"A journey of a thousand miles begins with a single step." (Chinese proverb)

June 11
Hope

Romans 12:12
Be joyful in hope, patient in affliction, faithful in prayer.

Romans 15:4
For whatever was written in former days was written for our instruction, that through endurance and through the encouragement of the Scriptures we might have hope.

Hope. God uses difficulties in our lives to build our character. When we read the Scriptures, our faith in God grows as does our hope because we learn all that God has planned for us. We face difficulties every single day; no one is immune from trouble, but when we have hope, we are encouraged, we endure and our character is enhanced. The Old and New Testaments tell a beautiful story of hope. The more we know and learn about what God has done in the past it gives us hope for the present and future. Hope and faith in our loving God helps us to grow and learn. The Scriptures give us encouragement, and God's strength helps us to endure whatever we must each and every day. Hope for today, endurance and encouragement for tomorrow is a wonderful roadmap for our journey of life. We must never, ever lose hope because whatever we are facing today it is not the end of our story.

"God is good all the time. All the time God is good." (Author unknown)

"In three words, I can sum up everything I've learned about life. It goes on." (Robert Frost)

June 12
God's Grace

Philippians 4:23
The grace of the LORD Jesus Christ be with your spirit. Amen.

The true secret of joy and peace is imitating Christ and serving others. By focusing our minds on Christ, we will learn unity, humility, joy and peace. We will also be motivated to live for Him. We can live confidently for Him because we have "the grace of the LORD Jesus Christ" with us. Thank You, God, for Your Grace and for loving us so much. Thank You that we can put all of our cares at Your feet and focus on You and for the joy and peace that fill us as we obey You and love others as we love ourselves. Amen

"People were designed for accomplishment, engineered for success, and endowed with seeds of greatness." (Zig Ziglar)

"He climbs highest who helps another up." (George Matthew Adams)

June 13
God, Thank You for Our teachers

Psalm 25:4-5
Show me thy ways, O LORD; teach me thy paths. Lead me in thy truth, and teach me: for thou art the God of my salvation; on thee do I wait all the day.

After so many years, schooling ends but education does not. It lasts a lifetime and should be a continual process. When we have an attitude of learning, we will always remain inquisitive, and, in the process, acquire knowledge on new subjects. Education is what we glean from people, places and circumstances. Opportunities and experiences help us to learn about relationships, attitudes and perspectives. We will have many teachers throughout our lifetimes who enhance our minds. God is the greatest teacher. He educates and guides us when we seek Him, we learn from His Word and we obey His commands. God will show us the right way. God knows us and what we need to learn to grow. We should be students of life and learn what God has in store for us. In every situation, we should ask what the lesson is and what are we supposed to learn. We may be surprised to learn that the school of life never ends, because we have the greatest teacher in the world and His lessons are a lifelong process and tuition-free.

Thank a teacher today.
"Knowledge is knowing a tomato is a fruit. Wisdom is not putting it in a fruit salad." (Author unknown)

Teacher by Jessica Baldwin Hughes
God took one pair of angel wings,
And patience without measure.
Two eyes that see potential
Great wisdom from His treasure.
A smile to give encouragement
A truly heavenly feature...
He wrapped it up with tender care
And called this gift...a teacher!

June 14
The Presence of Jesus

Matthew 28:20
I will be with you always, to the very end of the age.

WHAT A PROMISE!!! Jesus is with us always through the Holy Spirit. He keeps His promises and we can count on Him every moment of every day. Jesus our King—*our Spiritual King* rules over all and is the ruler of our hearts. Thank You, LORD Jesus, for being the King of our hearts, Ruler of our lives and our Savior. We can count on You and Your Presence. We see You in the morning light and in the stars at night. We hear You in the voices of nature and the sounds of water. We feel You with the beat of our hearts and know You through Your Word. Thank You for Your very Presence in our lives.

"At the end of the day, faith means letting God be God." (John Blanchard)

"Commitment is what transforms a promise to reality." (Author unknown)

June 15
Conflict

John 14:27
Peace I leave with you; my peace I give you. I do not give to you as the world gives. Do not let your hearts be troubled and do not be afraid.

Philippians 4:4-7
Rejoice in the Lord always. I will say it again: Rejoice! Let your gentleness be evident to all. The LORD is near. Do not be anxious about anything, but in everything, by prayer and petition, with thanksgiving, present your requests to God. And the peace of God, which transcends all understanding, will guard your hearts and your minds in Christ Jesus.

We all experience conflict in our lives but the important question is how do we react to it? Some people react with anger. They say mean and hurtful things. Some people remain quiet and take all that is going on around them deep inside until it eats away at them, eventually coming out in destructive ways. What Jesus wants us to do is turn our conflicts and worry into prayers. He instructs us in Philippians 4 to not be anxious about anything but pray more! Just stop and pray. Yes, we do get discouraged about unpleasant circumstances, but we can be joyful in them because we have a God who is bigger than anything we face. We can be joyful in all things. Our inner attitude does not have to reflect what is going on around us. We can rejoice in our LORD, and when we do, there is a peace that passes all understanding that will fill us, surround us and emanate from us. We will have the joy of the LORD in our hearts. Ah conflict—no thank you, I have Jesus.

"How many cares one loses when one decides not to be something, but to be someone." (Coco Chanel)

"They always say that time changes things, but you actually have to change them yourself." (Andy Warhol)

June 16
Until We Meet Again

Matthew 5:4
Blessed are those that mourn for they will be comforted.

We've all been to that place of losing a loved one. Our hearts become heavy and hurt as we say, "So long, until we meet again." We pray that our loved one is in the Hands of God. We don't know our loved one's heart or their final words with God, but what we do know is that God knows. What we do know is that God will comfort us through the days and months ahead with memories and love. We send our loved one into the presence of God with the proclamation, "Go with God until we meet again."

"It is love that gives life meaning.
It is love that makes us care.
In our times of grief and sorrow
It is love we come to share.
It is love that brings us comfort.
It is love that helps us cope.
And in our darkest hours,
It is love that gives us hope." (Author unknown)

"What touches us are the joys we've experienced. What comforts us are the memories we share. What lasts...is love." (Author unknown)

June 17
We Have a Choice

Proverbs 15:13
A happy heart makes the face cheerful....

Proverbs 15:15
...but the cheerful heart has a continual feast.

To be or not to be happy—*it's our choice.* Each day, as we wake up and open our eyes, we have a choice to make. We can decide how we are going feel. We can be happy or gloomy. Before we get out of bed, we should thank our LORD for this day, no matter what comes our way. When we have the resolve to change our attitude, it is amazing how our day can turn out. Our attitude colors our whole personality. We cannot always choose what happens to us, but we can choose our attitude towards each situation. The secret of a cheerful heart is filling our mind with thoughts that are true, pure, and lovely, and thoughts that dwell on the good things in life. We should choose today to be happy no matter what comes our way. To be or not to be happy—*it's our choice.*

"To get up each morning with the resolve to be happy is to set our own conditions to the events of each day. To do this is to condition circumstances instead of being conditioned by them." (Ralph Waldo Emerson)

"There are two ways of spreading light: to be the candle or the mirror that reflects it." (Edith Wharton)

June 18
ASAP

Job 22:27
You will pray to Him, and He will hear you, and you will fulfill your vows.

Whenever most of us see ASAP, we think "as soon as possible." But there is another acronym for ASAP and that is "always say a prayer." That is what we should do every day, all day long—pray. No matter what we do or face, we should pray first. God is listening and He is waiting. He loves conversing with us and He wants to hear from us. God is always there and we can call on Him, day or night, even for the simplest tasks. He has the answer to every problem or obstacle. The next time we hear or see ASAP...STOP and say a prayer first because whatever is needed will be done with God's helping Hand.

"ASAP—*Always say a prayer,* all day long and begin it ASAP—*As soon as possible." (Author unknown)*

"Let prayer be the key to the day, and the bolt to the night." (Wanda E. Brunstetter)

June 19
GPS

John 14:6
Jesus answered, "I am the Way and the Truth and the Life. No one comes to the Father except through me."

John 6:27
"Do not work for food that spoils, but for food that endures to eternal life, which the Son of Man will give you. For on him God the Father has placed his seal of approval."

When we think of a GPS, we think of the item we place in our cars to guide us as we travel. GPS stands for Global Positioning System. We also have our own GPS built inside of us—God's Positioning System. It's a good acronym to keep handy whenever we feel alone or lost because we have a God who is looking out for us. Each day we can look to our God for guidance, wisdom and discernment. He is our Source to take us where He wants us to go. The Bible is God's roadmap. It's full of guidance and lessons which will take us to eternal life. Jesus is the way to get to God. He came to show us the way so when we make the choice to follow God, we will live eternally with Him. When He ascended into heaven, He sent the Holy Spirit to live in us so that we are never, ever alone. We have a Triune God (God the Father, Jesus the Son and the Holy Spirit, our Counselor.) We should take a few minutes and rest in God. We can rely on Him for all things. We should let God be our GPS—God's Positioning System—and follow His roadmap to eternal life.

"And our wise Father in heaven knows when we're going to need things too. Don't run out ahead of him." (Corrie ten Boom)

"Don't bother to give God instructions, just report for duty." (Corrie ten Boom)

June 20
Graduation

Matthew 14:29-30
"Come," He said. Then Peter got down out of the boat, walked on the water and came toward Jesus. But when he saw the wind, he was afraid and, beginning to sink, cried out, "LORD, save me!"

We graduate from many areas in our lives such as school and from different stages of our lives as we age. We even graduate from our work life to retirement, and, finally, we will graduate from this life to eternity. When we attend a graduation, especially one for our child, grandchild or ourselves, we are in the moment experiencing joy and celebrating the completion of hard work, perseverance and goals. If we stop to think about all that took place to get to that moment—the hard work, struggles, the arguments, the sleepless nights etc., etc., etc.—our joy would deflate like a balloon. There would be no joy or celebration in the moment. That is what happened to Peter as he was walking on the water. He had his eyes on Jesus and recognized Him as LORD. As long as he kept his eyes and focus on Jesus, Peter could walk on water. Once he took his eyes off Jesus and the fear of the roaring waves and storm overwhelmed him, he began to sink. Our troubles in life are very real but there is One who can help us. God is the only One who can guide us and help us achieve the goals that He has planned for us. The very power of God is what will help us walk through years of difficulties to our graduation day from earth to living eternally with Him. We must keep our eyes on Jesus and not let all that is going on around us deter us from our destination. We must cast our cares on Him. It is only through surrendering all to Him, abandoning ourselves and our circumstances to Him, that we will recognize Jesus. His power will help us overcome any obstacle. We can enjoy graduation and not dwell on the difficulties that got us here. We should dwell instead on the power of our LORD that got us through them.

"It is the constant and determined effort that breaks down all resistance, sweeps away all obstacles." (Claude Me. Bristol)

"Keep adding, keep walking, keep advancing; do not stop, do not turn back, do not turn from the straight road." (St. Augustine)

June 21
Be a Dreamer....

Zephaniah 3:17
The Lord your God is with you, He will take great delight in you, He will quiet you with His love, He will rejoice over you with singing.

Ephesians 3:30
Now to Him who is able to do immeasurably more than all we ask or imagine, according to His power that is at work within us.

We have dreams. We imagine, hope and aspire for things and we dream of something better than what we have. Some of our dreams are so big that they seem unimaginable, but we have a God who is bigger than our dreams and with God all things are possible. All we need to do is begin. God is the only One who can make us happy and the journey that we take to follow our dreams will only be successful when we allow God to be with us. When we faithfully follow Him, obey His commands and let Him be our Captain and Guide, we will reach the dreams He has for us. When we do, He will rejoice over us and our dreams will be realized in Him. Our dreams may change over time. When we trust Him and believe in Him, our dreams become His dreams for us. Let's be dreamers with our God.

DREAM (DaySpring—Holly Gerth message on a mug)
"higher than a mountain, deeper than the sea,
wider than the world- for the size of our
dreams tells not how big we are but how
big our God is."

"Life at its essence boils down to one day at a time. Today is the day!!!"
(Jim Stovall)

"Realize you are greater than you ever considered yourself to be."
(Author unknown)

June 22
Fathers

Exodus 20:12
"Honour thy father and thy mother: that thy days may be long upon the land which the LORD thy God giveth thee.

Matthew 6:9
"Our Father in heaven, hallowed be Your name, Your kingdom come, Your will be done on earth as it is in heaven."

Parents have a special place in God's heart. Imagine what He has given them to do. He has chosen them to raise His children here on earth so that they will know and accept Him as their LORD and Savior. He wants them to eventually live eternally with Him. What a job parents have to do and many, many, many of them do it very well as they love, teach, guide, play and above all, put God first. They set the example for all the children in their lives. We have a personal and loving father in our Heavenly Father. Many of us are remiss in remembering that He is our first Father. He created us and loves us so much. One of the greatest commandments is to love our God with all our heart, soul, mind and strength. He gave us the gift of our earthly fathers to watch out for us and to train us up in the way we should go. We should take time to thank our Heavenly Father and all the dads in our lives for teaching and setting good examples, for raising us and showing us our Heavenly Father.

"A father is...
Respected because he gives his children leadership,
Appreciated because he gives his children care,
Valued because he gives his children time,
Loved because he gives his children the one thing
they treasure most—himself." (DaySpring)

"There are a lot of ways to be a dad...But there's an amazing difference in those dads who choose to follow God's lead." (Author unknown)

June 23
Summer

Psalm 19:1-6
The heavens declare the glory of God; the skies proclaim the work of His hands. Day after day they pour forth speech; night after night they display knowledge. There is no speech or language where their voice is not heard. Their voice goes out into all the earth, their words to the ends of the world. In the heavens He has pitched a tent for the sun, which is like a bridegroom coming forth from his pavilion, like a champion rejoicing to run his course. It rises at one end of the heavens and makes it circuit to the other; nothing is hidden from its heat.

Today is the first full day of summer. The school year is ending, activities are slowing down, and the warmth of summer is upon us. Many of us are planning vacations or outdoor activities, and we are looking forward to rest, relaxation and more family time. This is a great time to see God and spend time with Him in all that is going on around us. God is everywhere. As we slow down with summer and enjoy the people around us, He's in their faces and voices. We can look for the excitement of children as they are having a great time playing, swimming, blowing bubbles and laughing—He's there. As we travel for vacation, He's in the creation of the mountains, the waters of the lakes and oceans. He is the moon, the stars and the heavens. God is everywhere. We should spend time with Him. We can get quiet and get in touch with Him. We can listen for and to Him. We will experience all that He has planned for us when we walk humbly with our LORD who created everything around us for our enjoyment and praise. We must seek the LORD and enjoy Him. He is an awesome God. Happy Summer....

"My favorite thing is to go where I've never seen before." (Diane Arbus)

"Night is the other half of life, and the better half. (Johann Wolfgang Von Goethe)

June 24
God's Great Love for Us

Psalm 103:2-5
Praise the LORD, O my soul, and forget not all His benefits—who forgives all your sins and heals all your diseases, who redeems your life from the pit and crowns you with love and compassion, who satisfies your desires with good things so that your youth is renewed like the eagle's.

Psalm 103:8
The LORD is compassionate and gracious, slow to anger, abounding in love.

What an awesome God we have because He loves us when we don't deserve it. He forgives our sins, heals our diseases, and redeems us from death, crowns us with love and compassion, satisfies our desires and gives righteousness and justice. We can always count our blessings no matter what we are going through. As we think about our past, present and future, we will always see God's hand in our blessings. We should be so very thankful that He is compassionate and gracious, slow to anger and abounding in love. It doesn't get any better than that. Praise the LORD, oh my soul.

"Accept what is, let go of what was and have faith in what will be." (Author unknown)

"Every sunrise is a new message from God, and every sunset His signature." (William A. Ward)

June 25
'Lachen ist gut medizin'—Laughter is the Best Medicine

Psalm 2:4
The One enthroned in heaven laughs;

Psalm 126:2
Our mouths are filled with laughter, our tongues with songs of joy.

Laughter is such a wonderful emotion. There is the chuckle and then there is the hee,hee type of laugh, but the best type of laughter is the deep belly laugh. There is the joyous sound of a deep belly laugh. It just makes our hearts overflow with love and joy. Laughter can bind family and friendships together with strength and memories. It softens the rough edges and is a formula for success in relationships. When people are laughing together, whatever barriers that separate them seem to disappear. There are many lessons to be learned in good moments of laughing together because arguments don't seem as important and taking ourselves too seriously seems to disappear. We can laugh at ourselves. We can learn to tease playfully without tearing down another's self-esteem. These are all lessons that will create wonderful and fond memories. Laughter is the best medicine, and all it takes is a lighthearted spirit and a lively attitude. When we make the effort, we will find that humor and laughter have a momentum that builds as others join in. Laughter is a joyful noise to the LORD. Let's have a good laugh today as we make memories with those around us and make God smile.

"Laughter and weeping are the two most intense forms of human emotion, and these profound wells of human emotion are to be consecrated to God." (Oswald Chambers)

"The most thoroughly wasted of all days is one on which a person has not laughed. Laughter is the sound of heaven. Blessed are they who can laugh at themselves for they shall never cease to be amused." (Author unknown)

June 26
God's Garden

John 15:1
"I am the true vine, and My Father is the gardener. He cuts off every branch in Me that bears no fruit, while every branch that does bear fruit He prunes so that it will be even more fruitful."

God unfolds our life as He does a tiny rosebud. We are like those tiny rosebuds that need unfolding so we can eventually become the roses that He has designed us to be. We trust Him, and, through His wisdom and guidance, we learn about Him and the life He has designed for us. Just as rose petals slowly open, we do the same as we learn about Jesus and His love until we are in full bloom. A rose in full bloom drinks in the water of the rain and opens up wide in full sunshine. We, too, learn to take in the rains of life and grow in His light as the Holy Spirit fills us and teaches us about Jesus. There is peace in His light. Roses have beautiful fragrances with so many glorious colors just as we are all different people with different lifestyles, thoughts and desires. Some roses last for a full growing season and then some are so delicate that they only last a few days. This is a cycle of life. This is the life of a child of God. We are God's garden that He grows and prunes, feeds and waters until we blossom into a beautiful bouquet to live eternally with Him.

"It is only a tiny rosebud,
A flower of God's design;
But I cannot unfold the petals
With these clumsy hands of mine.

The secret of unfolding flowers
Is not known to such as I.
GOD opens this flower so easily,
But in my hands they die.

If I cannot unfold a rosebud,
This flower of God's design,
Then how can I have the wisdom
To unfold this life of mine?

So I'll trust in God for leading
Each moment of my day.
I will look to God for guidance
In each step along the way.

The path that lies before me,
Only my LORD and Savior knows.
I'll trust God to unfold the moments,
Just as He unfolds the rose." (Author unknown)

June 27
Stand Firm

Psalm 27:4
One thing I ask of the LORD, this is what I seek: that I may dwell in the house of the LORD all the days of my life, to gaze upon the beauty of the LORD.

We must stand firm in the presence of the LORD. When we stand firm in the LORD's presence, we are able to enjoy a relationship with Him forever. We stand firm in His presence each time we pray, read scripture, attend church, communicate with Him in song and just talk to Him. He welcomes us as we worship Him, opening ourselves to His love. His beautiful love will enfold, engulf, endure, engage, enlighten, enchant and enhance us. We must stand firm in Jesus today because there is no better place to stand.

"Today, LORD, bless this place and time that I've set aside to be with You. And bless all those I pray for." (Patricia Lorenz)

"Be sure you put your feet in the right place, then stand firm." (Abraham Lincoln)

June 28
And the Answer is—Jesus!

Psalm 23
The LORD is my Shepherd, I shall not be in want.
He makes me lie down in green pastures,
He leads me beside quiet waters,
He restores my soul.
He guides me in paths of righteousness
For His name's sake.
Even though I walk
  through the valley of the shadow of death,
I will fear no evil,
  for You are with me;
Your rod and Your staff,
  they comfort me.
You prepare a table before me
  in the presence of my enemies.
You anoint my head with oil;
  my cup overflows.
Surely goodness and love will follow me
  all the days of my life,
And I will dwell in the house of the LORD
  forever. Amen.

The question is, "Who is the good Shepherd that handles everything in our lives?" As wayward sheep, we are completely dependent on Him for provision, guidance and protection. Our Good Shepherd is the God of life who offers us eternal life and comfort. We follow Him to the "green pastures" and "quiet waters" that will restore us when our souls are depleted. Jesus is contentment. We will dwell with Him forever and ever when we are obedient followers and let Him be our guide to walk us through the valleys in life. This Psalm is all about what God does for us when we follow Him. He is the Good Shepherd, and we are His wayward sheep who need the hook of the staff every now and then to keep us safe. We need the prod of the staff to keep us going when we would like to give up. The Shepherd makes, leads, restores, guides, protects, comforts, prepares and anoints. The Shepherd loves His sheep. The Good Shepherd is Jesus and He wants to take care of His sheep. We are those sheep who so desperately need Him. The answer is, JESUS!!!!

"Every outcome of every challenge should reveal how God supplies the grace to make it through the seemingly impossible." (Father Leo Patalinghug aka the "Cooking Priest")

"Life without Christ is a hopeless end. With Christ it's an endless hope." (Wanda E. Brunstetter)

June 29
The Good Shepherd

Psalm 23:1
The Lord is my Shepherd, I shall not want.

John 10:14
"I am the Good Shepherd; I know My sheep and My sheep know me—just as the Father knows Me and I know the Father—and I lay down My life for the sheep."

Jesus is the Good Shepherd and we are His flock. He is committed to us and loves us so much that He was willing to lay down His life for us. He is committed to protect and care for us. As sheep follow the shepherd, we are to follow Jesus. As sheep follow the voice they know, we, too, are to listen for His voice and follow Him. His voice is in the Bible as we read and learn about Him. His voice is in the hymns we sing and in the prayers we say. Our Shepherd wants us to hear Him, and most often He whispers so we will be still and listen. Why do we crave the peace and quiet of being in God's nature and creation? Maybe it's because we want to hear His voice. Maybe we hear or see Him in the beauty of a sunrise or sunset, as we walk along a beach at the ocean. We might see Him in the morning mist rising over a lake or meadow, or hear Him in the singing of birds in the morning. Jesus is in the beauty of a garden or in the colors of the sky or a rainbow. We must follow Him because Jesus is the Good Shepherd.

"To the lost sheep, He is the seeking Shepherd;
To the needy sheep, He is the providing Shepherd;
To the hurting sheep, He is the comforting Shepherd;
To the bruised sheep, He is the healing Shepherd;
To the anxious sheep, He is the peaceful Shepherd;
To the wandering sheep, He is the guiding Shepherd;
To the fearful sheep, He is the protecting Shepherd;
To the lame sheep, He is the carrying Shepherd;
To the discontented sheep, He is the fulfilling Shepherd;
To the parched sheep, He is the anointing Shepherd;
To the timid sheep, He is the reassuring Shepherd;
To the fallen sheep, He is the merciful Shepherd;
To the nervous sheep, He is the quieting Shepherd;
To the heavy laden sheep, He is the restful Shepherd;
To the lonely sheep, He is the ever-present Shepherd;
To the weary sheep, He is the restoring Shepherd;
To all His sheep, He is the Good Shepherd." (Roy Lessin—Meet Me In The Meadow)

"What does God require? EVERYTHING!" (Erwin Lutzer)

June 30
HELP!!!

Psalm 46:1
God is our refuge and strength, an ever-present help in trouble.

One crisis after another … isn't that how it sometimes seems in life? We just get through one thing when "oops" there is another. We have no control over the events that trigger the crisis, but we do have control over how we respond to them. Our reaction and response can make matters better or worse. We can be objective and let God be in the middle, directing us to overcome, get through and actually survive. He brings family and friends to help us endure and to be there for one another. Many times no words need to be spoken—just their presence is enough. Sometimes the phone will ring at just the right moment and there is a friendly, encouraging and comforting voice at the other end. That person may even be unaware that we are in desperate need. In the midst of a crisis, we can reconnect with God. In the good times we may become self-sufficient and He is often forgotten. Then when the "oops" of life happen, we turn to Him—the one constant we always have. No appointment is necessary; no voice mail is needed, no "push 5 if you'd like to speak to the receptionist," no taking a number and waiting in line because we can talk to Him directly. He is always available. Staying close to God means He will stay close to us. We journey through life's crisis by responding to everything with God by our sides as He promises to never leave us. Reacting and responding with God as our partner will help us face whatever comes our way with strength and perseverance. Crises in life will happen to everyone, but our reaction and response will determine our outcome.

"There's something about resurrections that requires crosses." (Robert Sloan)

"People were designed for accomplishment, engineered for success, and endowed with seeds of greatness." (Zig Ziglar)

July 1
Praise the LORD

Psalm 92:4-5
I sing for joy at the works of Your hands. How great are Your works, O LORD, how profound Your thoughts.

Lamentations 3:22-23
The steadfast love of the LORD never ceases, His mercies never come to an end; they are new every morning; great is Your faithfulness.

Our God is so awesome. As we begin our day, we should take time to praise Him for all of our blessings. I wonder if that is what the birds are doing in the early morn. At 4 a.m. one bird begins and then soon after there is a whole chorus of them tweeting at the sunrise. The early morning light and the break of dawn is such a hopeful and peaceful time of day. It is one of my favorite times to spend with God. The quietness as night passes into day, the dew upon the ground, the streaks of color in the sky as the sun begins to rise are all reminders of God and the beauty of His creation. It is a time of peace and reflection, a time of oneness with our LORD and Creator. He has created this time for us to enjoy Him. Let's be thankful for the early morning as we watch the beginning of a brand new day. We can praise the Lord all day long thanking Him for His creation and for allowing us to celebrate the start of a new day with Him.

"When morning gilds the skies, my heart awakening cries; may Jesus Christ be praised." (Joseph Barnby)

"Every sunrise is a new message from God, and every sunset His signature." (Wanda Brunstetter)

July 2
The LORD's Work

John 9:4
"As long as it is day, we must do the work of Him who sent Me. Night is coming, when no one can work."

Sometimes we don't realize that the work we do for our LORD can be as simple as a smile, a hug, spending time with a child, spouse or friend. The LORD's work can be accomplished in our home, workplace, church, neighborhood and community. We can further God's purpose and bloom where we are planted because His garden is in our own backyard. Sometimes God's plan for us is so simple that we miss it. We get caught up in the where and how, not realizing that He has made it so easy for us to show Him to those around us. We should take time to think about where we are planted and look for ways to share Him. It's amazing what He will do and show us once we open our hearts and minds to His bidding. We need to show God by what we say and do. Sometimes the smallest gesture can mean the world to someone and will show God in a big way. As we go about doing the LORD's work, we should tend to His garden and bloom where we are planted because the blossoms of His purpose will make a beautiful bouquet.

"Slow me down LORD, I am going too fast; I can't see my brother when he's walking past. I miss a lot of good things day by day; I don't know a blessing when it comes my way." (Brother John G. Ollis)

"Trying to do the Lord's work in your own strength is the most confusing, exhausting, and tedious of all work. But when you are filled with the Holy Spirit, then the ministry of Jesus just flows out of you." (Corrie ten Boom)

July 3
God Cares

John 19:26
When Jesus saw His mother there, and the disciple whom He loved standing nearby, He said to his mother, "Dear woman, here is your son," and to the disciple, "Here is your mother."

Often when we are going through a crisis or a trial, God will send someone to spiritually lift us up with his/her presence or words. He sends people into our lives who will enrich and help us. He knows what we need before we need it because He knows the end from the beginning. We are all family and His presence shows that Jesus is a caring and loving God. We never know where He will send us or who He will bring into our lives. Each day we should be on the lookout for God speaking to us through another person, nature, a song or maybe a written word. Even a smile and a laugh could be sent to us from Jesus to encourage and bring some sunshine and hope into our day. On the other hand, we could be that light in someone else's life and that opportunity will lift us spiritually. Let's go ahead and make someone's day....

"Be a rainbow in someone else's cloud." (Maya Angelou)

"You never know when a moment and a few sincere words can have an impact on a life." (Zig Ziglar)

July 4
The Fourth of July—Happy Birthday America!

I pledge allegiance to the flag of the United States of America, and to the Republic for which it stands, one nation under God, indivisible with liberty and justice for all.

Psalm 84:12
LORD Almighty, blessed is the one who trusts in You.

Psalm 91:1-4
He who dwells in the shelter of the Most High will rest in the shadow of the Almighty. I will say of the LORD, "He is my refuge and my fortress, my God, in whom I trust." Surely He will save you from the fowler's snare and from the deadly pestilence. He will cover you with His feathers, and under His wings you will find refuge; His faithfulness will be your shield and rampart.

Happy Birthday America! Our country was founded and based on the principles of the Bible. Our money has the words "In God we trust" on it. We are blessed to live in such a nation that gives us the freedom to worship our LORD, fly our flag, go to the church of our choice and read the Bible plus so many other freedoms. Let's take a moment today to thank our LORD, pray for our country and remember to thank and pray for our servicemen and women who have fought for us and these freedoms. God bless America from sea-to-shining sea. Dear LORD, thank You for being with this country and for providing so many opportunities for its people. Thank You for our leaders and our government. Please help them to make wise decisions and to be discerning in their leadership. Thank You for protecting us and keeping us steady as we go. Amen.

"Blessed is the nation who trusts in the Lord." (Author unknown)

"The God who gave us life gave us liberty at the same time." (Thomas Jefferson)

July 5
We're Late….

Psalm 31:15
My times are in Your hands;

Ecclesiastes 3:14
I know that everything God does will endure forever; nothing can be added to it and nothing taken from it. God does it so that men will revere Him.

The power was out during the night; we overslept; oh no we're late….sound familiar? One thing we know for sure is that God is never late. He is always on time at just the right time. We sometimes wonder where He is, when will He arrive or do something that we think should be done. We can be assured that He will arrive at the perfect time and will do the perfect thing in His own time, and it will be good because He gets the glory. Whenever our day begins with us being late or waiting on God to answer our prayers, we can trust that He is never late. He knows what we need, when we need it, and He is always on time. We need to be patient, slow down, trust and wait on Him, remembering always to give Him the glory. Any time we are late, we can take a deep breath and say a prayer. Yes, we may be a little late but with God as our Coach and Guide, we'll always be on time.

"Faith sees the invisible, believes the unbelievable, and receives the impossible." (Corrie ten Boom)

"Genius is the ability to reduce the complicated to the simple."
(C.W. Ceram)

July 6
Our Roots

Psalm 1:3
He is like a tree planted by streams of water, which yields its fruit in season and whose leaf does not wither.

Jeremiah 17:8
"He will be like a tree planted by the water that sends out its roots by the stream. It does not fear when heat comes; its leaves are always green. It has no worries in a year of drought and never fails to bear fruit."

When we trust in the LORD, we will flourish like trees planted by water. A well-watered tree will flourish at all times even in drought. When we trust in the LORD, we will have abundant strength, not only for our own needs, but even for the needs of others. The roots of a tree will go deep into the ground to reach water. Our roots must go deep into the Word of God so that whatever we face, we will have God's Word in our hearts to help us to have actions and attitudes that honor God. All of us need deep faith roots in our LORD to sustain us each and every day. When we look at an oak tree on a windy hill as it faces all types of weather, it bends a little in every direction, but its roots are deep and it remains stable and steady. That is what the Word of God does for us as we face unknown situations. God's Word will keep us steady and remind us that He is with us, and when He is with us, we will bear much fruit.

"Deep roots anchor us when surprises blow like strong, unruly winds. Deep roots hold us steady during the storm that didn't show up on the radar. Deep roots find nourishment when the surface gets awfully dry. Deep roots allow for growth not previously possible.
Deep roots yield rich fruit. So, I'm learning to not be so afraid of what might be around the next corner. Even if it does catch me off guard. I close my eyes and whisper ... deeper still." (Lysa TerKeurst)

July 7
Joy and Hope

Romans 15:13
May the God of hope fill you with all joy and peace as you trust in Him, so that you may overflow with hope by the power of the Holy Spirit.

Joy and hope go hand-in-hand. We have hope because we have joy in our hearts as we trust our God. When we face the challenges of day-to-day living, we have joy and peace walking with our God, trusting Him in all circumstances. In Communion the bread and wine symbolize Jesus' body and blood, and it reassures us of His forgiveness and peace. No matter what we face today, we have the hope of our LORD and the peace that only He can give that strengthens us in all circumstances. We should take everything to Him in prayer and let the power of the Holy Spirit strengthen us as we know that He works all things together for our good. May His will be done in every area of our lives as we are filled with joy and hope today and always.

"Joy is the echo of God's life within us. Joy is not happiness so much as gladness; it is the ecstasy of eternity in a soul that has made peace with God and is ready to do His will." (New Every Morning)

"Joy is really a road sign pointing us to God. Once we have found God...we no longer need to trouble ourselves so much about the quest for joy." (C.S. Lewis)

July 8
Refreshing Rain

Jude 1:12
These men are blemishes at your love feasts, eating with you without the slightest qualm—shepherds who feed only themselves. They are clouds without rain, blown by the wind; autumn trees, without fruit and uprooted—twice dead.

As we watch the news and see fires, dried crops, parched earth of neighborhoods, people watching as their water dries up, we cannot not help but wonder why there is no rain. The heat and humidity is overwhelming and the need for rain is great. Our lives are like that when we face difficult situations or problems. We, too, dry up and are parched without God's Word to sustain us. All of us go through life with difficulties, but when we face these head-on with God's Word in us, we are sustained and find our way through every situation. God's Word is like much-needed rain. We don't want to be like the "clouds without rain" billowing around us and like the "trees without fruit and uprooted." No, we want to be full of God's Word, glorifying Him in every circumstance, knowing that He is with us and will see us through until much-needed, refreshing rain comes and the parched earth becomes green and lush again. We can go to His Word, memorize a verse or read a chapter in our Bible. Let's learn how to remain in Him no matter what we face today because when we do, it will be like refreshing rain.

"Some people drink at the fountain of knowledge. Others just gargle." (Author unknown)

"Some people think they have burning ambition when it is merely inflammation of the wishbone." (William James)

July 9
FAITH—Reliance, Loyalty, or Complete Trust in God
Forwarding All Issues To Heaven

Psalm 124:8
Our help is in the name of the LORD, the Maker of heaven and earth.

Hebrews 11:1
Now faith is being sure of what we hope for and certain of what we do not see.

Faith combines assurance and anticipation. Faith is the conviction based on past experience that God's new and fresh surprises will surely be ours. Faith is sure and certain. God is who He says He is and will do what He says He will do. True faith believes that God will fulfill His promises even though we don't see those promises materializing when we think they should. Day by day, we pray to our LORD, trusting Him to answer our prayers or to comfort us in some way. No problem is too great for Him to solve; no circumstance is too difficult. Life without God is senseless, and, whatever we do in our lives, we must have God as a foundation. In every area of our lives we trust Him to see us through every decision we make and every event and circumstance we experience. When we pray there is a time that we must be quiet and listen for His answer. He will answer in His way, His will and His time. We need to be patient, quiet and to keep looking for His answer. Remember, sometimes His answer is "no." Sometimes it is "yes" and sometimes it is "wait." As we faithfully trust our LORD with all that is on our hearts and draw nearer to Him, let's take time to be still and listen. We should listen not only with our ears but in the silence of our hearts as He will answer us at just the right time—His time. Having faith in our loving and awesome God is like building our lives on a solid-rock foundation. He will bring us through tough times, and we will come out better than before.

"Before you speak, it is necessary for you to listen, for God speaks in the silence of the heart." (Mother Teresa)

"This life is not intended to be the place of our perfection, but the preparation for it." (Richard Baxter)

July 10
Fan or Follower

Matthew 16:24-25
Then Jesus said to His disciples, "If anyone would come after me, he must deny himself and take up his cross and follow me. For whoever wants to save his life will lose it, but whoever loses his life for me will find it.

A fan is someone enthusiastic about a specific sport, pastime or performer. A follower is someone who follows another's beliefs or teachings; a disciple, a servant or attendant.

Fan or follower? Do we do anything for Jesus that takes us out of our comfort zones or do we cheer Him on and talk about Him from the sidelines, not committing ourselves to take up His cross? Jesus says carry your cross and follow me. What does this look like for us? Are we truly following Him or are we wearing the t-shirts, sporting the bumper stickers and carrying the team coffee cup but not committing our time, treasures or spiritual gifts? Oftentimes in today's culture, people want to be sideline Christians. Fans are those who go to church, talk about God and cheer Him on, and will continue to do so as long as Jesus does not interfere in their lives, their finances or their plans. Jesus has a scheduled timeslot in their lives, and He cannot have any other time because it is filled up with other things. God wants committed followers not fans. We can love Jesus, live for Him, be a doer and a follower and have life in Him and with Him. Let's live out our faith by being a follower of Jesus, committing to Him and pledging our whole existence to God. Let's pick up our crosses and follow Him. We won't be alone because He will be right there beside us, guiding us on His journey. He has gone before us and knows what it will take for us to be His follower. By giving our lives wholly in service to Jesus, we will discover the real purpose for living. We should be followers and not fans. Let's live for Jesus every moment of the day not just on Sunday mornings between 8 and 10 a.m.

"You know you are old when you have lost all your marvels." (Merry Browne)

"Your greatness is measured by your horizons." (Michel Angelou)

July 11
Somebody Cares

Acts 10:38
Then Jesus went around doing good and healing all who were oppressed by the devil, for God was with Him.

Jesus' is the way, the truth and the life and His life was all about serving. Our lives should be about serving and helping others, thus showing our God living in us. Being a servant is all about caring. When we are Spirit-filled, Spirit-led and centered on Christ, we will show Jesus. As followers of Jesus, what we do and say will show others that He loves and cares for us and is working in us. We don't need recognition. We can be the people God means for us to be by showing Him in our words and actions.

"I like to show Jesus and sometimes, I use words." (St. Francis of Assisi)

"Somebody knows when your heart aches,
And everything seems to go wrong;
Somebody knows when the shadows
Need chasing away with a song;
Somebody knows when you're lonely,
Tired, discouraged and blue;
Somebody wants you to know Him,
And know that He dearly loves you." (Fannie Stafford)

July 12
Birthdays, Birthdays—a Day of Thanksgiving

Psalm 136:1
Give thanks to the LORD, for He is good. His love endures forever.

1 Thessalonians 5:18
Give thanks with a grateful heart.

I hear many people complain about their birthdays and getting older. That has never been the case for me. I love my birthday and I'm so grateful each year when it comes around. My attitude of gratitude begins each morning as I wake up, especially on my birthday, to thank my LORD for this new day, new year, new opportunities and whatever experiences He has in store for me. I'm thankful that He gives me opportunities to give back and to be a good steward. His love is amazing and He surrounds me with wonderful family and friends who show their love each and every day. I'm thankful as I remember those who have gone ahead to be at home with Jesus. I'm thankful for laughter and love, my family and other past birthdays through the years. I know that I am a child of God, and that no matter what changes take place, He lives in and through me. I am His vessel and may all who come in contact with me see Him and not me. I love presents and I get daily presents of love, grace, mercy and peace. As I embark on another year, please know that I am so very thankful for every reader of these devotions. What a year it has been and it will only get better as I embark on another year with an attitude of gratitude.

"My goal is God Himself, not joy nor peace, nor even blessing, but Himself, my God." (Oswald Chambers)

G—*Gratitude is heaven itself*
R—*Remember, a thankful heart is the parent of all virtues*
A—*An attitude of gratitude*
T—*There is no joy without gratitude*
I—*Inhale love, exhale gratitude*
T—*Thankfulness turns whatever we have into enough*
U—*Uplifting moments become cherished memories*
D—*Daily giving thanks*
E—*Express gratitude for your blessings*

July 13
Presents or Presence

2 Timothy 1:12
I know whom I have believed, and am convinced that He is able to guard what I have entrusted to Him for that day.

Birthdays are not so much about "presents" but about the "presence" of the love of God and the love of those around us. All of us are very appreciative of "presents" and we love opening gifts that someone has specifically chosen for us. However, what we are most thankful for is the "presence" of Jesus Christ in our lives. We are thankful for the blessings of His grace, mercy, peace, and love, the blessings of family, friends, good health and all that He has brought into our lives. We feel cherished by our LORD. We feel His "presence" each day which is a "present" from Him. Yesterday is the past, today is the "present" (called the gift) and tomorrow is the future. We can't do anything about the past except to forgive others and ourselves. We can only live for today and do all we can to share Jesus and that is the gift. Tomorrow isn't here yet so there is no need to worry because everything is in God's Hands and our worries may never materialize. We should remember to always trust in the LORD because He has us in the palms of His Hands and will take care of all that we need. Let's look forward to the "presence" of today.

"Trust the past to God's mercy, the present to God's love and the future to God's providence." (St. Augustine)

"Never be afraid to trust an unknown future to a known God." (Corrie ten Boom)

July 14
A Brand New Day

Lamentations 3:22-23
The steadfast love of the LORD never ceases, His mercies never come to an end; they are new every morning; great is Your faithfulness.

God's love and mercies are new every morning. As a new day dawns, we get to begin again and to experience God's new life for us. We are so very blessed because we are His beloved children. May we be strong in the LORD and embrace each new morning with thanksgiving and excitement as we wait for all that He has in store for us this day. There are mysteries of life to be learned and He plans for us lives full of abundant blessings. We should enjoy today—feel the coolness of the early morn, see the dew upon the grass, hear the chirping of the birds, watch for the pinks and purples of the rising sun in the sky, smell the garden flowers as they awake to the day, listen for a morning rain to quench the dry earth, and know that our God created it all for our enjoyment and appreciation. We thank and praise You, LORD, for loving us so much that we can see You in each new day.

"Morning Has Broken" is a popular and well-known Christian hymn first published in 1931. It has words by English author Eleanor Farjeon and is set to a traditional Gaelic tune known as "Bunessan." Sung by Cat Stevens in later years.

Morning has broken, like the first morning
Blackbird has spoken, like the first bird
Praise for the singing, praise for the morning
Praise for them springing fresh from the Word.

Sweet the rain's new fall, sunlit from heaven
Like the first dewfall, on the first grass
Praise for the sweetness of the wet garden
Sprung in completeness where His feet pass.

Mine is the sunlight, mine is the morning
Born of the one light, Eden saw play
Praise with elation, praise every morning
God's recreation of the new day.

July 15
God is the God of Second Chances

Nehemiah 9:17
They refused to listen and failed to remember the miracles you performed among them. They became stiff-necked and in their rebellion appointed a leader in order to return to their slavery. But You are a forgiving God, gracious and compassionate, slow to anger and abounding in love. Therefore You did not desert them ...

Our God is a patient God. He is the God of second chances. No matter what we do and how many times we disappoint Him, He is patient and ready to pardon and instruct us on the way we should go. He is a forgiving God and because of His forgiveness of our sins, He wants us to forgive others "seventy-seven times." In other words, we should always forgive. God puts no limits on how many times we can go to Him for mercy, but the key is that we must go to Him, repent and ask for His mercy. He will guide and help us, but we must be willing to change our attitude and behavior. His mercies are new every morning. Let's not miss this opportunity to have a second chance. God is waiting. It's a new day. Are we willing to go to Him, ask for His forgiveness and to begin again?

"A life transformed by the power of God is always a marvel and a miracle." (Geraldine Nicholas)

"Even as the angry vengeful thoughts boiled through me, I saw the sin of them. Jesus Christ had died for this man; was I going to ask for more? LORD Jesus, I prayed, forgive me and help me to forgive him....Jesus, I cannot forgive him. Give me Your forgiveness....And so I discovered that it is not on our forgiveness any more than on our goodness that the world's healing hinges, but on His. When He tells us to love our enemies, He gives along with the command, the love itself." (Corrie ten Boom)

July 16
Be an Encourager

Colossians 3:17
And whatever you do, whether in word or deed, do it all in the name of the LORD Jesus, giving thanks to God the Father through Him.

Hebrews 3:13
But encourage one another daily...

As Christians, we represent Christ at all times—wherever we go and whatever we say. When we do it all in the name of the LORD Jesus, we bring honor to Him in every aspect and activity of daily living. Let's represent Him by being an encourager and sharing His love. It is easier than we think. We can encourage with a smile, a kind word, a simple prayer, a thank you, a listening ear, a compliment or a simple note. Encouraging people are those who, when they leave, there is a void. People want to be around an encourager. A kind word can lift someone's spirits and it will remain with them for a long time. We should encourage those we meet daily with love and concern. As we go through our day, let's stop to think about how we can deliberately encourage someone else. It's not about us but about them. We can make an impact on someone's day and give them something to think about and just maybe, they will encourage someone else. Kind words are like building a foundation on solid rock and by doing this, we can make someone's day brighter.

"Be a reflection of what you'd like to see in others. If you want love, give love. If you want honesty, give honesty. If you want respect, give respect. You get in return what you give." (Author unknown)

"Don't worry—God is never blind to your tears, never deaf to your prayers and never silent to your pains. He sees, He hears and He will deliver." (Author unknown)

July 17
God's Rest and God's Peace

Hebrews 4:16
Let us then approach the throne of grace with confidence, so that we may receive mercy and find grace to help us in our time of need.

James 4:8 Draw near to God and God will draw near to you.

Whenever we face impossible situations and circumstances, do we fret, complain, worry, try to take matters into our own hands or do we go to God? Nothing is impossible with Him. Jesus knew that. In the garden He knew what lay ahead, but He prayed and even asked in Matthew 26:30: Going a little farther, He fell with His face to the ground and prayed, "My Father, if it is possible, may this cup be taken from Me. Yet not as I will, but as You will." Jesus was God and He was human, too. He knew anguish and He suffered. Because of that, He can relate to all that we are experiencing. His strength to obey came from His relationship with His Father and we, too, can have that strength as we draw near to God who is the source of our strength. In order to go through whatever lies ahead, we should take everything to the LORD in prayer. God loves us. Jesus is our High Priest and He is sitting at the right hand of God. We can go to God in prayer with confidence, asking Him to meet us in our time and place of need. We can be confident in His love and know that He hears us when we pray. He is our King, our Father, our Savior and our Friend. Let's go to God and find rest and peace in Him.

"Need a break? Try Jesus." (Thrivent Financial)

"Actions are seeds of fate. Seeds grow into destiny." (Harry S. Truman)

July 18
Trust Him for Protection

Psalm 5:11
But let all who take refuge in You be glad; let them ever sing for joy. Spread Your protection over them, that those who love Your name may rejoice in You.

Psalm 91:4
He will cover you with His feathers, and under His wings you will find refuge; His faithfulness will be your shield and rampart.

God is our protector, our refuge, our ever-present port in a storm. Trusting Him during the raging seas of life can be one of the hardest things to do. We want to calm the seas, but, unfortunately or maybe fortunately, only He can do that. What we can do as we ride the waves of uncertainty, fear and doubt is TRUST Him by praying that He will meet us in our need. We should trust Him to take us through every storm with a peace and comfort that only He can give. No matter how intense our fears, we can trade them for faith in God. We must let Him carry us through all the raging storms and seas of life because He is trustworthy and certain. We can TRUST HIM in everything because He is our protector.

"Trust Him when dark doubts assail thee. Trust Him when thy strength is small. Trust Him when to simply trust Him seems the hardest thing of all." (Author unknown)

Prayer of protection by James Dillet Fremman
"May the light of God surround me (you, us).
May the love of God enfold me (you, us).
May the power of God protect me (you, us).
May the presence of God watch over me (you, us).
Wherever I am (you/we are), God is.
And all is well. Amen"

July 19
We are Healed

Isaiah 53:5
But He was pierced for our transgressions, He was crushed for our iniquities; the punishment that brought us peace was upon Him, and by His wounds we are healed.

Jeremiah 17:14
Heal me, O LORD, and I will be healed; save me and I will be saved, for You are the One I praise.

God came and lived as man named Jesus so that we would know that He is God. He is the Messiah and gave His life for us so that we would be forgiven of all our sins and will eventually live eternally with Him. We all need healing of one sort or another. We have a Savior who understands our suffering as He has suffered too. We can go to Him and know that He understands our illnesses, our fears and whatever we are going through. We are all assailed with some sort of illness or problem, and it's our responsibility to trust and rely on God so that His will can be accomplished. When we are rooted in the love of God, we know that we are not alone. We know that Jesus will have compassion on us, give us strength and peace. No matter what we face today, we should set our minds on Him because He is our anchor. *"By His stripes, we are healed."*

"Trust Me in the midst of a messy day. Your inner calm—your Peace in My Presence—need not be shaken by what is going on around you." (Sarah Young)

"When you seek Me instead of the world's idols, you experience My Joy and Peace." (Sarah Young)

July 20
We are More Than Conquerors

Romans 8:28
And we know that in all things God works for the good of those who love Him, who have been called according to His purpose.

Romans 8:37-39
No, in all these things we are more than conquerors through Him who loved us. For I am convinced that neither death nor life, neither angels nor demons, neither the present nor the future, nor any powers, neither height nor depth, nor anything else in all creation, will be able to separate us from the love of God that is in Christ Jesus our Lord.

We are God's—plain and simple. We are His called children and He loves and knows us. No matter what we face, we are not alone and we know that He works in all things for our good and His glory. Because we are His children, everything that happens to us happens to fulfill His purpose. We trust and love Him but He loves us more. God is with us in all circumstances. It is impossible to be separated from Christ. He died for us and He conquered sin for us, proving that His love is steadfast and perfect. Because of His great love, we can feel secure in Him in any circumstance. We are "Rooted and established in love." (Ephesians 3:17) Because of God's love, we have strong, deep roots and we have the strength to face whatever the day brings. We are anchored in the love of God, and, with Christ we are more than conquerors, so let's bring it on.

Quotes from Charles Spurgeon (1834-1892)
"Trials teach us what we are; they dig up the soil, and let us see what we are made of.

The Lord gets his best soldiers out of the highlands of affliction.

As sure as God puts His children in the furnace of affliction, He will be with them in it."

July 21
Don't be bullied by doubts and fears

Romans 8:31
"What, then, shall we say in response to these things? If God is for us, who can be against us?"

Romans 8:37 (I am a conqueror because He loves me.)
No, in all these things we are more than conquerors through Him who loved us.

At one time or another we have been bullied with doubts and fears. We don't sleep, we don't eat or we overeat; we get cranky. The attacker is Satan and he is constantly attacking us in our most vulnerable states. We have an advantage because we have a God who is in control and will guide us through these quagmires. Our job is to trust and rely on Him to build us up. We can Fully Rely On God (FROG) and His truth by surrendering every thought, doubt and fear to Him. He will handle it and He will give us the strength we need. We can live confidently in Him by spending time with Him. We must be intentional about praying, reading His Word, listening to uplifting music and spending time with Christian friends and should memorize Bible verses that will help when doubts and fears assail us. We can just say STOP and repeat a promise verse over and over again. We should make God's promises our promises by changing them into the first person. As an example, "I will be rooted and established in God's love." (Ephesians 3:17)

"Of whom shall I be afraid? One with God is a majority." (Martin Luther)

"Fear. His (Satan) modus operandi is to manipulate you with the mysterious, to taunt you with the unknown. Fear of death, fear of failure, fear of God, fear of tomorrow—his arsenal is vast. His goal? To create cowardly, joyless Christians. He doesn't want you to make that journey to the mountain. He figures if he can rattle you enough, you will take your eyes off the peaks and settle for a dull existence in the flat lands." (Max Lucado)

July 22
The Morning Star—God's Light

Psalm 119:105
Your Word is a lamp to my feet and a light for my path.

2 Peter 1:19
And we have the word of the prophets made more certain, and you will do well to pay attention to it, as to a light shining in a dark place, until the day dawns and the morning star rises in your hearts.

This morning when I woke up at 4 a.m., the moon was brightly shining and everything was surrounded by a lovely soft hue. What a comfort for us when night seems so dark and then there is this beautiful soft light of the moon illuminating the shadows. This is what the light of Jesus does for us when we go through difficult circumstances. During those deep, dark times, a light shines just as the moon rises or the sun comes up at the breaking of dawn. Jesus Christ is the light of the world that shines in our lives because He is God's Word. His light will shine when a friend reaches out with a helping hand, a hug, sends a card or gives us a call. Whenever the light of Jesus, the "Morning Star" comes, it is our hope that we're not alone and that God is watching over us. We can be confident that He will see us through the dark and bring us into the light of His love and grace. My prayer for us is that we will see the light of Jesus' love today and always. I pray that His light will live in us and through us for all to see His glory.

"Seeing how God works in nature can help us understand how He works in our lives." (Janette Oke)

"LORD, Jesus Christ, You are the sun that always rises but never sets. You are the source of all life, creating and sustaining every living thing ... May I walk in Your light, be nourished by Your food, be sustained by Your mercy, and be warmed by Your love." (Erasmus)

July 23
LORD, Take My Hand

Isaiah 52:7
How beautiful on the mountains are the feet of those who bring good news, who proclaim peace, who bring good tidings, who proclaim salvation, who say to Zion, "Your God reigns!"

Luke 1:38
Mary responded, "I am the LORD's servant. May everything you have said about me come true.

What a comfort to know that we have a God who will lead us in the way He would have us go. Of course, we must let Him, but, when we do, our lives will never be the same and will be oh so glorious. Mission team members are called to go to the mission fields and are open to God's leading, serving Him and helping others. Each of these diverse and courageous children of God step out of their comfort zones, trusting our LORD to show them where there are needs and how they are to help. We pray for safe travels and thank them for sharing Jesus with all those they meet. We, too, can reach out and let God take our hands and lead us. We can trust Him and ask for His discernment and guidance on our paths. Our journeys can be in our own homes, communities and our own backyards. God bless us as we trust, serve and bring the Good News of Jesus to all we meet.

"LORD, Take My Hand and Lead Me (Hymn)
LORD, take my hand and lead me upon life's way;
Direct, protect, and feed me from day to day.
Without Your grace and favor I go astray;
So take my hand, O Savior, and lead the way."

"True willpower and courage are not on the battlefield, but in everyday conquests over our inertia, laziness and boredom." (D.L. Moody)

July 24
Reach up, Reach out—Rejoice!!!

Psalm 118:24
This is the day the LORD has made; let us rejoice and be glad in it.

Psalm 118: 28-29
You are my God, and I will give You thanks; You are my God, and I will exalt You. Give thanks to the LORD, for He is good; His love endures forever.

Let's rejoice in the LORD, worshipping and praising Him—rejoice! He has given us life and has taken our sins to the cross. We are now forgiven. We must reach up, reach out—rejoice! He is alive. We should worship His Holy name and reach up to heaven, praising and worshipping our LORD, Jesus Christ. When we worship and praise our God, our hearts become full of thanksgiving and love so that we want to reach out to others to share Jesus with them. Let's rejoice that He has given us this day to live and to serve Him! We must reach up, reach out and share the Good News of Jesus Christ.

"Come to Me. Come to Me. Come to Me. This is My continual invitation to you, proclaimed in holy whispers." (Sarah Young)

"Love is larger than the walls which shut it in." (Corrie ten Boom)

July 25
Milky Way
The Milky Way is a barred spiral galaxy 100,000-120,000 light-years in diameter containing 200-400 billion stars.

Proverbs 27:17
As iron sharpens iron, so one man sharpens another.

Sometimes at 4:30 in the morning, I will stand on our patio enjoying the cool refreshing air of an early summer morning. What a blessing it is to feel the coolness and see a dark sky sparkling with stars shining like diamonds in a jeweler's showcase. One star shines brightly, but when you see millions of them together, what a beautiful display. Our God gives us the peacefulness of the morning and the last few minutes of darkness before the breaking of dawn for our enjoyment. It takes many people to be a church just as it takes many stars to make a Milky Way. In the church, we all come together to do the work of God. We work together to sharpen ideas, stimulate thoughts and shape them into God pleasing displays just as a beautiful array of stars is showcased in a dark night. We are our Father's house. We have the Holy Spirit living in us to show us the best way to work together as a church family. We are His shining stars. Whatever we do today we must shine brightly and do it with other brothers and sisters in Christ because we are God's Milky Way in an often dark world.

"Today I know that such memories are the key not to the past, but to the future. I know that the experiences of our lives, when we let God use them, become the mysterious and perfect preparation for the work He will give us to do." (Corrie ten Boom)

"Bring Me the sacrifice of thanksgiving. Take nothing for granted, not even the rising of the sun." (Sarah Young)

July 26
Making Deposits

Romans 5:5
God has poured out His love into our hearts by the Holy Spirit, whom He has given us.

When we encourage others we are making deposits into our own lives. God loves us and He wants us to share His love with others. In doing so, we are making deposits into our own lives because when we need a word of encouragement, hope or love someone will share it with us. It may be someone we don't know or someone very close to us. We should never be hesitant to be an encourager because when we plant a seed of encouragement, it will grow and blossom in another's life. The fruit of it may be something shared with us one day in our time of need. Let's make a deposit today in someone's life and watch the interest grow in our lives.

"Kind words can be short and easy to speak, but their echoes are truly endless." (Mother Teresa)

"Let Christ's beauty shine through me, for all the world to see." (Author unknown)

July 27
The Wonder Of It All....

Exodus 15:11
"Who among the gods is like you, O LORD? Who is like You—majestic in holiness, awesome in glory, working wonders?"

Psalm 40:5
Many, O LORD my God, are the wonders you have done. The things you planned for us no one can recount to you; were I to speak and tell of them, they would be too many to declare.

We all have the love of wonder—it is in our hearts. We wonder at the stars and the amazement of God's creation. We gaze at the ocean and wonder at the waves as they crash against the rocks and shore. We have this child-like appetite for what's next and the joy of living. A child-like sense of wonder is in us at the delights of our Creator's world and the beauty all around us. A rainbow against a dark sky after a storm, the dew on the flowers in the early morn, the majesty of mountains as the fog lifts and the mist rising off a lake all speak to us of You, LORD. The wonder of it all....

"You do not know what you are going to do; the only thing you know is that God knows what He is doing....It is this attitude that keeps you in perpetual wonder." (Oswald Chambers)

"Never be afraid to trust an unknown future to a known God."
(Corrie ten Boom)

July 28
We Have Today

Psalm 118:24
This is the day the LORD has made; let us rejoice and be glad in it.

Psalm 47:1-2
Clap your hands, all you nations; shout to God with cries of joy. How awesome is the LORD Most High, the great King over all the earth!

Congratulations! We have today! It is called the present. Yesterday is gone and tomorrow is not yet here. Rejoice because we have today, and it is a beautiful gift. God is the author of creation, and He provides so many gifts for us every day. Our lives are filled with beauty but they are not perfect. It is our choice as to how we look at our situations as we wait for God's timing. God is good all the time; all the time God is good. He is worthy of our praise.

Summer is a season of growing. The ground is flourishing with beautiful flowers that are God's gifts to us to appreciate. Let's embrace the early morning quiet and the peacefulness of a sunrise and enjoy the way the clouds play across the sky and the colors of the sun peek through as the earth awakes for another day. We can embrace all the beautiful gifts of God and remember what a good and loving God we have. As we look at all the beauty around us, we know that because we place our hope and trust in Him, this is but a glimpse of a more beautiful life in store for us.

"Faith is the art of holding on to things in spite of your changing moods and circumstances." (C. S. Lewis)

"The first principle to making life matter is to value the beautiful people and places in your life. God has given those places to us as gifts and with the understanding that how we treat these things in our journey determines, ultimately, what we value in God." (Shane Stanford)

July 29
Good Morning

Lamentations 3:22-24
Because of the LORD's great love we are not consumed, for His compassions never fail. They are new every morning; great is Your faithfulness. I say to myself, "The LORD is my portion; therefore I will wait for Him."

Good morning. A new day is upon us and God's compassions are new each day. His love and mercy are upon us and He is faithful. When we trust in God's faithfulness day by day it makes us confident in His great promises for the future. Good morning and let's enjoy today with the hope of the LORD in our hearts.

"Each dawn holds a new hope for a new plan, making the start of each day the start of a new life." (Gina Blair)

"In the morning let our hearts gaze upon God's love and the love He has allowed us to share, and in the beauty of that vision, let us go forth to meet the day." (Roy Lessin)

July 30
Believe

Mark 9:24
"I do believe; help me overcome my unbelief!"

John 11:25-26
Jesus said to her, "I am the resurrection and the life. The one who believes in Me will live, even though they die; and whoever lives by believing in Me will never die. Do you believe this?"

In the dictionary, the meaning of the word *believe* (as a verb) is to have confidence in the truth, the existence, or the reliability of something, although without absolute proof that one is right in doing so.

To *believe* is more than intellectual agreement that Jesus is God. It means to put our trust and confidence in Him that He alone can save us. It is to put Christ in charge of our present plans and eternal destiny. Believing is both trusting His words as reliable and relying on Him for the power to change. When we trust Christ, the promise of everlasting life will be ours and we can believe. Jesus Christ, our LORD and Savior, has the power over life and death as well as the power to forgive our sins. He is the Creator of life. He who is life can surely restore life. We have the assurance that when we believe in Christ, we have a spiritual life that death cannot conquer or diminish in any way. We don't know the future but God does. When we live by His standards, He will not leave us; He will come to us, be in us and show Himself to us. We need not fear whatever the future holds because He will be with us through it all. We must believe in God and have faith in Him to be secure about the future.

"You never know how much you really believe anything until its truth or falsehood becomes a matter of life and death to you. It is easy to say you believe a rope to be strong and sound as long as you are merely using it to cord a box. But suppose you had to hang by that rope over a precipice. Wouldn't you then first discover how much you really trusted it? . . . Only a real risk tests the reality of a belief." (C. S. Lewis, A Grief Observed)

"Because He lives, I can face tomorrow.
Because He lives, All fear is gone.
Because I know He holds the future,
And life is worth the living just because He lives." (Bill & Gloria Gaither)

July 31
Get Energized Today!

2 Corinthians 12:9
But He said to me, "My grace is sufficient for you, for my power is made perfect in weakness." Therefore I will boast all the more gladly about my weaknesses, so that Christ's power may rest on me.

There are times in our lives where we need a jolt of energy to keep us going. God can energize us with His power and grace. He told Paul that His power is made perfect in weakness. Remember those times when we've felt that kind of weakness and we thought we couldn't go on or accomplish some difficult task. When we believe in Jesus Christ, He will step in through the Holy Spirit to energize us to succeed. Jesus, our LORD and Savior, is so big, so powerful, and so awesome that His power can take us at our weakest and make us strong. Grace will meet us at those times and energize us to accomplish the tasks He has prepared for us. His Grace is more than enough. Let's get energized today and go to the LORD for He will lead us to the most effective pathway with His strength. We can experience the power of the Holy Spirit in our lives. Jesus will give us the courage, boldness, confidence and ability to be witnesses for Him in all that we do and say. He will energize us to move forward or give us the patience to wait on Him and not get ahead of Him. When we are weak, He is strong. Let's get plugged into Jesus today and be energized for all that He has planned for us to accomplish in His glorious name.

"This life was not intended to be the place of our perfection, but the preparation for it." (Richard Baxter)

"Success is the maximum utilization of the ability that you have." (Zig Ziglar)

August 1
Peace Like a River

John 14:27
Peace I leave with you; my peace I give you. I do not give to you as the world gives. Do not let not your hearts be troubled and do not be afraid.

The peace that we receive from the Holy Spirit is a deep and lasting peace. Christ's peace is confident assurance in any circumstance. We have no need to fear the present or the future when we accept God's peace that is comforting and lasting. True peace is knowing that God is in control. We should turn whatever is worrying us into prayers and feel the peace that passes all understanding—God's peace.

When Peace, like a River (Horatio G. Spafford)
When peace, like a river, attendeth my way;
When sorrows, like sea billows, roll;
Whatever my lot, Thou hast taught me to say,
It is well, it is well with my soul.

August 2
Touching Him

Luke 8:44
She came up behind Him and touched the edge of His cloak...

John 12:3
Then Mary took about a pint of pure nard, an expensive perfume; she poured it on Jesus' feet and wiped His feet with her hair.

Imagine what it would be like to touch the hem of Jesus' garment, wash His feet as He did the disciples' feet, or witness Mary washing His feet with the perfume, and wiping them with her hair. It is comforting to know He is present at the altar when we take communion. It is comforting to know He is present every moment of every day. In faith, we reach out to Him and in faith, we do touch Him. We touch Him whenever we help someone, when we hold a baby in our arms and when we hug someone. We touch Him when we see the beauty of His creation in a sunrise, a sunset or hear the waves of the ocean lapping against the shore. We touch Him in so many ways, every moment of every day. He is with us and He is present. We touch Jesus by faith in every way as we share Him with others.

"All that we love deeply becomes a part of us." (Helen Keller)

"Dear Jesus, help us to spread Your fragrance everywhere we go. God is everywhere and in everything and without Him we cannot exist. I see God in the eyes of every child..." (Mother Teresa)

August 3
A Breath of Fresh Air

Isaiah 41:10
So do not fear, for I am with you; do not be dismayed, for I am your God. I will strengthen you and help you; I will uphold you with my righteous right hand.

We just returned from a few days away. We traveled to Niagara Falls and then to the St. Lawrence Seaway where we spent time with friends on their island. Yes, they own an island and it is paradise. The air there is so fresh that it was literally a "breath of fresh air." As we prayed together, we realized that God is our daily "breath of fresh air and life." He refreshes us each day with love, hope and His promises. Because of our faith in Him, we can go through our day with assurance that we have a relationship with Him. He knows us—the real us. Oftentimes that may be frightening because we feel unworthy and truthfully, we are. However, because of what Jesus did on the cross, we are forgiven and redeemed. God has a purpose for us. He will show us what He wants us to do, and He will bring people into our midst that He wants us to meet. He is our LORD, Savior and Friend—our breath of fresh air. Let's go to Him in prayer, trusting Him to guide us through our day. Our relationship with God depends on our prayers and conversations with Him. Just as we open our doors and windows to breathe in the fresh cool air, we should open our hearts and minds to God and breathe in His love, peace, mercy and grace.

"Opportunities are seldom labeled." (Claude McDonald)

"One learns people through the heart, not the eyes or the intellect." (Mark Twain)

August 4
Waiting Means to Patiently Anticipate

Isaiah 40:31
Those who wait on the LORD shall renew their strength; They shall mount up with wings like eagles, They shall run and not be weary, They shall walk and not faint.

Technology and the information age have brought everything to us instantly and quickly. Anything we want to know or purchase can be done via the iphone, ipad or whatever new gadget is out there. In other words, the world is now at our fingertips and people are always in a hurry. They do not want to wait for anything. The information highway is fast and we are impatient when we have to wait longer than a nanosecond. We can only imagine what would be the reactions and responses of people today if they had to spend 40 days with Moses in the dessert only to learn from their "information highway" that the trip should have taken 11 days on foot or camel or an hour or less by today's modes of transportation. Poor Moses would have suffered more rebellion for sure than what had already taken place. There are lessons to be learned as we wait. Often we receive blessings that we would not have otherwise had if we weren't in that place at that moment. God may be teaching us something. We must slow down, be patient and share the fruits that He has given us with others. As we wait, we should be the people God wants us to be by showing Him in the way we act, love, share, give and speak.

"Bearing your circumstances bravely—even thanking Me for them—is one of the highest forms of praise. This sacrifice of thanksgiving rings golden-toned bells of Joy throughout heavenly realms. On earth, also, your patient suffering sends out ripples of good tidings in ever-widening circles." (Sarah Young)

"Pause before responding to people or situations, giving My Spirit space to act through you." (Sarah Young)

August 5
Waiting on God

Psalm 27:14
Wait for the LORD; be strong and take heart and wait for the LORD.

Micah 7:7
As for me, I watch in hope for the LORD, I wait for God my Savior; my God will hear me.

Romans 12:12
Be joyful in hope, patient in affliction, faithful in prayer.

Waiting on God means to rest in Him, trusting Him to take us where He wants us to go. He is the object of our waiting and we know He will never leave us nor forsake us. We expect Him to act in our lives, give us the strength to endure whatever we face, help us with decisions we need to make and answer our prayers in His due time. We look for God everywhere and wait for Him to renew us, strengthen us and give us the peace that only He can give. How do we wait? We wait patiently for Him. We listen for His whispers as He guides us through His Word. God speaks to us in nature and in song. When we wait upon the LORD, we soar like an eagle. We rise above life's difficulties and distractions as He renews us and shows us the way to Him and His promises. Waiting is good and waiting patiently is even better.

"It is not the load that breaks us down. It's the way we carry it."
(Wanda E. Brunstetter)

"God runs the show. Completely. Life proves it every day: He runs the show." (Mariska Hargitay)

August 6
Shining for Jesus

Matthew 5:14-16
You are the light of the world. A city on a hill cannot be hidden. Neither do people light a lamp and put it under a bowl. Instead they put it on its stand, and it gives light to everyone in the house. In the same way, let your light shine before men, that they may see your good deeds and praise your Father in heaven.

We all have the ability to bring Jesus' light into the world. When we live for Christ, we will glow like lights in a dark night showing others what Christ is like. Let's be a beacon of truth for Jesus Christ, showing others His light of love and truth. We can be like a lighthouse on a rocky cliff showing sailors a port in a storm and guiding them away from danger. We, too, can be a light in a dark world, showing others the safety of His loving arms. Jesus loves us so much. Let's be who God wants us to be in all we say and do. We must keep polishing our lights by studying His Word and serving Him. Let our lights shine for Jesus and let's continue shining brightly for our Savior.

"Temptations are sure to ring your doorbell, but it's your fault if you invite them for dinner." (Wanda E. Brunstetter)

"As you live in close contact with Me, the Light of My Presence filters through you to bless others. Your weakness and woundedness are openings through which the Light of the knowledge of My Glory shines forth." (Sarah Young)

August 7
Forgiveness

Matthew 18:21-22
Then Peter came to Jesus and asked, "LORD, how many times shall I forgive my brother when he sins against me? Up to seven times?" Jesus answered, "I tell you, not seven times, but seventy-seven times."

Jesus was saying that we should never keep track of how many times we forgive someone, and that we should always forgive those who are truly repentant. We are to forgive ourselves as well. Instead of berating and beating ourselves up over a side step or a misstep in our journey, we need to remember what Jesus said about forgiveness, 77 times—meaning always and forever. Sometimes it's easier to forgive others rather than ourselves. Our frustrations could include any number of things such as our desire to be who God wants us to be, our quest for health, the development of our financial stewardship and goal setting, our attitude adjustments and our reactions to situations—all these things and more require us to learn that there are things we can change and there are things we cannot change. We need to know the difference. With God anything is possible and once we know what we can change, we can do it with His help and love. We must ask for His wisdom and discernment. We should ask God for His help to forgive others and to forgive ourselves.

"God, grant me the Serenity to accept the things I cannot change, the Courage to change the things I can and the Wisdom to know the difference." (Serenity Prayer)

"Living one day at a time;
Enjoying one moment at a time;
Accepting hardships as the pathway to peace;
Taking, as He did, this sinful world
as it is, not as I would have it;
Trusting that He will make all things right
if I surrender to His Will;
That I may be reasonably happy in this life
and supremely happy with Him
Forever in the next.
Amen" (Author unknown)

August 8
Over the Edge

Psalm 121:2
My help comes from the LORD, the Maker of heaven and earth.

There are times that we all go "over the edge." Many times my youngest brother has rappelled down 18 stories of a local hotel to raise money for Special Olympics. Now that's what I call going "over the edge." I'm glad he can do it but it is certainly not for me. There are times when we all go over the edge in some area of our lives, especially when we face difficult situations or when we go above and beyond what we think we are capable of doing. What we need to remember is that our harness is Jesus Christ. Whatever we do, our help comes from Him. He is our Creator, our LORD, the Maker of heaven and earth. We can lean on Him, trust Him and know that whatever we are doing Jesus is there to help. We just need to ask. Whatever "over the edge" situation we are facing today, we need to call on Jesus. He's there and He'll help. His help may come in many different forms. He may send someone to give us the extra strength we need or give us the peace to continue. Let's go "over the edge" with Jesus.

"When everything seems to be falling apart, consider that maybe it's not. Maybe it is really just falling into place." (Karen Berg)

"As a bright sunbeam comes into every window, so comes a love born of God's care for every need." (Wanda E. Brunstetter)

August 9
Our Creator

Genesis 1:1
In the beginning God created the heavens and the earth.

God is the Creator. He had a purpose and a plan for His creation. The earth was not created by blind chance but by God's choice. He created the earth and every living thing in it as a deep expression of His love. He created all that we see, created man and woman in His own image, and wanted us to know Him, come to Him and have a relationship with Him. We are valuable to Him. God came in the person of His Son Jesus Christ, so that we would know Him in a more personal way. Now that is love. Thank You, LORD, for loving us so much. We will praise You all the day long.

"I can see how it might be possible for a man to look down upon the earth and be an atheist, but I cannot conceive how he could look up into the heavens and say there is no God." (Abraham Lincoln)

"Whoever loves much does much." (Thomas á Kempis)

August 10
Resting in Jesus

Matthew 11:28
"Come to Me, all you who are weary and burdened, and I will give you rest."

I can certainly appreciate a good night's rest. Resting in Jesus is like waking up after a good night's sleep, feeling refreshed and ready to tackle the day. When we are weary and heavy-burdened, it disturbs our rest in Him, our completeness in Him. No matter what situation we face, He will give us His rest. It will feel like waking up from a delicious nap. When we ask God for help, it makes us aware of Christ in our lives. He will steady us, give us peace and we will find wholeness in Him. We are complete in Him no matter what we face on a day-to-day basis. He is all we need and He will provide all we need as we abide in Him. We should not let anything come between us and our LORD. We want "Christ-awareness" in every area of our lives. The rest that Jesus promises is love, healing and peace with God. Let's go get some rest.

"Great works are performed not by strength but by perseverance."
(Samuel Johnson)

"Choosing to suffer means that there must be something wrong with you, but choosing God's will—even if it means you will suffer—is something very different. God places His saints where they will bring the most glory to Him, and we are totally incapable of judging where that may be."
(Oswald Chambers)

August 11
Our Father

Matthew 6:9
" 'Our Father which art in heaven, hallowed be thy name, . . .'"

Who is our Father in heaven? This first line of the Lord's Prayer indicates that God is not only majestic and holy but also personal and loving. We praise Him and commit to keep His name hallow (holy) and honor Him by respectfully using His name. As we pray to "Our Father," we should think about the way Jesus described God, as His Father and ours, being personal, all loving, forgiving and providing for us. God gave us earthly fathers to guide us, take care of us and be role models, but, occasionally, they disappoint us. We must remember that they are human and not perfect. Sometimes when we pray, their image comes to mind and that is not the image that Jesus describes. *"Our Father which art in heaven,"* You are holy and loving—we praise You and Your holy name.

"Prayer immediately turns us into something greater than ourselves."
(Cardinal Timothy Dolan)

"Feed your faith and your doubts will starve to death."
(Debbie Macomber)

August 12
Trust Me

Psalm 37:3
Trust in the LORD and do good; dwell in the land, and feed on His faithfulness.

Proverbs 3:5-6
Trust in the LORD with all your heart and lean not on your own understanding; in all your ways acknowledge Him, and He will make your paths straight.

We have an important decision to make—to trust God or not. Often we feel that we cannot trust anyone, not even God but He knows what is best for us and He is a better judge of what we want even more than we are. We must trust Him completely in every choice we make. That means trusting Him with every area of our lives to provide and protect us and our families. We should think carefully and use our God-given abilities to reason, but we should not trust our own ideas to the exclusion of all others. We should not be wise in our own eyes. It is important to always bring our decisions to God in prayer and use the Bible as our guide to follow God. We also need to be willing to listen to and be corrected by God's Word and wise counselors. We must acknowledge God in all our ways by turning every area of our lives over to Him. We should make God a vital part of everything we do, trusting Him to guide us so that we will accomplish everything for His purpose. God will make our paths straight by both guiding and protecting us. We can trust Him.

"There is one thing God says to every believer, regardless of his circumstances—Trust Me." (DaySpring)

"When I try, I fail. When I trust, He succeeds." (Corrie ten Boom)

August 13
Spending Time with God

Psalm 119:105
Your Word is a lamp to my feet and a light for my path.

John 15:15 "I have called you friends ..."

With the busyness of each day we need to take time to be with God. Sometimes we get to the end of our day and realize that the most important being in our lives has been totally left out. We haven't talked to Him all day. We haven't read His Word nor have we spent time with Him. No wonder our days go awry and feel so empty because our Captain hasn't been invited to share the day with us. The most important relationship we will ever have is our relationship with God, our LORD and Savior. The Holy Spirit is with us each day to guide and help us and we need to spend time with Him. We should take time for God today and every day. He is the best friend we'll ever have. His Word will guide us and take us to places we can't even imagine.

"Our friendship with Jesus is based on the new life He created in us, which has no resemblance or attraction to our old life but only to the life of God. It is a life that is completely humble, pure and devoted to God." (Oswald Chambers)

"I don't know what the future holds, but I know who holds the future." (Author unknown)

August 14
All by Myself

Proverbs 3:5-6
Trust in the LORD with all your heart and lean not on your own understanding; in all your ways acknowledge Him, and He will make your paths straight.

Let's think about the many times we have heard toddlers say, "I can do it myself" and the many times we have said the same thing. Unfortunately, they can't and neither can we. We cannot go it alone on this journey of life without the love, help and guidance of our LORD. He knows us and what we need each and every day. He allows experiences and He puts people on our journeys of life so that we will learn and grow. We are not all by ourselves because when we lean on and trust Him, our God will guide us and show us the way He wants us to go. He knows the future and exactly what we need each day. It's our choice to try to do it all by ourselves or to trust a loving God who has a Master Plan that will take us on an incredible journey.

"Every experience God gives us, every person He puts in our lives is the perfect preparation for the future that only He can see."
(Corrie ten Boom)

"Wisdom is knowing the right path to take ... integrity is taking it."
(Author unknown)

August 15
God is Light

John 8:12
When Jesus spoke again to the people, He said, "I am the light of the world. Whoever follows Me will never walk in darkness, but will have the light of life."

1 John1: 5
This is the message that we have heard from Him and declare to you: God is light; in Him there is no darkness at all.

Jesus Christ is the Creator of life, and His life brings light to mankind. Jesus lights the path ahead of us so that we can see how to live. God came into the world as a human through His Son, Jesus, who was God in the flesh. Jesus brings life and light into a dark world and He is eternal. Light represents what is good, pure, true, holy and reliable. Jesus died for our sins and we are forgiven. In order to have a relationship with God, we must put aside our sinful ways of living because darkness cannot exist in the presence of light, and sin cannot exist in the presence of a holy God. We all sin but we have a forgiving and loving God who forgives us and will help us to resist temptation. We cannot have fellowship with God and still walk in darkness. Jesus is the light of the world. When we look up and see Him, we let the light of Jesus shine in our lives.

"Run your day by the clock and your life with a vision." (Zig Ziglar)

"Even if you are on the right track, you'll get run over if you just sit there." (Will Rogers)

August 16
Grace

Psalm 84:11
For the LORD God is a sun and a shield: the LORD will give grace and glory: no good thing will He withhold from them that walk uprightly.

God does not promise to give us everything we think is good, but He will not withhold what is permanently good. He will give us the means to walk along His paths, but we must do the walking. When we obey Him, He will not hold anything back that will help us serve Him. God is enough and is our keeper. God's living presence is our greatest joy. God is grace and He never fails.

"God has not promised skies always blue, flower-strewn pathways all our lives through; God has not promised sun without rain, joy without sorrow, peace without pain. But God has promised strength for the day, rest for the labor, light for the way, grace for the trials, help from above, unfailing sympathy, undying love." (Annie Johnson Flint)

"Let God's promises shine on your problems." (Corrie ten Boom)

August 17
God Is the Heart of Everything

John 10:29
My Father, Who has given them (His followers/His sheep) to me, is greater than all; and no one is able to snatch them out of my Father's hand.

As followers of Jesus, the Spirit of God lives in us and He is our heart. We must keep our eyes on Him and not on our problems or the problems of the world. If we take our eyes off Jesus and focus on all that is going on around us, Satan will be able to choke out our spiritual life and squeeze our hearts until they hurt. God, help us keep close to You and keep the unsavory work of Satan from growing in our hearts and choking out Your Word. LORD, transform our hearts and lives so that we may do Your will and be Your light.

"As a bright sunbeam comes into every window, so comes a love born of God's care for every need."(Wanda E. Brunstetter)

"The center of God's Heart
In the center of His hand
*you find the center of **His Will**;*
In the center of His will
*you find the center of **His Peace**;*
In the center of His peace
*you find the center of **His Love**;*
In the center of His love
*you find the center of **His Heart**." (Author unknown)*

August 18
God Is ... in the House

Joshua 24:15
But as for me and my household, we will serve the LORD.

1 Corinthians 6:19
Do you not know that your body is a temple of the Holy Spirit, who is in you, whom you have received from God? You are not your own;

The church is not just a building but it is the people of God. The dwelling place of God is the people of God. God is in the house because He is lives in all of us in our bodies and hearts. The body of Christ is God's temple and the way we live shows others the strength of our commitment to serve Him. God is very present in our lives and we can trust Him to be with us. He is our hope and we can give Him complete control over everything. God is in the house; we should serve Him, worship Him and give Him the praise and glory that He deserves. Let's glorify God and take good care of His house.

"The first and fundamental law of nature is to seek out peace and follow it." (Thomas Hobbes)

"Darkness cannot drive out darkness: only light can do that. Hate cannot drive out hate: only love can do that." (Martin Luther King Jr.)

August 19
Plan A or Plan B

Psalm 20:4
May He give you the desire of your heart and make all your plans succeed.

Jeremiah 29:11
"For I know the plans I have for you," declares the LORD, "plans to prosper you and not to harm you, plans to give you hope and a future. Then you will call upon Me and come and pray to me, and I will listen to you."

When something doesn't work, we often go to Plan B. We think that we are Plan A and when all else fails, God is Plan B. This is backward thinking. God should always be our Plan A. Whatever we do, we should go to God first and include Him in all of our plans and decisions. When we include Him and ask for His wisdom and discernment, it is amazing how things will work out—actually better than we expect. When we surrender control to Him and follow Him, He opens doors and pathways for us that we, in our "infinite" wisdom, would never see or know about. God is Plan A. We should go to Him first before we begin anything because when we work closely with Him, we will succeed and can accomplish anything. We will never need a Plan B when we have God as Plan A.

"Let God carry your worries and stress today." (Thrivent Financial)

"Stay within whispering distance. If you stray, you won't hear His voice." (Author unknown)

August 20
God Is Our Refuge

Psalm 46:1
God is our refuge and strength, an ever-present help in trouble.

Psalm 91: 1-4
He who dwells in the shelter of the Most High will rest in the shadow of the Almighty. I will say of the LORD, "He is my refuge and my fortress, my God, in whom I trust." Surely He will save you from the fowler's snare and from the deadly pestilence. He will cover you with His feathers, and under His wings you will find refuge; His faithfulness will be your shield and rampart."

The dictionary describes "refuge" as a shelter or protection from danger, difficulty, etc.; a person or thing that gives shelter, help or comfort; a place of safety; shelter; safe retreat. God is our refuge. Our help comes from our LORD. He is always there and is our strength through all dangers and fears. He provides security, shelter and peace. He will not fail to rescue those who love, believe and trust Him. We can be confident in God's ability because He is our eternal refuge and will provide us with strength in any and every circumstance. We must trust in the LORD, trade in our fears and dwell and rest in Him. When we entrust ourselves to His protection and pledge our daily devotion to Him, He will keep us safe.

"Trust the LORD to calm troubled waters. At the end of the day may we all say, "I have kept the faith." (Thrivent Financial)

"Got no checkbooks, got no banks. Still I'd like to express my thanks—I got the sun in the mornin' and the moon at night." (Irving Berlin)

August 21
Jesus Is Our Friend

John 15:13
Greater love has no one than this, that he lay down his life for his friends.

What a friend we have in Jesus! We may not have to lay down our lives for our friends, but there are times that we can put aside our desires. When they need us, we put our friends first. In certain situations we may need to listen and not say a word. We can love, help, encourage or give them a shoulder to cry on, a listening ear, a hand to hold, or a smile to brighten their day. It can be a simple gesture that will give them hope. Jesus loved us enough to sacrifice His life for us. All He is asking us to do is to love others by serving Him. Jesus is our friend beyond and above all friends.

"The golden rule of friendship is to listen to others as you would have them listen to you." (David Augsburger)

"We are cups, constantly and quietly being filled. The trick is, knowing how to tip ourselves over and let the beautiful stuff out." (Ray Bradbury)

August 22
God Is Good All the Time. All the Time God Is Good

Psalm 46:10
"Be still, and know that I am God;"

God is good all the time. God loves us and He is always there to help us, but we need to take time to be still with Him during our day. He provides refuge, security and peace. His power is complete and His ultimate victory is certain. God will not fail to rescue those who love Him. As we worship God, we praise and thank Him for all that we experience. We thank Him that we are not alone on our journeys because He is with us. It's often hard to be still and talk to God as there are so many outside influences, but, when we do, we will not be disappointed. This does not mean that we won't ever experience hardships, but what it does mean is that our defender and guide will be with us in all those deep valleys. He will give us wisdom and discernment to see our way clear. We should take time, be still in God, get to know Him and sing praises to Him. All the time God is good.

"Love Him in the morning when you see the sun arising. Love Him in the evening cause He took you through the day. And in the in-between times when you feel the pressure coming, remember that He loves you and He promises to stay." (John Fischer)

"When you know how much God is in love with you then you can only live your life radiating that love." (Mother Teresa)

August 23
For the Love of God

1 John 4:7, 8
Beloved, let us love one another, for love is of God; and everyone who loves is born of God and knows God. He who does not love does not know God, for God is love.

Romans 5:8
God demonstrates His own love toward us, in that while we were still sinners, Christ died for us.

Innately, we all have the desire to be loved. God loves us and His love is magnificent, deep and everlasting. We are His children and belong in His family. He is constantly drawing us near to Him and He only wants the best for us. God loves us even when we don't know Him, don't turn to Him or don't deserve it. God's love is the source of our love. He loved us so much that He sacrificed His Son for us. Jesus is the ultimate example of what love is like, and everything He did in life and death was supremely loving. God's love is a source of strength for us as we face each day with the knowledge that we are not alone. We also are commanded to love others as God loves us. It's a choice, our choice, but, it is one we must make because He wants us to love as He does—unconditionally and totally. As difficult as this may be, we can do it because He first loved us. We should love Him right back because there is no greater love than the love of God.

"When all else is gone, God is left, and nothing changes Him."
(Hannah Whitall Smith)

"God's promises are like the stars; the darker the night the brighter they shine." (David Nicholas)

August 24
His Promise

Romans 8:38-39
For I am convinced that neither death nor life, neither angels nor demons, neither the present nor the future, nor any powers, neither height nor depth, nor anything else in all creation, will be able to separate us from the love of God that is in Christ Jesus our LORD.

These verses contain one of the most powerful and comforting promises—that it is impossible to be separated from Christ. His death for us is unequivocal proof of His unconquerable love. Nothing can stop His constant presence with us, and we can be secure in His love and promise. The love of Christ will sustain us as we encounter Satan and his evil desires. No matter what happens or where we are, we are never lost to the love of Christ. Whenever we go through tough situations, we have a God who loves us very much. During tough times we need to draw near to Him and not away from Him. We can believe these assurances that God is with us and He loves us—it's His promise... and He keeps His promises.

"You cannot control what happens to you, but you can control how you respond to what happens to you." (Zig Ziglar)

"To reach a great height a person needs to have great depth." (Author unknown)

August 25
Getting in "Sync" with God

2 Corinthians 10:5
We demolish arguments and every pretension that sets itself up against the knowledge of God, and we take captive every thought to make it obedient to Christ.

I often see on my computer the word "synchronizing" and I begin to wonder with whom or what I'm "synchronizing." Computer terminology is totally foreign to me and please don't tell me it's my age or I'll "delete" you. I do know about "deleting" in the computer world. Getting in "sync" with God means to bring every thought and decision to Him and to be obedient to Him. Obeying Christ in every area of our lives is a very important aspect of being a Christian. Getting in "sync" with God means to turn our natural life into a spiritual life. This is not easy and it is done only through a series of choices. What we do should never be done on impulse, but everything we do should be aligned with the will of our LORD. Jesus is our example because there was never the slightest tendency to follow the impulse of His own will as distinct from His Father's will—"the Son can do nothing of Himself." (John 5:19) When we are committed to Jesus and His view of God, we must renew our thoughts and ideas by being in "sync" with Jesus and God. We need to take those thoughts and ideas "captive" and ask ourselves, "What would Jesus do?" Let's get in "sync" with God. He's waiting.

"The more aware you are of My Presence, the safer you feel. This is not some sort of escape from reality; it is tuning in to ultimate reality."
(Sarah Young)

"There is a blessing in the air, which seems a sense of joy to yield to the bare trees, and mountains bare, and grass in the green field."
(William Wordsworth)

August 26
We Can Be Spiritually Fit Every Day with Jesus

John 1:48
"How do You know me?" Nathanael asked. Jesus answered, "I saw you while you were still under the fig tree before Philip called you."

We need Jesus every day. How we face challenges and handle situations is determined by how we worship God in our personal life. Our personal worship is God's training ground because it enables us to have the relationship with Him that we need in order to be ready for any battle that will surely come. Crisis always reveals a person's true character—character that is already in place because of our personal and private worship. A private relationship with God is the greatest essential element of spiritual fitness. Being spiritually fit is just like being physically fit—it's a daily thing. We can't go out and run a marathon without practicing. We need to slowly work up to it by being physically fit. Neither can we face a crisis or a major life-changing event without being spiritually fit. Jesus knows the real us through and through and wants us to follow Him. Spending time with Jesus every day equals spiritual fitness so we will be ready when we are called upon to face whatever we need to face. God's training ground is our private, hidden worship of Him, so let's get spiritually fit by spending time with Him.

"If the devil cannot make us bad, he will make us busy."
(Corrie ten Boom)

"As you rest at night, give your soul and God a time together; meditate on these things and commit with a conscious peace your life to God during hours of sleep. May God write over your heart and life each night. Sleep is God's celestial nurse that croons the consciousness away and deals with the unconscious life of the soul in places where only God and His angels have charge." (Oswald Chambers)

August 27
God Is Our Partner and We're a Majority

Philippians 4:6-7
Do not be anxious about anything, but in everything, by prayer and petition, with thanksgiving, present your requests to God. And the peace of God, which transcends all understanding, will guard your hearts and your minds in Christ Jesus.

God and us—we're a team and we are a majority. We are partners in everything and because we are, we can turn our worries and anxieties into prayers. In order to worry less, we pray more. It doesn't have to be a long prayer because sometimes we can just say, *"Jesus."* That's it—one word, one name. He hears us and we've surrendered those anxious thoughts to Him. That is the peace of God. True peace comes from knowing that God is in control and His peace will guard our hearts against anxiety. We must trust Him, as we capture and bring all thoughts to Him. We are children of a loving and caring Heavenly Father who is our partner in everything. Remember, with God we are a majority. We can have peace because we know that He hears us and will give us the peace that only He can give. We should turn ALL worries and cares over to Him. I dare you to know the peace of God. Together, we're a team and with Him all things are possible. God is our partner in everything and with Him on our side, who can be against us because together we are a majority.

"The only distance between you and God is the thought that there is distance between you and God." (Phil Bolsta)

"A prayer can inspire an act, but the act can be the prayer itself." (Rick Hamlin)

August 28
Our Perspective

Proverbs 17:22
A merry heart does good, like medicine, but a broken spirit dries bones.

What is the first thought that enters our minds when we wake up in the morning? Is it "Ugh, another day?" or is it "Thank You, LORD, that I have another day." Our attitude determines how we see things. It is our perspective and how we choose to see things because we look as much with our minds as with our eyes. We tend to "see" what we expect to see or want to see. Changing our perspective calls for a willingness to see things differently. It's the key to developing a positive attitude regardless of what happens to us. We have a choice. When things happen to us that are unplanned, we have a choice about how to react. We can learn to develop a positive, God-centered attitude or approach to life that takes the good and the bad that comes our way regardless of what happens to us. We can develop a positive attitude as we go through the hard times and look for something good. No, it is not always easy, and, no, we can't deny the seriousness of certain situations, but with God all things are possible. When we walk with Him or run to Him, He will help us. It's all about how we see things and our perspective. When we wake up and hear the rain falling and see that it's a cloudy, gray day, will we say, "This is terrible; I had plans to be outside today" or will we grab an umbrella and take a walk in the rain, being thankful that the earth is getting a drink and flowers will bloom. It's our perspective and choice.

"Happiness isn't something that depends on our surroundings...it's something we make inside ourselves." (Corrie ten Boom)

Zig Ziglar! A human exclamation point! The world's most popular motivational speaker, as he was often described, was always excited because "you never judge a day by the weather!"

August 29
Believe

Ephesians 1:4-8
For He chose us in Him before the creation of the world to be holy and blameless in His sight. In love He predestined us to be adopted as His sons (daughters) through Jesus Christ, in accordance with His pleasure and will—to the praise of His glorious grace, which He has freely given us in the One He loves. In Him we have redemption through His blood, the forgiveness of sins, in accordance with the riches of God's grace that He lavished on us with all wisdom and understanding.

We are not saved because we deserve it but because God is gracious and freely gives salvation. Grace is God's voluntary and loving favor given to those He saves. We cannot save ourselves, and the only way to receive this loving favor is through faith in Christ. To "believe" is more than intellectual agreement that Jesus is God. It means to put our trust and confidence in Him that He alone can save us. It is to put Christ in charge of our present plans and eternal destiny. Believing is both trusting His words as reliable and relying on Him for the power to change. If we have never trusted Christ, let this promise of everlasting life be ours—and believe.

"I Believe Jesus is my redeemer and He has redeemed me through His shed blood. His redemption means that He has bought me at a great price, the highest price that could be paid for my ransom. I believe that His ransom means that I am no longer in bondage to Satan, stuck in a horrible pit of despair, or a slave to sin. I Believe that my redemption means that I am no longer my own, and that my purpose is to serve Jesus and glorify Him, not unwillingly, but from the heart, as His bondservant. I count it a privilege to serve Him for love's sake. I Believe His ownership of my life brings me great comfort, deep peace, and overflowing joy."
(Roy Lessin)

August 30
The Fingerprints of God

Daniel 3:25
He said, "Look! I see four men walking around in the fire, unbound and unharmed, and the fourth looks like a son of the gods."

Feelings of awe alert us to the fingerprints of God. Whether we feel it in response to a sunset, the rushing of a waterfall, or the majesty of angels, it's easy to be swept up in the moment and to forget the Creator behind the breathtaking beauty. Jesus is our Jehovah-Jireh. He is the provider of every need, every day. How comforting to know that Jesus will always find a way of being with His people. Even now He is present by His Holy Spirit, and He constantly speaks to us through His Word. We have a Savior who is always near and always dear. As we see in the scripture above, He's the fourth man in the furnace, but He's first in our hearts. As we look around us, we see the fingerprints of God, and, if we look inside ourselves, we will see where He has left fingerprints on our hearts.

"To throw the Christian into the furnace is to put him into Christ's parlor; for lo! Jesus Christ is walking with him." (Charles Spurgeon)

"Life is a succession of lessons, which must be lived to be understood." (Ralph Waldo Emerson)

August 31
Jesus Is the Soul Winner

John 4: 10
"If you knew the gift of God and who it is that asks you for a drink, you would have asked Him and He would have given you living water."

John 4:13-14
Jesus answered, "Everyone who drinks this water will be thirsty again, but whoever drinks the water I give him will never thirst. Indeed, the water I give him will become in him a spring of water welling up to eternal life."

Throughout the Gospels, we read stories of encounters with Jesus. His purpose on earth was to win the souls of people; thus, He is called the "Soul Winner." God is called the "fountain of life" and the "spring of living water." Here in these verses, Jesus was claiming to be the Messiah. Only the Messiah could give this gift that satisfies the soul's desire. Our souls hunger and thirst as do our bodies. Our souls need spiritual food and water. The living Word, Jesus Christ, and the written Word, the Bible, can satisfy our hungry and thirsty souls. He came to change us on the inside and to empower us to deal with problems from God's perspective and not to take away the challenges we face on a daily basis. When Jesus wins our souls, then we can carry His message to others and spread the news of a wonderful LORD and Savior. We have been given the priceless gift of the "living water" of the Gospel. We can share His story, His love and forgiveness. Jesus working through us is the "Soul Winner."

"A real Christian is the one who can give his pet parrot to the town gossip." (Billy Graham)

"Nobody worries about Christ as long as He can be kept shut up in churches. He is quite safe inside. But there is always trouble if you try and let Him out." (Geoffrey A. Studdert-Kennedy)

September 1
Repent to Be Refreshed

Acts 3:19
Repent, then, and turn to God, so that your sins may be wiped out, that times of refreshing shall come from the presence of the Lord.

James 4:8
Humble yourselves before the LORD, and He will lift you up. (Draw near to God and God will draw near to you.)

When we repent, God promises not only to wipe out our sins but also to bring spiritual refreshment. Repentance may at first seem painful because it is hard to give up certain sins, but God will give us a better way. We can get refreshed because our LORD is near. Jesus will touch our hearts in ways that no one else can with a tenderness that only He can bring. He will refresh our hearts as we turn to Him and lean on Him. The LORD is near—let Him refresh us. Let's repent and go to God because He will forgive us and we will be refreshed.

"The greatest use of life is to spend it for something that will outlast it." (William James)

"We are always in the forge, or on the anvil; by trials God is shaping us for higher things." (Henry Ward Beecher)

September 2
May the LORD Bless You Today and Always!

Numbers 6:24-26
The LORD bless you, and keep you.
The LORD make His face shine on you and be gracious to you.
The LORD look upon you with favor and give you peace.

"The Lord bless you
with the riches of His *grace*;
with the treasures of His *love*;
with the comfort of His *mercies*;
with the strength of His *presence*;
with the touch of His *care*." *(DaySpring)*

Just when
Everything
Seems hopeless God
Unselfishly
Sacrificed His Son

"You don't always need to understand your journey in life, you just need to trust that you're going in the right direction." (Steven Aitchison)

September 3
Be Strong and Take heart—HOPE in the LORD

Psalm 31:24
Be strong and take heart, all you who hope in the LORD.

"Continue to turn to Him...
His heart is toward you.
Continue to look to Him...
His eyes are upon you.
Continue to lean upon Him...
His arms are around you
Continue to trust in Him...
His hope is within you." (DaySpring)

HOPE. Happily Overcoming with Patient Expectation—*HOPE.* All of us need hope. Thank You, LORD, for reminding us to turn to You, to look to You, to lean upon You and to continue to trust You. You are our HOPE in all situations. Your HOPE lives in us and what a blessing it is. Thank You, Jesus, for You are our HOPE.

"Glory not in what is made but in the Maker, not in being saved but in the Savior." (Thrivent Financial)

"Let my soul take refuge ... beneath the shadow of Your wings: let my heart, this sea of restless waves, find peace in You, O God."
(Augustine)

September 4
God Is the Source

Romans 11:36
For from Him and through Him and to Him are all things. To Him be the glory forever! Amen.

All of us are absolutely and totally dependent on God. He is the Source of all things including us. He is the power that sustains and rules the world in which we live. God works out all things to bring glory to Himself. The all-powerful God deserves our praise.

"We must drink deeply from the very Source—the deep calm and peace of interior quietude and refreshment of God, allowing the pure water of divine grace to flow plentifully and unceasingly from the Source itself."
(Mother Teresa)

"He is the Source. Of everything. Strength for your day. Wisdom for your task. Comfort for your soul. Grace for your battle. Provision for your need. Understanding for each failure. Assistance for every encounter."
(Jack Hayford)

September 5
Getting to Know God

Matthew 6:6-8
"But when you pray, go into your room, close the door and pray to your Father who is unseen. Then your Father, who sees what is done in secret, will reward you. And when you pray, do not keep on babbling like pagans, for they think they will be heard because of their many words. Do not be like them, for your Father knows what you need before you ask Him."

When we pray, we must keep our eyes on God not on people. The essence of prayer is not public praying but private communication with Him. There is a time for public praying, but private prayer is talking to God one-on-one. Often when people pray in public, their audience is not God but other people. Praying to God in secret means getting to know Him, keeping His will, learning who He is and what He has planned for us and our lives. Prayer is coming into perfect fellowship and oneness with Him. Yes, we can take our concerns and cares to Him, and that is what He wants us to do, but, more importantly, it is mostly getting to know Him. He is not our "fairy godfather." He is God and He has a plan for our lives. Jesus encourages us to be persistent in our praying. We must be sincere in our prayers and talk to Him just as we would our best friend because that is what He is—our best friend. Let's have a talk with Him in a quiet place—He already knows our needs but He wants us to talk to Him about them.

"When you do not know what more to do, you must go and tell everything to God." (from the book Heidi)

"Good judgment comes from experience and a lot of that comes from bad judgment." (Will Rogers)

September 6
Today Is a Delight, Celebrate It with God

Psalm 118:24
This is the day the LORD has made; let us rejoice and be glad in it.

Psalm 23:6
Surely goodness and mercy (love) shall follow me all the days of my life: and I will dwell in the house of the LORD forever.

God is our Shepherd and He promises to love, guide and protect us and bring us into His house forever. Sometimes the last thing we want to do is rejoice. Sometimes as we go through situations, we want to grumble but as we turn our faces toward God and talk honestly to Him, we find that He somehow gives us reason to rejoice. Often, we see the beauty of His creation or we hear His whisper that says, "Everything will be alright." We should remember that He has given us this day and wants us to serve Him. Let's rejoice and be glad that we have this day. We should not regret yesterday; it's done and gone and don't worry about tomorrow; it's not here yet. We just have today, so let's rejoice in it and serve our LORD. We can rejoice and have a delightful day filled with joy as the love of God surrounds and guides us.

"Experience God in the breathless wonder and startling beauty that is all around you. His sun shines warm upon your face. His wind whispers in the treetops. Like the first rays of morning light, celebrate the start of each day with God." (Wendy Moore)

"Keep your face to the sunshine and you cannot see the shadow." (Helen Keller)

September 7
School Has Begun

Colossians 3:23-24
"Whatever you do, work at it with all your heart, as working for the LORD, not for men, since you know that you will receive an inheritance from the LORD as a reward. It is the LORD Christ you are serving."

Even though summer is not technically over until September 22, for many of us summer is over once school begins. The busyness of life increases when children go to school. Children need to go to bed early, get up early, do homework, participate in sports and music lessons. Parents are busy making lunches, laying out clothing, keeping schedules, preparing meals, making family time, Sunday school and church a priority. Plus many of us work fulltime jobs. Even if we don't have children in school, we all usually get busy this time of year. Sometimes, in all of this, we get overwhelmed and maybe a little lost. The one thing to remember is that we have a God who loves us. We must rely on Him daily in order for us to get through each day. When we put Him first and serve Him, we see that His love is greater than any love we have ever known. We should not let the noise of busy and difficult days make it a little hard to hear Him. Let's listen closely—the Heart of Heaven is cheering us on and so are others who love us too.

"I dare you to...Do less.
Laugh more. Stop trying so hard.
Be gentler with yourself.
Lay down those expectations and embrace grace.
Just for this week.Or just for this day.
Maybe just for this minute.
Take a deep breath. Know you're loved. And live like you believe it."
(Author unknown)

"A good thing to remember and a better thing to do, is work with the construction gang and not with the wrecking crew." (Author unknown)

September 8
This Is a Test

Jeremiah 31:34
"I will forgive their wickedness and will remember their sins no more."

Matthew 5:44
But I tell you: Love your enemies and pray for those who persecute you.

Every day is a test because we face situations where Satan can attack us. We start out with good intentions and something will trigger a reaction that is certainly not the reaction we intend. In traffic, another driver cuts us off; someone is rude on the phone; whatever, we lose sight of Jesus and our feathers are ruffled, and, oftentimes, things come out of our mouths that we don't intend. This is a test and that may be a good phrase to say to ourselves before we let those thoughtless words leave our mouths. Jesus tells us to love our enemies and to pray for them so that we can overcome evil with good. He tells us to forgive. By following His example, we can show that Jesus is LORD of our lives. Oh, how hard this is because sometimes when we are angry, it feels good to let go, but that is not what our LORD wants from us. We must trust the Holy Spirit to help us show love to those for whom we may not feel love. Our tendency to sin must never deter us from striving to be more like Christ. We should show others what God has shown to us—love and forgiveness. By the Grace of God, our true character is God-likeness as we face all types of situations in life. This is a test.

"God is not forgetful, but He chooses in Christ not to remember our sins." (Thrivent Financial)

"Let no one ever come to you without leaving better and happier. Be the living expression of God's kindness: kindness in your face, kindness in your eyes, kindness in your smile." (Mother Teresa)

September 9
Jesus, Where Are You?

Revelation 3:20
Here I am! I stand at the door and knock. If anyone hears My voice and opens the door, I will come in and eat with him, and he with Me.

Often we are so busy with life that we shut Jesus out of ours. Let's remember that He's there knocking on our hearts. We should always leave the door of our hearts open to Him, and we never need to worry about hearing His knock. It's our decision to let Him in and answer His persistent knocking.

Jesus, Are You There?
  By Char Gaylord
God, I need You, are You there?
Do You know my thoughts and hear my prayer?
In Your Word I believe and trust.
I surrender my life and put You first.
I know Your promises are true.
My deepest desire is to know You.
I hunger for Your forgiveness and peace.
I long for Your mercy and grace.
You love me Your Word says so.
My sins are forgiven and salvation is won.
Jesus, You lived and died on a cross for everyone.
Lord, where are You and why don't You answer?
Please take away this illness, tribulation and fear.
Oh, there You are, right where You've always been.
In my heart, walking beside me, carrying me often.
Jesus, You are my confidant and friend.
You are the beginning and the end.
I love, believe and trust You.
In me the Holy Spirit lives, the three in One.
Your answer to my prayer will come.
In Your time, Your will be done. Amen

September 10
Patiently Waiting

Isaiah 40:31
But those who hope in the LORD will renew their strength. They will soar on wings like eagles; they will run and not grow weary, they will walk and not be faint.

We should ask our LORD, teach us to wait. Oh no, who wants to pray this prayer? We do. God's power and strength never diminish. He is never too tired or too busy to help and listen. His strength is our source of strength, and we can go to Him and call upon Him to renew our strength. He will help us patiently wait and rise above what is going on in our world. Waiting on God also means trusting Him. As we trust Him while we wait patiently, He is preparing us so that when He does speak to us, we will hear Him. Often, when He speaks to us, He asks us to wait a little bit longer. Hopefully, as we patiently wait for Him to fulfill His promises we will find the answers in His Word. LORD, teach us to patiently wait for You.

"If you walk with the LORD, you will never be out of step."
(Author unknown)

"Think not of what belongs to you, but to whom you belong."
(Thrivent Financial)

September 11
Remembering

Job 19:25
Job testified: "I know that my Redeemer lives, and at the last He will stand upon the earth."

Revelation 21:4
"He will wipe every tear from their eyes. There will be no more death or mourning or crying or pain."

September 11, 2001 is a day etched in history, in our memories and hearts. We can remember where we were and what we were doing when we learned of the horrific evil that descended upon our country. Everyone was touched. We may not have known anyone personally who died or was injured that day, but we grieved and hugged our loved ones a little bit tighter and longer, and we prayed. There were questions as to where God was during this tragedy. God was right where He was supposed to be—with each and every one of us and with those who were injured and those whose lives were taken. He loved, comforted, healed and helped. Over 2,000 years ago, Jesus laid down His life for all of us on the cross. He suffered all things for this world and died but, then on the third day, He rose from the grave and lives for us. Our Redeemer lives. He is present with us in the Holy Spirit. That's His promise and His promises are true. Jesus is King of our lives—our Savior and LORD. As we remember that tragic day, we have hope because we have Jesus who promises to never leave us nor forsake us. He is a God who loves us. We should remember September 11, 2001—with hope.

"Through faith in our loving Savior, we have the hope of eternal life."
(Thrivent Financial)

"Courage is the decision to place your dreams above your fears."
(Author unknown)

September 12
A Threesome with God

Ecclesiastes 4:12b
A cord of three strands is not quickly broken.

1 John 4:19
We love because He first loved us.

Today, my husband and I celebrate our wedding anniversary. From our very first date, God has been a part of our relationship, and I know that, without His Divine intervention, we would not be who we are today as people and as a couple. I married my best friend. We both wanted "happily ever after" but joy and closeness don't come from just wishing. They come from being together every day, working hard through good and bad times and from faith and trust in our God. He is the third person in our marriage guiding and providing for us. Tim is my best friend, my partner, the love of my life. As we grew together and deepened our relationship, we realized that we needed God more and more. We realized that in order for us to make this marriage work, we wanted and needed Him to be first, us second, our children third and everyone and everything else must come after that. God brought us together, He joined us together and He has been with us every step of the way. We are a threesome. We are threads that are intertwined or braided together. As we celebrate the anniversary of our marriage, we are so very thankful for all of our blessings and most especially that we are a threesome with our Heavenly Father. We are learning not to get ahead of God and to wait patiently for Him. He is our Pilot and will guide us wherever He wants us to go, and He gives us a peace that only He can give. LORD, thank You for loving us and teaching us to love each other. Thank You for being a part of our relationship and life. Your love binds us together. Thank You for our family and many blessings. We look forward to many more years of love and memories. Amen

"In the end, it's not the years in your life that count. It's the life in your years." (Abraham Lincoln)

"A home is a house with a heart inside." (Author unknown)

September 13
God's Children

Matthew 19:14
Jesus said, "Let the little children come to me, and do not hinder them, for the kingdom of heaven belongs to such as these."

As I watch babies being baptized, I think about how all of us are children of God as well. We're not helpless like they are at this time or maybe we are but in different ways. Babies need their parents to carry them to the altar, but most of us can take ourselves there. Babies are so innocent and trusting but we are not so innocent and are less trusting. As babies grow, it becomes all about "me" instead of all about "Jesus." We always want more. God wants us to be like little children in our faith. He wants our humility and complete trust. God wants us to have simple childlike attitudes as we trust Him. We must remember, He is our Father in Heaven and on earth and we are His children. It's not about us; it's all about Him. We should take whatever is troubling us to the altar, lay it all at the feet of Jesus and the cross, and surrender all to Him as we worship, praise, pray and trust Him in all things. We are loved by our Heavenly Father; let's love Him right back.

"For all that I see that You do for me, I thank You. For all that I do not see that You do for me, I praise You." (Christopher De Vinck)

"Life in the presence of God should be known to us in conscious experience. It is a life to be enjoyed every moment of every day."
(A. W. Tozer)

September 14
Faith As Small As a Mustard Seed

Matthew 17:20
He replied, "Because you have so little faith. I tell you the truth, if you have faith as small as a mustard seed, you can say to this mountain, 'Move from here to there' and it will move. Nothing will be impossible for you."

The definition of "faith" is reliance, loyalty, or complete trust in God or something or someone else. It doesn't matter how big or small our faith is because what matters is what or who our faith is in. Our God is all-powerful and He can do anything. There is great power in even a little faith when God is with us. It is through our faith in His power that we can do anything. No matter if we have great or small faith, we must make sure that our faith is in Him and not in our own abilities. God is able and with Him we are able, too. When we face a mountain, we should turn to Jesus because with Him all things are possible.

"We desire many things, and God offers us only one thing. He can offer us only one thing—Himself. He has nothing else to give. There is nothing else to give." (Peter Kreeft)

"We are made for God, and nothing less will really satisfy us." (Brennan Manning)

September 15
The Bible

2 Timothy 3:14-17
But as for you, continue in what you have learned and have become convinced of, because you know those from whom you learned it, and how from infancy you have known the Holy Scriptures, which are able to make you wise for salvation through faith in Christ Jesus. All Scripture is God-breathed and is useful for teaching, rebuking, correcting, and training in righteousness, so that the man of God may be thoroughly equipped for every good work.

The Bible is not just a nice book, possibly dusty or brand new, that sits on a nightstand or used as a bookend on a shelf for all to see. The Bible is not a dictionary or a book of geography where we look up interesting words or places. It is our daily guide to life and should be opened every day and not just at Christmas or Easter. Its pages need to be used and possibly become tattered and torn. The Bible is filled with wisdom, history and inspiration. It is God-breathed. The Bible is God's inspired and living Word and it is trustworthy. We want to know God so the Bible is where we need to spend our time because He is in there. He wrote it through others. It is our source of knowledge about how we can be saved and how we can do Christ's work in the world. When we spend time in God's Word, we will learn how He wants us to live and how much He loves and forgives us. Spending time with God by reading the Scriptures will prepare and strengthen us every day to do all that He wants us to do so that we can help spread the Good News of Jesus Christ. Let's make a plan to read the whole Bible so that we will know God's truth. Then we will have the confidence and faith to share it with others and do the work that He would have us do. What is the Bible to us—it is God's truth and living Word.

"To nourish your body, give it wholesome food. To nourish you soul, read your Bible." (Author unknown)

"The soul is the fingerprint of God." (Iyanla Vanzant)

September 16
Washed and Renewed

Romans 12:2
Do not conform any longer to the pattern of this world, but be transformed by the renewing of your mind. Then you will be able to test and approve what God's will is—His good, pleasing and perfect will.

God wants us to be transformed people with renewed minds, living to honor and obey Him. The Holy Spirit renews, reeducates and redirects our minds. We are renewed when we read God's Word, attend Bible studies, worship and spend time with other Christians and follow the Holy Spirit. Let's get washed in the Word. Learn the boundaries that God has set for us to help us live the lives that He wants us to live. We should let the words of Jesus wash over us, refresh us, give us hope, transform us and renew us in every area of our lives. We will be washed and renewed in the love of Jesus.

"It's not what you know or who you know. It's what you are that finally counts." (Zig Ziglar)

"There is wisdom of the head, and . . . there is wisdom of the heart." (Charles Dickens)

September 17
God's Promise and Prayer

Psalm 98:1-3
Sing to the LORD a new song, for He has done marvelous things; His right hand and His holy arm have worked salvation for Him. The LORD has made His salvation known and revealed His righteousness to the nations. He has remembered His love and His faithfulness to the house of Israel; all the ends of the earth have seen the salvation of our God.

God's promise and prayer is to love us at our worst and our best, save us and return again. He is perfectly loving and perfectly just. God is victorious over evil; all those who follow Him will be victorious with Him when He judges the earth.

"If you are seeking after God, you may be sure of this: God is seeking you much more. He is the Lover, and you are the beloved. He has promised Himself to you." (John of the Cross)

"Faithful, O LORD, Thy mercies are, A rock that cannot move! A thousand promises declare Thy constancy of love." (Charles Wesley)

September 18
Prayer Is All about Love

1 Thessalonians 5:17
pray continually;

Prayer is all about having a relationship with God and becoming more like Him every day. It is about communicating with our Heavenly Father and experiencing Him. When we pray and read Scripture, we will hear His voice. He will speak to us about sin, forgiveness, healing and love. When we pray, His love fills us and overflows to those around us. Jesus took time to pray because He knew how essential it was to be in constant communion with His Father. We, too, can be in constant communion with God in prayer. We say prayers of thanksgiving, prayers of need and prayers for family and friends. Jesus is always ready and willing to extend His arms to us in a warm embrace, and all we need to do is reach out to receive His touch. Jesus gave us a wonderful gift in His death and resurrection: His life for our life; His unchanging, healing love forever. Prayer is all about the love of Jesus filling us, healing us and being with us always.

"Prayer is as natural as breathing. Think of prayer as the breath in our lungs and the blood from our hearts. Our blood flows and our breathing continues 'without ceasing'; we are not even conscious of it, but it never stops ... Prayer is not an exercise; it is the life of the saint. [It] is coming into perfect fellowship and oneness with God." (Oswald Chambers)

"As a bright sunbeam comes into every window, so comes a love born of God's care for every need." (Wanda E. Brunstetter)

September 19
Our "To-Do lists"

Isaiah 40:25-26
"To whom will you compare Me? Or who is My equal?" says the Holy One. Lift your eyes and look to the heavens: Who created all these? He who brings out the starry host one by one, and calls them each by name. Because of His great power and mighty strength, not one of them is missing.

Many of us have a daily "to-do list" that changes in a nanosecond with distractions, phone calls or someone else's ideas or plans. First and foremost, we need to remember that Jesus is in charge of everything, and He may have a reason or a bigger "to-do list" for us. We must decide what our response will be to these daily changes. Do we surrender our day to Him and ask for His guidance through prayer and the Word or do we get frustrated and stressed? Above all, our days should be dedicated to Jesus, His will and plan for us. We must spend time with Him in His Word and in prayer and not let a change in our day change our attitudes. We must let Him be in charge of our lives. He will make order out of chaos and bring calm to every situation. We need to let Him in and ask Him to take care of our days. We should dedicate today and every day to Him and watch what He will do with it. With Jesus on our side, every day will be successful. At the end of the day when we lay our heads on our pillows, we should remember to thank Him for another day of living with Him. We may be surprised that with Jesus in charge, this day was the best day ever. Our "to-do lists" will be there tomorrow—they always are... Maybe that is where the saying "tomorrow is another day" comes from.

"The purpose of life is not to be happy. It is to be useful, to be honorable, to be compassionate, to have it make some difference that you have lived and lived well." (Ralph Waldo Emerson)

"God is everywhere and in everything and without Him we cannot exist." (Mother Teresa)

September 20
Be Strong And Courageous

Joshua 1:9
Be strong and courageous ... The LORD your God is with you wherever you go.

Our LORD tells us that no matter what we face we should be strong and courageous because He promises to be with us in every situation. The greatest gift we have ever received is the gift of salvation. Our LORD loves us so very much that He gave His own life for us and our sins. Jesus was strong and courageous on the cross. Let's remember to thank Him today for what He did on that cross for us. He has saved us and made us saints because of the cross. Sometimes we get stuck in our lives and in our situations and trials. Adversities are temporary and can lead us to the changes that God wants in our lives. Oftentimes, it seems like we will be stuck in that place forever but we won't. God is with us on our journey through everything. Our book is not finished because there are more chapters to write. We can be strong and courageous because God is with us wherever we go. We will know that He is with us because a friend will stop by or we will recognize Him in a verse we read in our devotions. Encouragement can be found in the sun or the rain falling upon our faces. God is there; look for Him. He has not forsaken us. We can be strong and courageous because He is and His promises are true. Whenever we face tough situations, we should remember the cross and lean on God.

"God is watching out for you. Call on the LORD for help."
(Thrivent Financial)

"Some people grumble that roses have thorns; I am grateful that thorns have roses." (Alphonse Karr)

September 21
We Are Like Onions

Matthew 5:8
Blessed are the pure in heart, for they shall see God.

Onions, really? I bet we never thought of ourselves as onions with their smelly, strong, stringent odors but, yes, we are like onions because we have many layers. There are layers of temptation, unforgiveness, anger, unhappiness, offensiveness and so many more. God peels away those layers as He walks with us through many situations to bring us closer to Him. As each layer is removed, there is a lesson to be learned. As He peels away each one, He shows us how we can overcome so that we will be the people He wants us to be. He wants to get to our core so we will be closer to Him, see Him more clearly and love Him unconditionally. If we want to go forward with God, we must allow Him to work in our lives to help us reach the ultimate goal which is to put Him first above everything and to live the life that He wants us to live. Jesus Christ is our core and Shepherd. As God peels away the layers of the Vidalia onions of our lives, we must trust Him and let Him purify our hearts so that we can spend eternity with Him.

"Christ is the unseen head of every house, the unseen guest at every meal and the silent listener to every conversation." (Author unknown)

"God takes our sins – the past, present, and future, and dumps them in the sea and puts up a sign that says NO FISHING ALLOWED."
(Corrie ten Boom)

September 22
Onions Part Two

Matthew 5:8
Blessed are the pure in heart, for they shall see God.

I know yesterday was a stretch as we thought about our comparison to onions. Then again, as we think about all the layers that are in our makeup as human beings, maybe it was not such a stretch after all. As God peels away each of our individual layers, He allows us to go deeper into our hearts so that we will know Him. We have layers of love that He peels away. The love we feel can be a guarded love because of our experiences. Sometimes we love material things more than we love God, and our priorities are in the wrong things or people. God wants us to love as He loves us so He peels away each layer of misdirected love so that we can see His love as He teaches us how to love ourselves and others. He will also peel away the layers of hurt and anger to teach us how to forgive. He forgives us and commands us to forgive ourselves and others. He wants to get to our core which should be Him. He wants us to have a pure heart so that we can have clarity with Him and be able to hear Him. The more we forgive and learn about His forgiveness and the more we learn about His love, the closer we will get to a pure heart. The more we have God, the more we want Him and want to know Him. Let's go deeper with God and let the peeling begin. We should trust Him to lead us to a place where He wants us to be by putting Him first above everything and everyone, loving others as ourselves and forgiving others as we want Him to forgive us. The sweet smell of onions flavors our food and pallets. When we recognize and experience God's love, grace and mercy, that, too, will flavor our lives forever.

"What you see depends on where you are standing." (Author unknown)

"Looking back over a lifetime, you see that love was the answer to everything." (Author unknown)

September 23
Blooming Onions

Galations 5:1
It is for freedom that Christ has set us free. Stand firm, then, and do not let yourselves be burdened again by a yoke of slavery.

There is a local restaurant well-known for its blooming onions that are huge, sweet, dipped in batter, deep fried to a golden brown and served with a spicy dressing. At first, they were all the rage until we started to realize how unhealthy they are for us, but, oh, they are delicious. We are "blooming onions" as well because we get bathed in the world and deep fried in our sins, enjoying the spicy flavor and behavior of sinful living. Then along comes Jesus and He starts to peel away at those sins by loving and forgiving us along the way. He lets us see Him and His way of life, free of the heavy batter and grease of disappointment, anger, stress and sinful living. As we mature in Him, He rewraps us with grace, love, blessings, strength and joy so that we don't spoil. Because of Jesus and what He did on the cross, we become the righteousness of God. Then when something goes awry, we may still get unwrapped or unraveled, but we will blossom in His love and forgiveness enjoying the flavor of life that only He can give. We will have joined our lives with Him and have what is promised in Galatians 5:22: "the fruit of the Spirit, which is love, joy, peace, patience, kindness, goodness, faithfulness, gentleness and self-control." We have freedom in Christ and are new creations in Him, and we will blossom where we are planted, sharing Him with those who we meet. Being a "blooming onion" may not be so bad after all because our core is Jesus Christ and with Him every day is a good day.

"Listen. Acknowledge. Solve. Thank." (Author unknown)

"What gives me the most hope every day is God's grace; knowing that His grace is going to give me the strength for whatever I face, knowing that nothing is a surprise to God." (Rick Warren)

September 24
Getting Our Wonder Back

Matthew 18:3-4
"I tell you the truth, unless you change and become like little children, you will never enter the kingdom of heaven. Therefore, whoever humbles himself like this child is the greatest in the kingdom of heaven. And whoever welcomes a little child like this in My name welcomes Me."

Let's get our wonder back. Little children are curious and look at the world with joy and adventure. They capture the wonder that we as adults have missed. Children are wired to enjoy life with humble and sincere hearts and get excited about the day ahead. As adults, we have responsibilities and our noses are to the grindstone providing for our families. Heartaches and the daily grind of life have knocked the wonder out of us. If we want to get our wonder back we should ask a child to help. It will take energy but it certainly will not be dull. Children take discovery seriously and imagination is one of their best tools. We should remember what thrilled us, challenged us and called to us as children. God was in the midst of play as well. He was smiling and laughing right along with us in our child play. We just didn't recognize Him at the time. Let's get our wonder back by remembering that each day is a gift from God, and we can rest in Him, knowing that He is in control. We are His children forever, and He is a loving parent who finds pleasure in us just as we love our children and find pleasure in them. Let's go play and get our wonder back.

"God provides the wind, man must raise the sail." (Augustine of Hippo)

"If you are lucky enough to do well, it's your responsibility to send the elevator back down." (Kevin Spacey)

September 25
Go Forth and Meet the Day

Psalm 118:24
This is the day the LORD has made; let us rejoice and be glad in it.

John 15:11
I have told you this so that My joy may be in you and that your joy may be complete.

Each new day is a day of discovery because each new dawn holds new hope for a new plan and possibly the start of a new life. Our hope and joy are in Christ. With Him, life is eternal, both in quality and length. What joy we glean and experience when we discover something new from God and about God. Joy and hope come from a constant relationship with Jesus Christ. As we continue to discover, learn, and live a God-fashioned life, joy and hope blossom in our hearts and grow in our lives. As we go forth and meet the day with God, He will reproduce His character in us. Let's live close to Him and experience God in everything. We are loved, accepted, and set free to live our lives to the fullest in Him. We will find joy and hope when we go forth and meet the day—with Jesus.

"Without hope, people are only half alive. With hope, they dream and think and work." (Charles Sawyer)

"It is pleasing to God whenever you rejoice or laugh from the bottom of your heart." (Martin Luther)

September 26
Don't Worry, Be Prayerful

Matthew 6:34
Therefore do not worry about tomorrow, for tomorrow will worry about itself. Each day has enough trouble of its own.

Philippians 4:6
"Do not be anxious about anything, but in every situation, by prayer and petition, with thanksgiving, present your requests to God."

We all have worries and there are things that trouble us, keep us awake, and plague us throughout the day. Jesus tells us to only consider today and take all our worries and troubles to Him in prayer. He is telling us that He is in control and that He can take care of everything better than we can. We can be joyful because we can turn to Jesus and let Him work everything out. We can turn to Jesus in prayer every minute of every day and not get stuck in worries beyond today. We should not worry, but be prayerful and joyful no matter what is going on in and around us. Jesus has us and we need to let Him be in control.

"Yesterday is gone. Tomorrow is not here yet. All we have is today, which is a gift and that is why it's called 'the present.'" (Author unknown)

"No man ever sank under the burden of the day. It is when tomorrow's burden is added to the burden of today that the weight is more than a man can bear. Never load yourself so." (George MacDonald)

September 27
Open Hands, Open Hearts

Jeremiah 24:7
I will give them a heart to know Me, that I am the LORD. They will be my people, and I will be their God, for they will return to me with all their heart.

Matthew 7:11
If you, then, though you are evil, know how to give good gifts to your children, how much more will your Father in heaven give good gifts to those who ask Him!

The definition of *gift* "is anything given, a present, a sacrifice; anything given voluntarily, at no cost." God gives us life now and in eternity because He loves us so much. It is a gift. Our job is to open our hearts and hands to Him, His gifts, His blessings and to receive all from Him. Even in our troubles, He is with us making us stronger. In our prosperity, we can do His work by taking care of and serving others. Our Heavenly Father is a loving, kind God who understands, cares and comforts His children. I saw in a movie once in which a Rabbi was dying. He said when he was younger, he always had his hands closed and palms down, not receiving what God had for him. Now that he was older, he had his hands open, palms up ready to receive what God had in store for him. We should have open hands, palms up and open hearts that receive all that God has planned for us. He wants to bless us but we must be ready.

"God is always trying to give good things to us, but our hands are too full to receive them." (St. Augustine)

"When Jesus Himself fasted, He was not fasting to repent or to bring His desires under control, of course, but to demonstrate His absolute dependence upon His Father." (Peter C. Moore)

September 28
The Everlasting Arms of God

Deuteronomy 33:27
The eternal God is your refuge, and underneath are the everlasting arms.

Imagine that! The everlasting arms of God are underneath us, holding us up through life's experiences. God is our refuge and our only true security—not our money, family, friends, careers, causes or lifelong dreams. He is our eternal God who is our only true refuge. He always holds out His arms to catch us when the shaky supports of other things we trust collapse and we fall. We can take refuge in Him, dare to be bold, and be who He wants us to be in His everlasting arms.

The Everlasting Arms of God (Text by Elisha A. Hoffman)
1) *What a fellowship, what a joy divine, leaning on the everlasting arms; what a blessedness, what a peace is mine, leaning on the everlasting arms.*

Refrain:
Leaning, leaning, safe and secure from all alarms; leaning, leaning, leaning on the everlasting arms.

2) *O how sweet to walk in this pilgrim way, leaning on the everlasting arms; O how bright the path grows from day to day, leaning on the everlasting arms.*

Refrain:

3) *What have I to dread, what have I to fear, leaning on the everlasting arms? I have blessed peace with my LORD so near, leaning on the everlasting arms.*

Refrain:

"Character is what you are in the dark." (Dwight Moody)

September 29
For the Love of God

Luke 6:36
Be merciful, just as your Father is merciful.

Ephesians 5:1-2
Be imitators of God, therefore, as dearly loved children and live a life of love, just as Christ loved us and gave Himself up for us as a fragrant offering and sacrifice to God.

God's love takes action by our meeting specific needs of people around us, even those who dislike us or plan to hurt us. We are to love others, not judge them. God's love isn't about feelings but is about giving. When we run out of human love, we must ask God for His love. In our surrendered hearts, His love pours out of us in so many different ways such as when we are praying, listening, serving and speaking kind words of encouragement. We are instructed to imitate Christ, just as children imitate their parents. He loved us so very much that He was willing to sacrifice Himself so that we might live forever. He wants us to love others the same way—a love that goes beyond affection to self-sacrificing service. God's love is not contingent on our capacity to love Him back. It's called grace which is totally unmerited love. We all need it and it carries us through each day. For the love of God, we can do what He asks because He is with us and won't forsake us. God is loving and merciful. Thank You, LORD!

"As long as we're alive, God will call us to new ways of loving, and none of them are easy." (Virelle Kidder)

"We make our friends, we make our enemies, but God makes our next-door neighbor." (G. K. Chesterton)

September 30
Due North

Hebrews 13:20-21
May the God of peace, who through the blood of the eternal covenant brought back from the dead our LORD Jesus, that great Shepherd of the sheep, equip you with everything good for doing His will, and may He work in us what is pleasing to Him, through Jesus Christ, to whom be the glory for ever and ever. Amen.

A compass gives us direction and allows navigators to determine their direction quickly and accurately. The LORD Jesus Christ has given His people something even greater: navigational tools that transform our relationship to Him and the world we live in today. As followers of Jesus Christ, we use our God-given tools to help us navigate our lives. Our world is changing rapidly, and we are bombarded with updates, new ways of doing things, and new technology that seems endless. The good news is that we have a God who is our "due north." He has shown us how to navigate these waters, He has provided for us by leaving directions in the Bible and has given us His Holy Spirit. He wants to use each of us to further His kingdom and purpose. The LORD has taught us to navigate our lives by trusting Him and keeping our focus on Him. He is our living LORD. We will navigate our way to our eternal home with His help and His indwelling Spirit. We must remember, Jesus Christ is our "due north."

"When all else is gone, God is left, and nothing changes Him."
(Hannah Whitall Smith)

"God's promises are like the stars; the darker the night the brighter they shine." (David Nicholas)

October 1
Goliath

1 Samuel 17:45, 47
45 David said to the Philistine, "You come against me with sword and spear and javelin, but I come against you in the name of the LORD Almighty, the God of the armies of Israel, whom you have defied.

47 All those gathered here will know that it is not by sword or spear that the LORD saves; for the battle is the LORD's and He will give all of you into our hands.

We've all heard of Goliath who was a giant of a man, over nine feet tall, and a seasoned warrior. When dressed in all his armor and with his booming voice, he struck fear into the Israelites. Then along came David, a shepherd boy who decided that he could defeat Goliath armed with only his slingshot and a few smooth stones. This is almost laughable as we picture it. The whole Israelite army wouldn't go against Goliath, but David had an advantage. He had God on his side. David put the situation into perspective. Everyone saw Goliath as a giant who was a bully, but David saw him as a mere man, defying almighty God. David went into battle with God on his side and he won!

We all have Goliaths of our lives, and, most often, we deal with them by worrying and fretting. We complain and talk about them, and, as we do, our Goliaths become bigger and bigger. We can face each of them with God on our side. Once we see the situation from God's point of view, we can put the problem into perspective and fight more effectively. Nothing is impossible with God. NOTHING!!! He and His opinion matters most. David wasn't perfect by any means but He walked with the LORD and knew and trusted Him. Let's take our Goliaths to God and ask for His help. As we acknowledge Him as our LORD, we will be stronger because we are not alone in our battle, "for the battle is the LORD's ..."

"God gave us a gift of 86,400 seconds today. Use one to say thank You." (Author unknown)

"Feed your faith and your doubts will starve to death." (Debbie Macomber)

October 2
God's Grace—God's Riches At Christ's Expense

Psalm 51:10
Create in me a pure heart, O God, and renew a steadfast spirit within me.

Titus 3:5-7
[God] saved us, not because of righteous things we had done, but because of His mercy. He saved us through the washing of rebirth and renewal by the Holy Spirit, whom He poured out on us generously through Jesus Christ our Savior, so that, having been justified by His grace, we might become heirs having the hope of eternal life.

God's Grace is new every day and He continually renews our hearts. Each morning is a new chance for change and a new life. We don't deserve it because of our sinful lives, but Christ freed us from the desires and control of sin. We move from a life full of sin to one where we are led by God's Holy Spirit. All our sins are washed away in the waters of our baptism, a sign of salvation. We haven't earned this or deserve it but it is all God's gift. We can receive His Grace that is new every day, all day. It's God's gift to us and what we do with it is our gift back to Him.

"For God is, indeed, a wonderful Father who longs to pour out His mercy upon us, and whose majesty is so great that He can transform us from deep within." (Teresa of Avila)

"Every sunrise is a new message from God and every sunset His signature."(William A. Ward)

October 3
A New Paint Job

Psalm 51:2
Wash away all my iniquity and cleanse me from my sin.

Psalm 51:7
Cleanse me with hyssop, and I will be clean; wash me, and I will be whiter than snow.

It is amazing what a little soap, water and paint will do to clean up and refresh a room or anything, for that matter. Afterward everything takes on a new, brighter look. That is what happens to us when we go to God to confess our sins. By the blood of Jesus on the cross we are forgiven. He is the bread of life and His blood is life. God wants us to be intimate with Him, but that is impossible when we have unconfessed sin. It's between us and God but once we talk to Him and ask for His forgiveness, we are painted with the fresh paint of peace. We become cleaner and brighter, wanting to share Him with others. There is no greater peace than a fresh coat of Jesus' "paint of joy" washing over us. We should go pick out our favorite color and thank God for His love, grace, mercy and peace. Let the peace of God color our lives and world.

"Out of clutter, find simplicity." (John Archibald Wheeler)

"The more you lose yourself in something bigger than yourself, the more energy you will have." (Norman Vincent Peale)

October 4
Our Daily Walk with God

Genesis 5:24
Enoch walked with God....

It is painful work to get in step with God and to keep pace with Him because it means getting our second wind spiritually. In learning to walk with God, there is always the difficulty of getting into His stride, but, once we have done so, He lives in and through us. The individual person is merged into a personal oneness with God and God's stride and His power are exhibited in us. Just like Jesus, we must never work from our own standpoint but always work from God's standpoint. It is God's Spirit that changes our way of looking at things. Things then become possible which before seemed impossible. Walking with God means nothing less than oneness with Him and it takes a long time to get there. We must keep walking with God and have a blessed day.

"Keep looking up, for God is looking down." (Wanda Brunstetter)

"You can never learn that Christ is all you need, until Christ is all you have." (Corrie ten Boom)

October 5
True Joy

Philippians 4:4
Rejoice in the LORD always. I will say it again: Rejoice!

While Paul was in prison, he wrote the book of Philippians, a letter filled with joy. Imagine writing about joy from prison. All of us have experienced some sort of prison in our lives. Our prison doesn't have to be a building with barbed wire, electric fences and armed guards. We often make our own kind of prison in our minds and hearts. We, too, can rejoice despite whatever we face and whatever prison we have created for ourselves. Inner joy is the quiet, confident assurance of God's love and work in our lives—that He will be with us no matter what! Happiness depends on happenings but joy depends on Christ. When happiness flees and despair sets in, Christ still reigns and we know Him. We can rejoice at all times and in all circumstances. Paul learned to be content no matter what he experienced because He found real joy as he focused all of his attention and energy on Christ—knowing Him and obeying Him. The secret of Paul's joy is grounded in his relationship with Christ. As we read this beautiful letter written by Paul, it is a lesson for us to keep our eyes and hearts on Jesus, rejoice in Him, and know Him so that we can know the pure joy that only He can give. Paul says, *"Rejoice in the LORD always. I will say it again: Rejoice!"* These are beautiful words to inspire us each day and to help us to find real joy in Christ. We experience many blessings each day as we rejoice in our LORD!

"How truly is a kind heart a fountain of gladness, making everything in its vicinity to freshen into smiles." (Washington Irving)

"When joy and prayer are married, their first born child is gratitude." (Charles Spurgeon)

October 6
We Are Parched

Psalm 42:2
My soul thirsts for God.

Isaiah 55:1
Come, all you who are thirsty, come to the waters;

John 4:13-14
Jesus answered, "Everyone who drinks this water will be thirsty again, but whoever drinks the water I give him will never thirst. Indeed, the water I give him will become in him a spring of water welling up to eternal life."

Do we thirst after God as we thirst for water? Jesus is the Messiah and only He gives the gift that satisfies one's soul forever—living water. God is in the soul business and our souls need spiritual food and water. The spiritual food we need comes from the living Word—Jesus Christ and the written Word—the Bible. Just as our bodies need water, our lives depend on God who is called the fountain of life and the spring of living water. We can drink from the fountain because the waters are cleansing. We can ask Jesus for His forgiveness and receive the salvation that He won for us on the cross. God forgives all our sins. When we are parched and thirsty, we should go to the well because Jesus is waiting. We must saturate our souls by drinking of the living water that only He can give because our very lives depend on that. We'll never be thirsty again.

"What makes a river so restful to people is that it doesn't have any doubt—it is sure to get where it is going, and it doesn't want to go anywhere else." (Hal Boyle)

"Live in the sunshine, swim in the sea, drink the wild air's salubrity" (Ralph Waldo Emerson)

October 7
Our Prayer Life

Matthew 11:28-29
"Come to Me, all you who are weary and burdened, and I will give you rest. Take My yoke upon you and learn from Me, for I am gentle and humble in heart, and you will find rest for your souls. For my yoke is easy and my burden is light."

Luke 6:12
One of those days Jesus went out to a mountainside to pray, and spent the night praying to God.

Our prayer life should reflect the prayer life of Jesus. Sometimes He went away to a quiet place to pray but He communed with His Father constantly throughout His day. Jesus' life was all about the Father, His will and His mission for Jesus. As we read below, it isn't so much about our prayers as it is our life and our relationship with Jesus and our Heavenly Father. God is always ready and willing to listen to us as we talk to Him. The most important thing is that we know we can go to Him at any moment of the day with whatever is on our hearts and minds. We should also remember that important decisions should be grounded in prayer. A relationship with God changes meaningless, wearisome toil into spiritual productivity and purpose. We should always take all our cares to the LORD in prayer!

"What matters to God is not the words we pray, or the amount of time we spend praying, but the life of the pray-or. Praying revealed Jesus' relationship with His Father. For us, prayer is also a relationship, one that grows as we spend time with Jesus daily. Prayer is also an attitude, a response, and a commitment but most of all, it is practicing the presence of God daily, worshipping Him continually, and depending upon His power completely. That's what Jesus did." (Rebecca Barlow Jordan)

"Is prayer your steering wheel or your spare tire?" (Corrie ten Boom)

October 8
Never Alone

Genesis 28:15
I will not leave you.

Psalm 23:4
Thou art with me;

Psalm 46:1
God is our refuge and strength, a very present help in trouble.

Acts 17:27
He is not far from each one of us.

The Lord is near us every moment, every second, every nanosecond and He is even closer than that. God is with us, and, because He is, everything is different. Whatever we face, we are not alone—ever. Even in death, He is there. We are not alone because He is with us. Because we can speak to Him face to face, it's personal, friend to friend. As we read the Bible, we are assured and reassured that the Lord is present in our lives every day because we stay connected to Him in prayer. Jesus was called Immanuel—God with us. He was God in the flesh and was literally among us, "with us" and today He is present with every believer through the presence of the Holy Spirit. In Hebrews 13:5, God said, "Never will I leave you; never will I forsake you." We have His promise and assurance of His presence in every challenge, valley, highs and lows. He will provide for all of our needs. He provides help, refuge, security and peace. God's power is complete and His ultimate victory is certain. He will provide strength in any circumstance and be our eternal refuge. We are assured that He is with us and we are never alone.

"Eyes that look are common; eyes that see are rare." (J. Oswald Sanders)

"If we truly love people, we will desire for them far more than it is within our power to give them, and this will lead us to prayer."
(Richard J. Foster)

October 9
The Twenty Third Psalm

Psalm 23
The LORD is my Shepherd;
I shall not want.
He maketh me to lie down in green pastures;
He leadeth me beside the still waters.
He restoreth my soul;
He leadeth me in the paths of righteousness
For His name's sake.
Yea, though I walk through the valley of the shadow of death,
I will fear no evil;
For Thou art with me;
Thy rod and Thy staff, they comfort me.
Thou preparest a table before me
in the presence of mine enemies;
Thou anointest my head with oil;
My cup runneth over.
Surely goodness and mercy shall follow me
All the days of my life:
And I will dwell in the house of the LORD forever. (NKJV)

Every verse of Psalm 23, every phrase, every promise, every image, every word was purchased and paid for by the blood of Jesus Christ. And the Bible tells us we must confess Him as Lord and know in our hearts that He died and rose again for us. (Robert J. Morgan)

The 23rd Psalm. "Written by a Shepherd who became a King—because He wanted us to know about a King who became a Shepherd." With this Psalm of comfort, you can release your burdens, cast away your fears, and rest safely in the Shepherd's arms. When you have the Shepherd, you have everything you need. God will lighten our loads. (Max Lucado)

October 10
Our Shepherd

Psalm 23:1-3
The LORD is my Shepherd;
  I shall not want.
He maketh me to lie down in green pastures;
  He leadeth me beside the still waters.
He restoreth my soul;
  He leadeth me in the paths of righteousness
  For His name's sake.
Yea, though I walk through the valley of the shadow of death,
  I will fear no evil;
  For Thou art with me;

The LORD is our Shepherd—forever! He makes. He leads. He restores. He is a sure God and we will dwell with Him forever. We should invite Him into our hearts. He gently knocks and waits but few hear His voice and fewer still open the door. He is still there as He never leaves. He is our Lord and Shepherd who seeks to find, love, guard, guide and bless us. The Lord is our Shepherd—that's enough! We don't need anything else. The Psalm begins with "The Lord is my Shepherd" and ends with "forever" and it doesn't get any better than that.

"The Lord is my Shepherd….forever and ever." (Author unknown)

"God has promised us even more than His own Son. He's promised us power through the Spirit—power that will help us do all that He asks of us." (Joni Eareckson Tada)

October 11
God Is Prepared

Psalm 23:4
Thy rod and thy staff, they comfort me.

Isaiah 49:16
I have written your name on My hand.

Our Shepherd comes prepared because He brings His equipment—a rod to drive off predators and enemies. He has a staff with a hook at the top so that He can snatch us if we get too close to the edge or begin to fall. He will protect us from ourselves and our missteps. He is carefully watching and constantly guarding us. Our God is ever-present and ever-protecting and what a comfort that is for us. The Good Shepherd is in life's valleys with us. He has brought His equipment—His rod and His staff—and we are in His line of sight. We can talk and pray to Him always with just a whisper. It doesn't need to be a term paper. He is ever-present and He knows us, so take comfort—He is right alongside of us. Our names are written on God's Hand and our names are on His lips. Everything that matters to us matters to Him. God cares for us, He is a faithful Father and we are His children. We can trust Him. We can take 100 percent of Him and that helps us deal with whatever else comes our way. Thank You, Jesus, thank You!

"Pray, hope, don't worry." (Saint Padre Pio)

"Faith believes in spite of the circumstances and acts in spite of the consequences." (Adrian Rogers)

(Paraphrased from *Safe in the Shepherd's Arms by Max Lucado* and *The LORD is my Shepherd* by Robert J. Morgan)

October 12
God's Perfect Provision

Psalm 23:5
Thou preparest a table before me in the presence of mine enemies:

Colossians 1:13
You are delivered from the power of evil.

We have three kinds of enemies: (1) enemies of our nation who are constantly trying to destroy us; (2) personal enemies who are people we don't get along with; and (3) Satan, our greatest enemy, who is constantly looking for ways to trip us up and lead us away from God. However, we have the Good Shepherd who has, by His own death, defeated Satan. He keeps us safe by delivering us from certain situations and taking us through others. We'll never know how many times Jesus has protected and delivered us. The LORD is able to provide for us throughout life and eternity. He keeps us safely in His hands and invites us to take a permanent place at His table. Jesus teaches us how to get along. In Isaiah 7:4 He tells us, "Be careful, keep calm and don't be afraid. Do not lose heart...." He is telling us to stay calm in the storms of life, keep things in perspective, and not let bitterness take root in our hearts. We should do what we can and leave the rest in the LORD's hands. Our Shepherd knows about enemies because He faced them all and has already defeated every one of them. Our Lord prepares a table of safety and victory for us. He will lead us in the presence of our enemies to the safety of eternal life with Him. He will reign forever and ever.

"God is the Shepherd who guides, the Lord who provides, the Voice who brings peace in the storm." (Max Lucado)

"Christ is the unseen head of every house, the unseen guest at every meal, and the silent listener to every conversation." (Author unknown)

October 13
God Anoints

Psalm 23:5
Thou anointest my head with oil.

Psalm 100:3
He made us, and we belong to Him; we are His people, the sheep He tends.

Sheep need a shepherd to tend to them and we too need a Good Shepherd to stay with us through all the experiences in life. In ancient Israel shepherds used oil on the sheep for three purposes: to repel insects, to prevent conflicts when rams fought and to heal wounds. The shepherd doesn't want today's wound to become tomorrow's infection. We, too, have wounds of the heart that come from disappointment after disappointment which can lead to bitterness. We, too, need preventive care and a healing touch from the day-to-day frustrations, mishaps and heartaches. Sometimes our wounds come from everyday living such as aging, loss, and illness or from dealing with difficult people. The good news is that we have a Shepherd who will tend to us. He will anoint us and take care of us. God "heals the brokenhearted" (Psalm 147:3). We must go to Him with our hurts and not run to anyone else, but go to Him, bow to Him and trust Him. Jesus is the "anointed One." The Lord knows how to heal our hurts and bind our wounds. He rubs the soothing oil onto the rough spots of life. In order for us to be anointed, we must let the Shepherd do His work. It's often during life's hurts that we come to understand the heart of the Shepherd as we learn to accept His care and trust His heart. We fall in love with Him as He tends and mends us and anoints us with the "oil of His Spirit" and we receive the comfort, joy, peace, healing, strength and power that only He can give.

"When we come to God ... we come with high hopes and a humble heart." (Max Lucado)

"Follow hard after Him, and He will never fail you." (C. H. Spurgeon)

(Paraphrased from *Safe in the Shepherd's Arms* by Max Lucado and *The LORD is my Shepherd* by Robert J. Morgan)

October 14
Overflowing with Blessings

Psalm 23:5
My cup runneth over

Romans 15:13
"May the God of hope fill you with all joy and peace as you trust in Him, so that you may overflow with hope by the power of the Holy Spirit."

Whenever I say this part of the 23rd Psalm, I cannot help but think of and be thankful for all the blessings God has poured into my life. The love, grace, mercy and peace that He bestows on me every day are unimaginable. I can't absorb or contain all of the blessings that He sends my way. These blessings in our lives should overflow into the lives of others. We pray for God's love and light to live in us and through us for all to see His glory. This is Christ living in us and overflowing to those we meet. We go to God in prayer and Bible study to get filled up and overflow with His love and Spirit so we can share His hope and love with others. The Good Shepherd laid down His life for His sheep (us). He drained His cup so ours can overflow. Jesus blesses our lives to overflowing with joy and peace. May our cups overflow with the hope and power of the Holy Spirit.

"It is not the things we get, but the hearts we touch, that will measure our success in life."(Author unknown)

"Keep adding, keep walking, keep advancing; do not stop, do not turn back, do not turn from the straight road." (St. Augustine)

(Paraphrased from *Safe in the Shepherd's Arms by Max Lucado* and *The LORD is my Shepherd* by Robert J. Morgan)

October 15
Surely Goodness And Mercy

Psalm 23:6
Surely goodness and mercy shall follow me all the days of my life,

Romans 8:38-39
"I am persuaded that neither death nor life, nor angels nor principalities nor powers, nor things present nor things to come, nor height or depth, nor any other created things, shall be able to separate us from the love of God which is in Christ Jesus our Lord."

There is no doubt about it: our God is a "sure" God who makes "sure" promises and provides a "sure" foundation. God does not change or shift. He is who He promises to be and who He says He is—a faithful and sure God who promises goodness and mercy. God is with us always through the good and challenging times that lie ahead—all the days of our lives. He doesn't pick and choose which day because every single day God is by our side, following us. He is near. "How," we ask? A friend calls, a stranger speaks a kind word to us, a sermon touches us down deep, a beautiful song makes our hearts fill with joy and we look at His creation. God is near and we surely do not want to miss Him. God gave first and continues to give of Himself. He pursues us with goodness and mercy. He never leaves us, never forces us and He is patient and persistent. God transforms us from the inside out as we discover that the joy of the Lord is the strength of our lives. We should trust Him because surely, He is a "good" God who is full of mercy, and He will lead us home. Psalm 100:5 says, "For the Lord is good and His love endures forever; His faithfulness continues through all generations."

"Goodness to supply every want. Mercy to forgive every sin. Goodness to provide. Mercy to pardon." (F. B. Meyer)

"It's in God's nature to be merciful, forgiving, and benevolent. He surrounds our lives with acts of grace we could never earn by our own efforts, all because of His loyal and steadfast love for us. Goodness represents all He bestows on us that we don't deserve. Mercy represents all He withholds that we do deserve." (Robert J. Morgan)

October 16
Forever And Ever

Psalm 23:6
And I will dwell in the house of the Lord forever.

Philippians 3:20
But our citizenship is in heaven.

Ecclesiastes 3:11
God has "set eternity in the hearts of men"

We belong to God and have our Heavenly Father's promise that we will one day live in His House with Him forever and ever. Forever—that's a very long time. We are not homeless because our home is not here. This home is only temporary. Our home is in heaven, our eternal address. Home is where our hearts are and our hearts are with our God. Daily we keep before us our eternal home knowing that one day we will reside there with our Lord—our Good Shepherd. That's where our journey on our earthly road will end. We will live in God's presence forever. John 14:1-2 says, "Let not your heart be troubled: ye believe in God, believe also in Me. In My Father's house are many mansions; if it were not so, I would have told you." Luke 23:43 says, "Today you will be with Me in paradise." What a promise. Our God, the perfect Shepherd and host, promises to guide and protect us through life and bring us into His house forever.

"God never said that the journey would be easy, but He did say that the arrival would be worthwhile. He will get you home. And the trials of the trip will be lost in the joys of the feast." (Max Lucado)

"Commitment is what transforms a promise to reality."
(Author unknown)

(Excerpts taken from *Safe in the Shepherd's Arms* by Max Lucado and *The LORD is my Shepherd* by Robert J. Morgan)

October 17
God Satisfies

Psalm 145:13-16
Your kingdom is an everlasting kingdom, and Your dominion endures through all generations. The Lord is faithful to all His promises and loving toward all He has made. The Lord upholds all those who fall and lifts up all who are bowed down. The eyes of all look to You, and You give them their food at the proper time. You open Your hand and satisfy the desires of every living thing.

God is the Source of our daily needs. He is righteous and loving in all His dealings. He remains near to us who call upon Him and never gives up. God satisfies all who come to Him.

"Whenever we feel doubt and uncertainty, look to the cross and remember where in holy blood is written the promise: "God would give up His only Son before He'd give up on you." God's faithfulness has never depended on the faithfulness of His children. He is faithful even when we aren't." (Max Lucado)

"The best gifts to give:
To your friend—loyalty
To your enemy—forgiveness
To your boss—service
To your child—a good example
To your parents—gratitude and devotion
To your wedded mate—love and faithfulness
To all men—charity
To God—your life." *(Author unknown)*

October 18
God's Footprints

Psalm 100
Shout for joy to the Lord, all the earth.
Worship the Lord with gladness;
Come before Him with joyful songs.
Know that the Lord is God.
It is He who made us, and we are His;
We are his people, the sheep of His pasture.
Enter His gates with thanksgiving and His courts with praise;
Give thanks to Him and praise his name.
For the Lord is good and His love endures forever;
His faithfulness continues through all generations.

God's footprints are on our hearts and are simple reminders that He is our Creator and gives us all we have. He is worthy of our praise and worship and is dependable, kind, patient, loving and forgiving. We have His Grace. All that He has brought to us are footprints on our hearts and reminders to pay it forward to others so that they, too, will know Him. We should remember His goodness and dependability and worship Him with thanksgiving and praise.

"Catalog God's goodness. Meditate on them. He has fed you, led you, and earned your trust. Remember what God has done for you."
(Max Lucado)

"A loving heart is the truest wisdom." (Charles Dickens)

October 19
God Is Always with Us

Psalm 46:10
Be still and know that I am God.

Psalm 145:5
I will meditate on the glorious splendor of Your majesty and on Your wondrous works.

Look all around and see God because He is in the heavens, the stars, the moon, the rainbows after a storm, the mountains, the clouds, the oceans, the flowers and all of nature. He created all of it for our enjoyment and as a reminder that we are never alone. He hasn't left. In the clamor of life, He is still here. God is everywhere and, most importantly, He is in our hearts, leaving His footprints and giving us hugs whenever we need Him. He is in the midst of all those voices, faces, memories, pictures and years. He is Divine and full of glorious splendor and majesty. God knows our beginning and our end, we should be still and know that God is always with us.

"Faith is the art of holding onto things in spite of your changing moods and circumstances." (C.S. Lewis)

"If you can't be a highway, then just be a trail. If you can't be the sun, be a star. It isn't by size that you win or fail—be the best of whatever you are." (Douglas Malloch)

October 20
We Have Value and We Matter

Psalm 119:73
Your hands made me and formed me; give me understanding to learn your commands.

Psalm 139: 23-24
Search me, O God, and know my heart; test me and know my anxious thoughts. See if there is any offensive way in me, and lead me in the way everlasting.

We are valuable to our Lord. He loves us just the way we are and our salvation does not depend on what we do for Him. We are valuable to Him simply because of who we are in Jesus Christ. We are His valuable children. We don't have to be like the world to have an impact on the world, and we don't have to be like the crowd to change the crowd. Holiness seeks to be like God. Every day our prayer should be, "God, examine us, know our hearts, and lead us on the road to everlasting life." Amen.

"With God, every day matters, every person counts. And that includes you." (Max Lucado)

"God takes you however He finds you. No need to clean up or climb up. Just look up." (Max Lucado)

October 21
The Ultimate Choice

Psalm 119:30
I have chosen the way of truth; I have set my heart on Your laws.

John 14:6
Jesus answered, "I am the way and the truth and the life."

There are many things in life that we can't control: the weather, the economy, or whether we are born with a big nose, blue eyes, or a lot of hair. We can, however, choose where we spend eternity. God urges us to love Him, but in the end, the choice is ours. Jesus is both God and man and is the way because He is the only path to God. By uniting our lives with His, we are united with God. As the truth, He is the reality of all God's promises and as the life, He joins His divine life to ours, both now and eternally. This ultimate choice is ours to make.

"When you have a choice and don't make it, that is in itself a choice." (William James)

"Actions are seeds of fate. Seeds grow into destiny." (Harry S. Truman)

October 22
Seeking God

Deuteronomy 4:29
But if from there you seek the Lord your God, you will find Him if you look for Him with all your heart and with all your soul.

Psalm 63:1
O God, You are my God, earnestly I seek You; my soul thirsts for You, my body longs for You, in a dry and weary land where there is not water.

Isaiah 58:2
For day after day they seek Me out; they seem eager to know My ways.

We seek God because we want a relationship with Him. God is knowable and wants to be known, but we have to want to know Him. We will find Him when we search for Him with all of our hearts and souls. Often we seek God out of tragic circumstances when we don't know where else to turn. We seek Him when we are looking for something more to life and are looking for answers to questions that constantly plague us. We seek Him for wisdom and discernment as we hunger for lessons that only He can teach us—lessons about love and wisdom, harmony and joy. He is our Heavenly Father and we are His children. As His children, we should seek Him daily, diligently and continuously and with all of our hearts. He's waiting and wants to have a conversation with us. Seeking Him will change us because we will lead deeper and richer lives which will be full of promise with our LORD. We should go, seek, find because He's waiting.

"We live in an uncertain world, but we serve a Savior who's unchanging. We may face hard times, but the Lord is our solid Rock. We don't know what the future holds, but we're sure Jesus has us in His hands."
(DaySpring)

"Wise men still seek Him." (Author unknown)

October 23
The Great House of God

Acts 2:28
You have made known to me the paths of life; You fill me with joy in Your presence.

1 John 3:24
Those who obey His commands live in Him, and He in them. And this is how we know that He lives in us: We know it by the Spirit He gave us.

There is a home for our hearts and it is the Great House of God. We long to be there and we have a lifelong residence. We live in Christ as He lives in us. We believe in Him, love others, and try to live morally upright lives. Our conduct verifies His presence in us and our mutual relationship with Him. The Great House of God is in us and we can be joyful for His presence. We can go to Him in prayer and have very intimate conversations with Him. We can express our hearts, our joys and our praises to the One who will never forsake us. What a delightful experience it is when He draws us in and we are in His presence. It is welcoming and refreshing when our souls can rest in Him. There is no better place to be than in the joyful presence of God.

"If you want to touch God's Heart, use the name He loves to hear. Call Him Father." (Max Lucado)

"Whoever loves much does much." (Thomas á Kempis)

October 24
God Loves Us Perfectly

1 John 4:14-16
And we have seen and testify that the Father has sent His Son to be the Savior of the world. If anyone acknowledges that Jesus is the Son of God, God lives in him and he in God. And so we know and rely on the love God has for us. God is love. Whoever lives in love lives in God, and God in him.

1 John 4:19
We love because He first loved us.

God loves us immeasurably and perfectly. His love will quiet our fears and give us confidence. He loves others through us because God is love. His love is the source of all human love. His love for us kindles a flame in our hearts so that we can love others and they will feel God's love through us. May God's love and light live in us and through us for all to see Him.

"Our love is a testimony to God's love for us." (Thrivent Financial)

"Grandmother/grandchild relationships are simple: grandmas are short on criticism and long on love." (Author unknown)

October 25
We Are Precious to Our God

Psalm 59:16
But I will sing of Your strength, in the morning I will sing of Your love; for You are my fortress, my refuge in times of trouble.

Psalm 89: 1-2
I will always be about the Lord's love; I will tell of His loyalty from now on. I will say, "Your love continues forever; Your loyalty goes on and on like the sky.

We are precious to God and are totally His. When we look deeply into the face of every human being on earth we will see His likeness. Though some people appear to be distant relatives, they are not. God has no cousins, only children. Incredibly we are the body of Christ. Though we may not act like our Father, there is no greater truth than this: We are His. He loves us unconditionally. Nothing can separate us from the love of Christ. We can rest today in the knowledge that we are precious to the One who matters most and there is nothing that can alter that fact. We are precious to God.

"The most important opinion is the one you have of yourself, and the most significant things you say all day are those things you say to yourself." (Zig Ziglar)

"If you do not hope, you will not find what is beyond your hopes." (St. Clement of Alexandria)

October 26
Pray Where We Are

Psalm 46:10
Be still and know that I am God; I will be exalted among the nations, I will be exalted in the earth.

Psalm 139: 23
God, examine me and know my heart; test me and know my anxious thoughts.

There are moments in our days when we are quiet. We wait at traffic lights, we stand in lines, we do the dishes, we walk the dog and we fold the laundry. We can use those moments to communicate with God and pray where we are by sharing with Him our thoughts, prayers and concerns because He is listening and wants us to talk to Him. Every quiet moment is a potential opportunity to communicate with God. We can take those moments when we are quiet to pray and be intimate with the Almighty.

"Within reach of your prayers is the maker of the oceans—God!"
(Max Lucado)

"God hears even when it's just a whisper of the heart."
(Author unknown)

October 27
The Plan

Psalm 119:105
Your word is like a lamp for my feet and a light for my path.

John 1:12-13
Yet to all who received Him, to those who believed in His name, He gave the right to become children of God—children born not of natural descent, nor of human decision or a husband's will, but born of God.

We all make plans, set goals, and have "to do" lists. God has a plan, too, and His plan is to save His children. The whole purpose and truth of the Bible is to show us His plan. We are lost and need to be saved. The Bible communicates the message that Jesus is God in the flesh sent to save His children. The Bible is like a compass that we must calibrate correctly. We can use God's Word as a road map for guidance and assurance to journey through life. As we go step-by-step through each page of the Bible, the way will be opened up to us. We need to let the journey begin and the plan which is God's plan will unfold before us.

"God leads us. He will do the right thing at the right time."
(Max Lucado)

"The beginning of a habit is like an invisible thread, but every time we repeat the act we strengthen the strand, add to it another filament, until it becomes a great cable that binds us irrevocably through thought and act." (Orrison Swett Marden)

October 28
Don't Be Late

Luke 22:38
There was a written notice above Him, which read: THIS IS THE KING OF THE JEWS. One of the criminals who hung there hurled insults at Him: "Aren't You the Christ? Save Yourself and us!" But the other criminal rebuked him. "Don't you fear God," he asked, "since you are under the same sentence? We are punished justly, for we are getting what our deeds deserve. But this man has done nothing wrong." Then he said, "Jesus, remember me when you come into Your kingdom." Jesus answered him, "I tell you the truth, today you will be with me in paradise."

Many times in our lives we can be late, but there is one date that we will not be late for and that is the date when we will come face-to-face with our LORD and Savior, Jesus Christ. Whether we believe in Him or not, it is a date when we will have to answer for our actions. The thief on the cross recognized Jesus, asked to be remembered in His kingdom and was granted forgiveness. This last moment of faith saved him and proved that it is never too late to turn to God. Even after all that Jesus taught and said, many who were at the cross that dark day had a different view of His kingdom. They thought the kingdom of Israel was finished, but the thief on the cross had a new-found faith in Jesus and was able to see beyond the shame of the day to the coming glory of spending eternity with "The King of the Jews." This is a beautiful lesson for all of us. Jesus came to save us, and all we need to do is believe, trust Him and love others as He has loved us. It's not too late because one day we will stand before God wanting to hear the words that we long to hear, "Well done, good and faithful servant! You have been faithful with a few things; I will put you in charge of many things. Come and share your master's happiness!" (Matthew 25:21)

"In the end, it's not the years in your life that count. It's the life in your years." (Abraham Lincoln)

"Your aspirations are your possibilities." (Samuel Johnson)

October 29
Real Change

Psalm 51:10
Create in me a pure heart, O God, and renew a steadfast spirit within me.

We all want real change in our lives especially when things go awry. We want to be better, do better and feel better. We have problems and try to resolve them ourselves. Real change is an inside job and is a matter of the heart. We are sinners and must ask God to forgive us and cleanse us from within by clearing our hearts and spirits to make way for new thoughts and desires. Right conduct can come only from a clean heart and spirit. God wants our hearts to be right with Him and we want real change that only He can affect. Only His Grace can save us and change us into who He wants us to be. Are we ready for real change? If so, let's go to the One who can make it happen from the inside.

"No matter how much we have failed, the love of God never ceases."
(Author unknown)

"A problem is no more a challenge to God than a twig is to an elephant."
(Max Lucado)

October 30
Dressed for Success

Psalm 23:3
He leads me in the paths of righteousness for His name's sake.

Isaiah 61:10
For He has clothed me with the garments of salvation; He has covered me with the robes of righteousness.

To be righteous means to act in a morally correct manner; correct by divine declaration. We are the righteousness of God through Jesus Christ. Clothed by Jesus, we are declared to be innocent of our sins. He provides the garments that cover us so when we appear before God we are totally blameless. Our appearance is beautiful to Him because it is an outward beauty that moves our inward being to serve our Lord and our neighbor with actions that bring glory to His holy name and serve the good of His creation. We wear the garments of salvation as we work for our LORD. The garments of salvation are our "work clothes." Our righteousness is adorned with good works that testify to a living, genuine faith. With Jesus, we are always dressed for success.

"The path of righteousness is a narrow, winding trail up a steep hill. At the top of the hill is a cross. We need a shepherd to care for us and to guide us. And we have One. One who knows us by name." (Max Lucado)

"Success is the maximum utilization of the ability that you have."
(Zig Ziglar)

October 31
God's Grace

Hebrews 12:15
See to it that no one misses the grace of God.

Galatians 2:20
Christ lives in me.

God's grace is His unconditional love and unmerited favor and it is often difficult for us to grasp even though each one of us is in desperate need of it. As Christians, each of us has experienced God's grace, mercy and forgiveness in our own times of failure and despair. God's grace is a kindness that comes from Him and is a gift to us. God's grace changes our lives and our stories and transports us into the peace of God's all-consuming embrace. We have a perfect God who truly delights in sinful people like us. God's grace is His unmerited favor that is unconditional and full of love. Jesus Christ is grace and He is truly the only hope that brings everlasting peace and He lives in us.

"God's grace is truly much more than we deserve and greater than we can imagine." (Max Lucado)

"The Christian is a man to whom something has happened."
(E. L. Mascall)

November 1
All Saints Day

Psalm 100:3
Know that the Lord, He is God! It is He who made us, and we are His; we are His people, and the sheep of His pasture.

1 Peter 2:10
Once you were not a people, but now you are God's people; once you had not received mercy, but now you have received mercy.

Protestants generally regard all true Christian believers as saints, and, if they observe All Saints' Day they use it to remember all Christians, both past and present. In many churches, All Saints' Day is celebrated on the first Sunday in November. It is held not only to remember Saints but also to remember all those who have died. We are considered saints because we have been chosen by God and have been called to represent Him to others.

"We have been declared innocent—we are saints—because of the gift of grace. We endure the taunts of a world that doesn't understand how we, who sin daily, could be called holy. They call us hypocrites. We are no less saints because of our sinner-actions. And although our failings make us appear hypocritical, they cannot, in themselves, make us unholy. Instead, they make us humble, repentant, and reliant on God's mercy for the sake of His Son. The world may accuse us, but we can rest assured that God has made us His saints. He has chosen us as recipients of grace; He has chosen us to be His own people." (Portals of Prayer)

"Holy God, defend me against my foes because of Christ's righteousness, not my own. O God, who has called me out of my darkness and into Your marvelous light, I give You resounding thanks for all whom You have chosen to be made holy—both past and present. What an indescribable joy to be counted among them for the sake of Your Son! Amen
 (Portals of Prayer)

November 2
Team Jesus

John 15:5
"I am the vine; you are the branches. If a man remains in Me and I in him, he will bear much fruit; apart from Me you can do nothing."

Romans 11:16
If the root is holy, so are the branches.

There are many types of fans in this world: football fans, baseball fans, soccer fans, Nascar fans, shopping fans, family fans, and many others, but the most important fan is the fan of Jesus Christ. We are fans of Jesus Christ because we are on His team—team Jesus. He is the root and we are His branches. We get our strength and nourishment from Him. We become His fan and remain in Him by: 1) believing that He is the Son of God; 2) receiving Him as Savior and LORD; 3) doing what He says; 4) continuing to believe the gospel; and 5) relating in love to the community of believers, Christ's body. The only way to stay close to Jesus is to be like a branch attached to the vine. Apart from Christ, we are nothing. When we remain in Him we will "bear much fruit" in our lives and in the lives of others. That is the joy of living with Jesus. He will walk with us through every situation. Yeah, Go Team Jesus!!!

A cheer for Team Jesus:
Give me a J—what's it stand for: Jesus
Give me an E—what's it stand for: Every day
Give me an S—what's it stand for: Savior
Give me a U—what's it stand for: United in Him
Give me an S—what's it stand for: Salvation won on a Cross.

"People are like sticks of dynamite. The power's on the inside, but nothing happens until the fuse gets lit. "(Mac Anderson)

November 3
God's Great Love for Us

Psalm 103:2-5
Praise the Lord, O my soul, and forget not all His benefits—who forgives all your sins and heals all your diseases, who redeems your life from the pit and crowns you with love and compassion, who satisfies your desires with good things so that your youth is renewed like the eagle's.

Psalm 103:8
The Lord is compassionate and gracious, slow to anger, abounding in love.

What an awesome God we have because He loves us when we don't deserve it. He forgives our sins, heals our diseases, redeems us in death, crowns us with love and compassion, satisfies our desires and gives us righteousness and justice. We can always count our blessings no matter what we are going through. As we think about our past, present and future, we will always find blessings for which to thank and praise our LORD. We should be so very thankful that He is compassionate and gracious, slow to anger and abounding in love. It doesn't get any better than that. "Praise the LORD, oh my soul."

"Accept what is, let go of what was and have faith in what will be." (Author unknown)

"The greatest thing you'll ever learn is just to love and be loved in return." (David Bowie)

November 4
We Are United in Him

1 Corinthians 12:12
The body is a unit, though it is made up of many parts; and though all its parts are many, they form one body. So it is with Christ. For we were all baptized by one Spirit into one body—whether Jews or Greeks, slave or free—and were all given the one Spirit to drink.

Ephesians 4:1-7
As a prisoner for the LORD, then, I urge you to live a life worthy of the calling you have received. Be completely humble and gentle; be patient, bearing with one another in love. Make every effort to keep the unity of the Spirit through the blood of peace. There is one body and one Spirit—just as you were called to one hope when you were called—one LORD, one faith, one baptism; one God and Father of all, who is over all and through all and in all. But to each one of us grace has been given as Christ apportioned it.

We are united in Jesus Christ. We are His prisoners and this is a sentence we should be happy to live out. We have the awesome privilege of being called Christ's very own. We are His representatives on earth and are one body united in Him: one body, one Spirit, one hope, one LORD, one faith, one baptism, one God! One of the Holy Spirit's important roles is to build unity and we must be willing to be led by Him. All believers belong to one body and are united under one head, Christ Himself. We all have unique abilities and gifts to use in God's service to build the strength and health of the body of believers. God is over all, through all and in all and this shows His active presence in the world in all believers. We are Christ's very own, united in Him, and we are responsible to use our different gifts together to spread the Good News of salvation.

"Success is the maximum utilization of the ability that you have." (Zig Ziglar)

"My life is a loan given from God. I will give this loan back but with interest…You love; you serve the brother or sister in front of you. That is how you have a happy life." (Andy Wimmer)

November 5
The Word of God

1 Peter 1:23-25
For you have been born again, not of perishable seed, but of imperishable, through the living and enduring word of God. For, "All men are like grass, and all their glory is like the flowers of the field; the grass withers and the flowers fall, but the word of the Lord stands forever." And this is the word that was preached to you.

The Word of God is the Bible. It is a most cherished book because it comes with a promise from God: "It shall accomplish that which I purpose and shall succeed in the thing for which I sent it." (Isaiah 55:11) It is the *living* word of God and can literally change those who read and study it. The change is an inside job because it is a Godly change. The Old Testament is filled with history and Jesus' footprints are everywhere. The New Testament is about Jesus being born a man but He is still God. It traces His footprints as He walked the earth, teaching and living as a sinless man—the only sinless person ever. It tells of His sacrifice for all, the salvation He won for us on the cross, and His promise to never leave us. Because of the promise, He sent the Holy Spirit to live in us. The Bible is a wonderful book full of stories about God's love for His people. It is full of lessons about how to live the life God wants us to live. The Bible guides us to the light of Jesus and His forgiveness and gives us hope because, when we believe in Him, trust and follow Him, we are saved and will live eternally with Him. There is no death because He conquered it for us. The Bible is God's living Word and is the best book we could ever read.

"The Bible is a tool with which God equips us to combat the sin in our lives. Every time we hear or read the Word, its living power works within us, equipping us to resist those sins we continually fall into and to do the things God wants us to do. The living Word will make a transformation in us, even in those areas in which we constantly fail. God's Word creates faith and creates change." (Portals of Prayer)

"I just came again to tell You, LORD, how happy I've been since we found each other's friendship and You took away my sin. I don't know much of how to pray, but I think about You every day. So, Jesus, this is me checking in today." (Author unknown)

November 6
God Has an Exchange Policy

2 Corinthians 5:21
God made Him who had no sin to be sin for us, so that in Him we might become the righteousness of God.

God has an exchange policy. When we trust in Christ, we make an exchange—our sin for His righteousness. Our sin was poured into Christ at His crucifixion. This is what Christians mean by Christ's atonement for sin. God offers to trade His righteousness for our sin—something of immeasurable worth for something completely worthless. Because of Thanksgiving in November, we tend to think more about being thankful than at other times of the year. We have good reason to be thankful every day to our LORD for His kindness to us and for His exchange policy. We can trust Christ to take away our sins so that we can become the righteousness of God. There is no other exchange policy that has more benefits than God's.

"Jesus took away what was wrong in us and gave us what is right in Him." (Thrivent Financial)

"Begin each new day as if it is the beginning of your life, for truly it is the beginning of what is left of your life." (Author unknown)

November 7
Vote for Jesus Christ

Romans 13:1
Everyone must submit himself to the governing authorities, for there is no authority except that which God has established. The authorities that exist have been established by God.

1 Timothy 2:1-2
I urge, then, first of all, that requests, prayers, intercession and thanksgiving be made for everyone—for kings and all those in authority, that we may live peaceful and quiet lives in all godliness and holiness.

One of our greatest freedoms is the freedom to vote, and on Election Day, that is what we must do—get out and vote. No matter how the elections turn out, we must remember that we have a God who is above all. We have elected officials who run our government, but we have a God who is our King and who is LORD and ruler of our lives. Our first allegiance is to Him but we must obey our government and leaders as well. We are Christ's ambassadors on earth and have to remember to keep our priorities straight because our duty to God comes before our duty to any government. We need to keep praying for our government and leaders, asking for wisdom and guidance for all. We must remember Jesus Christ is LORD. He is the Alpha and Omega, the Beginning and the End.

"Win without boasting. Lose without excuses." (Vince Lombardi)

"A good leader takes more than their fair share of the blame and gives more than their share of the credit." (Arnold Glasgow)

November 8
Welcome Home

John 15:4, 7
Remain in Me, and I will remain in you. No branch can bear fruit by itself; it must remain in the vine. Neither can you bear fruit unless you remain in Me... If you remain in me and My words remain in you, ask whatever you wish, and it will be given you.

Home is a place where our hearts beat because it's a place where our family lives and gathers. Home changes as time goes by because we and our families change. When we make our home with God and remain in Him, every place is home because He is there. Our hope is in our LORD because He is home for us. His heart is our heart. At difficult times people ask, "Where is God?" The answer is, "God is right where He has always been. He is right there in the midst of every storm. He's in our hearts and alongside us. He is in the hands of helping people—He is right where we let Him be."

God makes a home in our hearts when we ask Him to. Our home is not in a building full of things and memories—our home is in our hearts full of God's love, grace, joy, peace and mercy. A building can be destroyed but our hearts that belong to God cannot. Where is God? God is in our hearts and in our sacrificial love, listening, helping, encouraging and giving to those who are hurting and suffering. Home is where our hearts are and where our God lives. Welcome Home—what a beautiful place to be.

"This is and has been the Father's work from the beginning—to bring us into the home of His heart." (George MacDonald)

"God does not spare us trials, but He helps us overcome them." (Wanda E. Brunstetter)

November 9
Where is God?

Genesis 28:15
I am with you and will watch over you wherever you go.

Psalm 139:7-10
Where can I go from Your Spirit? Where can I flee from Your presence? If I go up to the heavens, You are there; if I make my bed in the depths, You are there. If I rise up on the wings of the dawn, if I settle on the far side of the sea, even there Your hand will guide me, Your right hand will hold me fast.

After tragedies, we ask, "Where is God?" The answer is: God is right where He has always been—in us and with us. God's hand is always there; once we grasp it we'll never want to let go. He is present everywhere so we can never be lost to His Spirit and His comforting presence. God is all-seeing, all-knowing, all-powerful, and present everywhere. God knows us, is with us, and His greatest gift is allowing us to know Him. He is in our beating hearts and walking beside us. We can reach out, take His Hand and never let go. We must trust Him and acknowledge Him as our LORD and Savior. God is in the air we breathe, in the blowing winds, the sea, the earth, the smiles of our children, the love of our spouses and the hugs of our friends. God is everywhere. Let's keep looking because we will see Him and know He is closer to us than our own skin. We should thank Him "for never leaving us nor forsaking us." (Hebrews 13:5)

"I believe that God is in me as the sun is in the color and fragrance of a flower—the Light in my darkness, the Voice in my silence."
(Helen Keller)

"Know by the light of faith that God is present, and be content with directing all your actions toward Him." (Brother Lawrence)

November 10
Searching

1 Chronicles 28:9
...for the LORD searches every heart...

Psalm 139:4
Search me, O God, and know my heart;

Romans 8:27
And He who searches our hearts knows the mind of the Spirit, because the Spirit intercedes for the saints in accordance with God's will.

As we walk through these last two months of the year, I realize that I need to be searching and thinking about a new word to focus on next year. My word last year was GRATITUDE. As I searched for that word, I prayed and asked God to show me what word He wanted me to focus on. It was amazing how many times the word GRATITUDE appeared in my day, either in things I read, in songs or in conversations. Finally, I realized that GRATITUDE was the word. I wrote an acronym for it and found Bible verses with the word GRATITUDE in them. Now GRATITUDE is a part of my every day as I find myself being thankful for little things all day long, especially now that we are in the month of "Thanksgiving." However, it is time to find a new word. So the search begins and as the days unfold, I'm anxious to see where God is going to lead me by way of verses and signs to the "word." I know that whatever word it is, it will help me grow and learn more about Him and eventually myself. It will help me share Him with others. He knows my heart and He knows me. I wonder what the new word will be: love, joy, peace, patience, forgiveness, serve or servant, prayer or maybe praise. The list is endless and I'll know the word because once I choose it, a peace will fill my soul.

"To handle yourself, use your head. To handle others, use your heart."
(Eleanor Roosevelt)

"God never measures the mind... He always put His tape measure in the HEART." (Corrie ten Boom)

November 11
Veterans Day

Psalm 91
He who dwells in the shelter of the Most High will rest in the shadow of the Almighty. I will say of the LORD, "He is my refuge and my fortress, my God in whom I trust." Surely He will save you from the fowler's snare and from the deadly pestilence. He will cover you with His feathers, and under His wings you will find refuge; His faithfulness will be your shield and rampart. You will not fear the terror of night, nor the arrow that flies by day, nor the pestilence that stalks in the darkness, nor the plague that destroys at midday. A thousand may fall at your side, ten thousand at your right hand, but it will not come near you. You will only observe with your eyes and see the punishment of the wicked. If you make the Most High your dwelling—even the LORD, who is my refuge—then no harm will befall you, no disaster will come near your tent. For He will command His angels concerning you to guard you in all your ways; they will lift you up in their hands, so that you will not strike your foot against a stone. You will tread upon the lion and the cobra; you will trample the great lion and the serpent. "Because he loves Me," says the LORD, "I will rescue him; I will protect him, for he acknowledges My name. He will call upon Me, and I will answer him; I will be with him in trouble, I will deliver him and honor him. With long life will I satisfy him and show him my salvation.

I've heard that this is often called the "military prayer." I love the verse, "He will cover you with His feathers, and under His wings you will find refuge." What a beautiful thought and picture—God's promise of protection and help in the midst of danger. He is our shelter and refuge, and no matter how intense our fears, we can trade them for trust and faith in Him. We do this by "dwelling and resting in Him." What a comfort to know that our Heavenly Father watches over us even in times of great stress and fear.

Veterans, THANK YOU for your service to God and our country. Thank you for your sacrifices, time and efforts. Thank you, too, to the families that serve along with you. Thank you to those who have served in years past and to those serving today. We pray for you and ask for God's love to surround you, protect you and give you peace.

"Faith believes in spite of the circumstances and acts in spite of the consequences." (Adrian Rogers)

"If your actions inspire others to dream more, LEARN MORE, do more, and become more, you are a leader." (John Quincy Adams)

November 12
Loved and Redeemed

Psalm 32:44
But the LORD redeems His servants; No one will be condemned who takes refuge in Him.

Psalm 103:2-5
Praise the LORD, O my soul; all my inmost being, praise His holy name. Praise the LORD, O my soul, and forget not all His benefits—who forgives all your sins and heals all your diseases, who redeems your life from the pit and crowns you with love and compassion, who satisfies your desires with good things so that your youth is renewed like the eagle's.

There is no greater love than God's love because He loves us so much that He has redeemed us from death, forgiven our sins, and healed and blessed us with love and compassion. We have so much to be thankful for because God is our Redeemer! He loves us so much that He sent His Son to die on the cross for our sins. God hears us when we pray to Him and pays attention to those who call on Him. We are loved by Him so we can take refuge in our LORD. No matter what we are facing or dealing with, we should go to Him and surrender to Him because He hears our cries. Thank You, LORD, for Your love and redemption.

"If there is righteousness in the heart, there will be beauty in the character. If there is beauty in the character, there will be harmony in the home. If there is harmony in the home, there will be order in the nation. If there is order in the nation, there will be peace in the world." (Confucius)

"Temptations are sure to ring your doorbell, but it's your fault if you invite them for dinner." (Wanda E. Brunstetter)

November 13
Living hope

1 Peter 1:3-4
Praise be to the God and Father of our LORD Jesus Christ! In His great mercy He has given us new birth into a living hope through the resurrection of Jesus Christ from the dead, and into an inheritance that can never perish, spoil or fade—kept in heaven for you, who through faith are shielded by God's power until the coming of the salvation that is ready to be revealed in the last time.

2 Corinthians 5:17
Therefore, if anyone is in Christ, he is a new creation; the old has gone, the new has come!

We are like caterpillars who live in cocoons until we accept Jesus and then break free to become beautiful butterflies brand new in Him. Our lives are transformed by the power of God. We are new people in Christ and recreated in Him—that is our hope. We are not alone because we have new life in Him and have the living hope of new birth in Jesus because of what He did on the cross. Our spirits are reborn in Him because of the Holy Spirit bringing us into God's family. This is our joy and hope because of what God has done for us in Jesus Christ. We will live with Christ forever and the Holy Spirit will live in us, giving us the ability to live life differently and faithfully, full of hope and trust in our LORD. He is KING over all. No matter what goes on around us, we have a brand-new life in Christ. We have a living hope.

"When others see you, let them also see Jesus in you."
(Thrivent Financial)

"When you know how much God is in love with you then you can only live your life radiating that love." (Mother Teresa)

November 14
The Master Craftsman

Isaiah 64:8
Yet, O Lord, You are our Father. We are the clay, you are the potter; we are all the work of Your hand.

Jeremiah 18:6
"O house of Israel, can I not do with you as this potter does?" declares the Lord. "Like clay in the hand of the potter, so are you in My hand, O house of Israel."

Romans 9:21
Does not the potter have the right to make out of the same lump of clay pottery for noble purposes and some for common use?

God, the Master Craftsman, has control over us—His created vessels. Our very existence depends on Him. Just as the potter has the power to reshape defects or let them remain in a vessel, God has the power to do so with us, and, as we trust and yield to Him, God reshapes us into valuable servants for Him. Yes, sometimes it hurts as He stretches, pushes, pokes and shapes us where we need it most, but the end result is a useful and wonderful creation for Him. He knows what is best and He is doing this so that we will become the people He wants us to be, eventually serving Him to the best of our ability. We should let the stretching and shaping begin; the Master Craftsman is at work. "Ooh, aah, ouch that hurts, Lord, please, is this necessary?" Yes, it is—just wait and see because it will be so worth it.

"For God is, indeed, a wonderful Father who longs to pour out His mercy upon us, and whose majesty is so great that He can transform us from deep within." (Teresa of Avila)

"God puts each fresh morning, each new chance of life, into our hands as a gift to see what we will do with it." (Author unknown)

November 15
The Master's Children

Romans 8:16-17
The Spirit Himself testifies with our spirit that we are God's children. Now if we are children, then we are heirs—heirs of God and co-heirs with Christ, if indeed we share in His sufferings in order that we may also share in His glory.

We are the Master's Children!!!! He has already given us His best gifts—His Son, forgiveness and eternal life. We can go to Him with our concerns, needs and prayers. There is privilege and responsibility in belonging to God's family. We have the privilege of being led by the Holy Spirit. He lives in us and encourages us with God's love. We also have a responsibility to share God with those around us, to show Him in all we do and say, and to do it without thinking or receiving credit. Being a parent takes a lot of love and brings much joy and many blessings. It is very comforting to think of God as our parent. The love we have for our children and grandchildren is beyond measure, and He loves us even more than we can imagine. He sacrificed so much to save and forgive us. Thank You, Lord, for bringing us into Your family and for enhancing our families with the many blessings You have given us. We are Your heirs and co-heirs with Christ. What a privilege and honor to be members of Your family. We are the "Master's Children."

"Following God is a journey best made in the company of others. ... Growth isn't always comfortable or easy, and it is good to have help along the way." (Pamela Kennedy)

"In God's family, we are joined with bonds as close as any blood ties or earthly genealogies. Sharing a heritage of faith, our hearts are knit together with that of Christ, our eldest brother. And the very best thing about our relationship is that it is eternal! This family is far greater than any we might have planned. " (Author unknown)

November 16
Grace: God's Redeeming Attributes in Christ for Everyone

Luke 2:40
And the child (Jesus) grew and became strong; He was filled with wisdom, and the grace of God was upon Him.

John 1:14
The Word became flesh and made His dwelling among us. We have seen His glory, the glory of the One and Only, who came from the Father, full of grace and truth.

The definition of "Grace": God's free and unmerited favor for sinful humanity; unmerited divine assistance given humans for their regeneration or sanctification; a virtue coming from God; a state of sanctification enjoyed through divine grace.

Jesus is Grace. He is God in the flesh and is both God and man. He is the perfect expression of God in human form. Jesus is God's only Son. He was perfect in every way and shows us how to live according to His plan. Jesus, the Lamb, became the perfect sacrifice for all sins, and His death satisfied God's requirements for the removal of sin. Jesus is Grace. He had all of God's redeeming attributes that He freely gave to everyone so that we as sinners are set free from the slavery of sin. Because of Jesus, our slate is wiped clean. Christ purchased our freedom and the price was His life. Thank You, LORD, for loving us so much. We should enjoy the GRACE of God because it came at a very high price.

O God, help me to see the good, the bright side and the reality of grace in every situation. Amen (Author unknown)

"If you are wearing out the seat of your pants before you do your shoe soles, you are making too many contacts in the wrong place."
(Author unknown)

November 17
GRACE 2
Grace: God's Redeeming Attributes in Christ for Everyone

Romans 5:15
But the gift is not like the trespass. For if the many died by the trespass of the one man, how much more did God's grace and the gift that came by the grace of the one man, Jesus Christ, overflow to the many!

The definition of *Grace* is "God's free and unmerited favor for sinful humanity; unmerited divine assistance given humans for their regeneration or sanctification; a virtue coming from God; a state of sanctification enjoyed through divine grace."

In the Bible Adam disobeyed God and was sinful, and, because we are descendents of Adam, we have his sinful nature and have reaped the results of Adam's sin. We have inherited his sin and God's punishment, BUT, because of Jesus, we can trade judgment for forgiveness and eternal life. Adam is the opposite of Jesus. When we come to God by faith, we have life through Christ. Thank You, Jesus, for Your life and death on the cross, for taking our punishment, suffering for us and for being raised from the dead. We are thankful that we have the Grace of God. We have been redeemed. Alleluia!!!

"God, who numbers the stars in the universe, also cares for you."
(Thrivent Financial)

"O Divine Master, grant that I may not so much seek to be consoled as to console; to be understood as to understand; to be loved as to love. For it is in giving that we receive; it is in pardoning that we are pardoned; and it is in dying that we are born to eternal life." (St. Francis of Assisi)

November 18
God Has a Plan

Jeremiah 29:11-13
"For I know the plans I have for you, "declares the Lord, "plans to prosper you and not to harm you, plans to give you hope and a future. Then you will call upon Me and come and pray to Me, and I will listen to you. You will seek Me and find Me when you seek Me with all your heart."

God gives us many promises in Scripture. During troubled times we can have hope and know that He will "never leave us nor forsake us." (Hebrews 13:5) We know that God has a plan for us and will see us through every situation. Because of this we have boundless hope. It does not mean that we will be spared from suffering but it does mean that we will not go through anything alone. He will be with us, and when we walk with Him and keep Him at the center of our lives, He prepares and helps us endure. We have a God who loves us and has a plan for every one of us. We can lean on Him and seek Him with all our hearts while reading His Word and trusting His promises.

"Every experience God gives us, every person He puts in our lives, is the perfect preparation for the future that only He can see."
(Corrie Ten Boom)

"We do not fill ourselves with the power of God. Instead, the LORD fills us by the Gospel promises. God, who numbers the stars in the universe, also cares for you." (Thrivent Financial)

November 19
God's Travel Plans—He Is Everywhere!

Exodus 33:14
The LORD replied, "My Presence will go with you, and I will give you rest."

Joshua 1:9
"Have I not commanded you? Be strong and courageous. Do not be terrified; do not be discouraged, for the LORD your God will be with you wherever you go."

God is everywhere and He is telling us to be strong and courageous. We will succeed because He is with us wherever we are and wherever we go. Our God rules over all, works through all and is present in all. He is Oneness and is in everything we think and do. He has travel plans to be everywhere we are because we have one God and He is Father of all. What an awesome God we have!!! May God be visible in us in everything we do and say for His Glory! If God brings us to it, He will bring us through it. We should trust God's travel plans.

"You already know that God is everywhere…And where God is, there is heaven—heaven! Where His Majesty reigns in glory." (Teresa of Avila)

"LORD, give me an open heart to find You everywhere, to glimpse the heaven enfolded in a bud, and to experience eternity in the smallest act of love." (Mother Teresa)

November 20
The Great *"I AM"*

Exodus 3:14-15
God said to Moses, "I AM WHO I AM. This is what you are to say to the Israelites: "I AM has sent me to you." God said to Moses, "Say to the Israelites, 'The LORD, the God of your fathers—the God of Abraham, the God of Isaac and the God of Jacob—has sent me to you.' This is my name forever, the name by which I am to be remembered from generation to generation."

John 14:20-21
"On that day you will realize that I AM in My Father and you are in Me, and I AM in you. Whoever has My commands and obeys them, he is the one who loves me. He who loves me will be loved by My Father, and I, too, will love him and show myself to him."

I AM—God's name describing His eternal power and unchangeable character. I AM is our stability and security in a world that changes by the nanosecond. The same God who appeared to Moses all those years ago is the same God that is alive in us today. God is stable and trustworthy. He is "the same yesterday, today and forever." (Hebrews 13:8) God has an unchanging nature so we can trust in and rely on Him. He is who He says He is. Jesus described Himself as "I AM." "I AM the bread of life." (John 6:35) "I AM the gate…" (John 10:9) "I AM the good shepherd; I know my sheep and my sheep know me…" (John 10:14) "I AM the true vine, and My Father is the gardener." (John 15:1) The Great I AM never changes. His promises are as true today as they were in the day of Moses and when Jesus walked the earth. He will never leave us nor forsake us. (Hebrews 13:5) The Great "I AM" is alive in us today. It doesn't get any better than that.

"Listening to God is a firsthand experience. God invites you to vacation in His splendor. He invites you to feel the touch of His hand. He invites you to feast at His table. He wants to spend time with you."
(Max Lucado)

"He is a God who can be found. A God who can be known. A God who wants to be close to us. That's why He is called Immanuel, which means "God with us." But He draws close to us as we draw close to Him."
(Stormie Omartian)

November 21
Being Restful with the "I Ams"

Job 33:14-15
For God does speak—now one way, now another—though man may not perceive it. In a dream, in a vision of the night, when deep sleep falls on men as they slumber in their beds...

Proverbs 16:9 "Life and death are in the power of the tongue."

I've heard that the last five minutes before we go to sleep is the most important time of our day. The reason for this is that once we go to sleep, whatever we've thought about or focused on in those last five minutes will marinate in our subconscious throughout the night. If we focus on all the troublesome things that happened in our day, that is what will go through our minds throughout the night. If we focus on God and His love, praying, forgiving others and asking for forgiveness, we will have a more peaceful and restful night's sleep. "The act of forgiveness can change your life. It will get the rage out of you and fill you with love. When you fill yourself with love, you become aligned with your Source—God." (Author unknown) Before we go to sleep we should be saying, "I am well"; "I am strong"; "I am healthy" and turn our negative "I ams" into positive "I ams." We should remember that our attitude determines our future.

Tonight have a more peaceful and restful night's sleep. *"Now I lay me down to sleep pray the LORD my soul to keep. Guide me safely through the night wake me at dawn's early light." (Author unknown)*

"Forgiveness is the fragrance that the violet sheds on the heel that has crushed it. It is the ability to send love when someone sends you what you think of as hatred or shortages or whatever it may be." (Mark Twain)

November 22
God Is Dependable

Psalm 121
I lift up my eyes to the hills—
Where does my help come from?
My help comes from the LORD,
The Maker of heaven and earth.
He will not let your foot slip—
He who watches over you will not slumber;
Indeed, He who watches over Israel
Will not slumber nor sleep.
The LORD watches over you—
The LORD is your shade at your right hand;
The sun will not harm you by day,
Nor the moon by night.
The LORD will keep you from all harm—
He will watch over your life;
The LORD will watch over your coming and going
Both now and forevermore.

God is dependable and is the Creator of everything. He is all-powerful and watches over us. Nothing diverts or deters Him so we are safe. We need His untiring watch over our lives. In everything, our help comes from Him and we can depend on Him. He is our dependable and everlasting LORD.

"I am a little pencil in the hand of a writing God who is sending a love letter to the world." (Mother Teresa)

"The man who walks with God always gets to his destination." (Author unknown)

November 23
We Are Conquerors

Romans 8:28-39
And we know that in all things God works for the good of those who love Him, who have been called according to His purpose. For those God foreknew He also predestined to be conformed to the likeness of His Son, that He might be the firstborn among many brothers. And those He predestined, He also called; those He called, He also justified; those He justified, He also glorified.

What, then, shall we say in response to this? If God is for us, who can be against us? He who did not spare His own Son, but gave Him up for us all—how will He not also, along with Him, graciously give us all things? Who will bring any charge against those whom God has chosen? It is God who justifies. Who is he that condemns? Christ Jesus, who died—more than that, who was raised in life—is at that right hand of God and is also interceding for us. Who shall separate us from the love of Christ? Shall trouble or hardship or persecution or famine or nakedness or danger or sword? As it is written: "For your sake we face death all day long; we are considered as sheep to be slaughtered."

No, in all these things we are more than conquerors through Him who loved us. For I am convinced that neither death nor life, neither angels nor demons, neither the present nor the future, nor any powers, neither height nor depth, nor anything else in all creation, will be able to separate us from the love of God that is in Christ Jesus our Lord.

The Promise! Did you ever hear the phrase, "Don't make a promise you can't keep?" Here is God's promise—we are His and we can never be lost to Him or His love. God is with us in every circumstance and His love is eternal. He is able to turn every circumstance around for our good—our long-range good. He is working to fulfill His purpose for those who love Him. His purpose is for us to be more like Christ every day in every way. We cannot be separated from Christ because after His death and resurrection, He sent the Holy Spirit to live in us. We can be totally secure in the fact that this promise is ours, and there is no need to be afraid. In Christ, we are more than conquerors. What a promise and what love!

"Keep my mind and thoughts clear, my speech soft and precise, never offensive; my work always worthy; my faith proud and strong."
(Author unknown)

"The quality of a person's life is in direct proportion to their commitment to excellence, regardless of their chosen field of endeavor."
(Vince Lombardi)

November 24
Thanks and Giving

Psalm 107:1
"Give Thanks to the Lord, for He is good; His love endures forever."

Psalm 128:5 (TLB)
"May the Lord continually Bless You with heaven's blessings as well as with human joys."

Every day we give Thanks to God for our many blessings. Every day is a day of Giving. We give love to others, we give forgiveness, we share what we have, we help when we can and care when we see a need. This is Thanks and Giving. As Christians, we thank our LORD every day and we give a part of ourselves to others. May our blessings be abundant and the love of God be overflowing in our hearts and homes as Thanks and Giving become a part of our every day.

"Praying You are
Blessed in a way that brings God's presence closer than you have ever known it...
Blessed in a way that assures you of the plans He has for your life...
Blessed in a way that fills your heart with a thousand "thank-yous" for all that His hand will bring your way." (DaySpring)

"The world rams at your door; Jesus taps at your door. There is never a time during which Jesus is not speaking nor a place in which Jesus is not present." (Max Lucado)

November 25
JOY

Jesus
Others
Yourself

Romans 15:13
May the God of hope fill you with all joy and peace as you trust in Him, so that you may overflow with hope by the power of the Holy Spirit.

I love the feel of joy overflowing in my soul and it's better than happiness. Happiness is fleeting but joy is deep within. Our joy comes from knowing that God has somehow touched us in our innermost being and we have the ecstasy of looking forward to eternity. We know that we've made peace with Him and are ready to do His will. Joy is the evolving manifestation of God in our lives as we walk with Him. On our worst day, we can still have joy because the joy of the LORD is deep within us and never goes away. We can always have abundant JOY as we walk with our LORD.

"Joy is really a road sign pointing us to God. Once we have found God…we no longer need to trouble ourselves so much about the quest for joy." (C.S. Lewis)

"A joyful spirit is like a sunny day; it sheds a brightness over everything; it sweetens our circumstances and soothes our souls." (Author unknown)

"Just slipping quietly into the presence of God can be so exotic and fresh that it delights us enormously." (Richard J. Foster)

"JOY is the echo of God's life within us." (Author unknown)

November 26
Who Inspires Us

1 Corinthians 1:21-25
Since God in His wisdom saw to it that the world would never know Him through human wisdom, He has used our foolish preaching to save those who believe. It is foolish to the Jews, who ask for signs from heaven. And it is foolish to the Greeks, who seek human wisdom. So when we preach that Christ was crucified, the Jews are offended and the Gentiles say it's all nonsense. But to those called by God to salvation, both Jews and Gentiles, Christ is the power of God and the wisdom of God. This foolish plan of God is wiser than the wisest of human plans, and God's weakness is stronger than the greatest of human strength.

The definition of "inspire" is: to cause, guide, communicate, or motivate as by divine or supernatural influence; to affect with a specified feeling or thought.

Knowing Jesus Christ personally is the greatest wisdom anyone can have because He is an inspiration to anyone who chooses to follow Him. In heaven, He had it all, but He gave it up to save us from our sins. He knew what was going to happen before He came here. Jesus knew the suffering He was to endure and knew we wouldn't appreciate it, but He agreed to do it anyway. Jesus Christ obeyed His Father and came as a humble servant into a world that thrived on power. He had power over death which He demonstrated in His resurrection. Jesus Christ is our power and our victory over death, and He will lead us to eternal life. Jesus inspires us to believe Him, trust Him and follow Him. Jesus is our inspiration.

"True self-discovery begins where your comfort zone ends."
(Adam Braun)

"When life gives you lemons, throw them back and pray for chocolate."
(Author unknown)

November 27
Take Hold of God's Hand

Isaiah 41:9-10
I took you from the ends of the earth, from its farthest corners I called you. I said, 'You are my servant'; I have chosen you and have not rejected you. So do not fear, for I am with you; I will uphold you with My righteous right hand.

There is something special about holding hands. Doing so with my husband, children and grandchildren warms my heart and fills me with joy. The love that flows through our hands to our hearts is so comforting and special. That's what it's like to take hold of God's Hand. As we worship and praise Him all day long, we should lift up our hands to Him and feel His love. God is with us, He is strong, and He is all powerful. We should take hold of His Righteous Right Hand because He has us and He will never let us go.

"All I have seen teaches me to trust the Creator for all I have not seen."
(Ralph Waldo Emerson)

"Kind hearts are the gardens, kind thoughts are the roots, kind words are the flowers, kind deeds are the fruits. Take care of your garden and keep out the weeds, fill it with sunshine, kind words and kind deeds."
(Henry Wadsworth)

November 28
Throne of Grace

Hebrews 4:15-16
For we do not have a high priest who is unable to sympathize with our weaknesses, but we have one who has been tempted in every way, just as we are—yet was without sin. Let us then with confidence draw near to the throne of grace, that we may receive mercy and find grace to help in time of need.

We have a High Priest who was tempted in every way throughout His life as a human being. Jesus can sympathize with us because He faced temptation but He did not give in to sin. We can approach God with confidence and get close to the throne of grace. There is no reason to fear God's judgment or Christ's nearness because as we get near to the throne of grace, Christ puts His cross-scarred arms around us, and we find where we truly belong—in the nearness of Christ with a never-ending supply of forgiveness. He has chosen to bring us near and does not judge us by our sins, but on the His merits. LORD, we come to You with reverence because You are our King. We come to You with bold assurance because You are our friend and counselor. Thank You, Jesus.

"Keep room in your heart for the unimaginable." (Mary Oliver)

"God protects us not by prohibiting anything bad from happening in our lives but by giving each and every one of us everything we need to handle anything that happens to us." (John E. Welshons)

November 29
Who and What Do We Worship?

Psalm 29:1-2
Ascribe to the LORD, O mighty ones, ascribe to the LORD glory and strength. Ascribe to the LORD the glory due His name; worship the LORD in the splendor of His holiness.

Psalm 100:2
Worship the LORD with gladness; come before Him with joyful songs.

Colossians 3:17
Whatever you do, whether in word or deed, do it all in the name of the LORD Jesus, giving thanks to God the Father through Him.

When we think of worship, who or what comes to our minds? The essence of worship is simply giving God the honor He deserves. To worship is to applaud the greatness of God. The definition of *worship* is "to attribute worth to someone or something." Worship is both an attitude and an action—a view of the heart and an event in life. Worship is a lifestyle because we represent Christ in everything we do and say. Worship is every deed and duty done in such a way that God receives credit and applause. He deserves the honor in every aspect of life and daily living. Worship begins as an attitude but is manifested in our actions. Worship has nothing to do with us; it has everything to do with God. He alone is worthy of being worshipped and deserves to receive it. Let's willingly and joyfully come into God's presence, worshipping Him with thanksgiving and praise.

> "Praise God, from whom all blessings flow;
> Praise Him all creatures here below;
> Praise Him above Ye heavenly host:
> Father, Son and Holy Ghost. Amen." (Hymn)

"Everything is God's to give and to take away, so share what you've been given, and that includes yourself." (Mother Teresa)

"The secret of happiness is to admire without desiring." (F. H. Bradley)

November 30
Finding Joy

James 1:2
Consider it pure joy, my brothers, whenever you face trials of many kinds, because you know that the testing of your faith develops perseverance. Perseverance must finish its work so that you may be mature and complete, not lacking anything.

James 1:12
Blessed is the man who perseveres under trial, because when he has stood the test, he will receive the crown of life that God has promised to those who love him.

Finding joy in trials and tribulations is not an easy task. We all have them, but the point is that, as we go through them, we must look for how they can enhance our lives. We can turn our hardships into times of learning because there are lessons to be learned in every situation. Tough times can teach us perseverance and develop our character. During these times, God wants to make us mature and complete but not keep us from all pain as these times are opportunities for growth. He is with us even during tough times to help us solve problems and give us strength to endure them. He will stay close and help us grow. When we look back on these situations, we can find the joy of overcoming circumstances with courage, integrity, faithfulness and perseverance. When we persevere, loving Him and staying faithful under pressure, our reward will be the "crown of life"—a victory wreath in God's winning circle of eternal life in heaven. We can do this. We can learn and we can find the joy of facing trials and tribulations with our LORD who carries us through. Yes, we can do this.

"O Divine Master, grant that I may not so much seek to be consoled as to console; to be understood as to understand; to be loved as to love. For it is in the giving that we receive; it is in the pardoning that we are pardoned; and it is in the dying that we are born to eternal life."
(St. Francis of Assisi)

"Courage is resistance to fear, mastery of fear—not absence of fear."
(Mark Twain)

December 1
Getting Prepared

Galatians 5:22-23
The fruit of the Spirit is "love, joy, peace, patience, kindness, goodness, faithfulness, gentleness and self-control."

Ephesians 5:18
…be filled with the Spirit.

Today is first day of December and we have several weeks to prepare for a peaceful celebratory season. Indeed, preparation is the key to preventing stress all year long. I'm sure we will all make our Christmas lists. We need to include on our lists reading our daily devotions so that we are in a peaceful place at the very beginning of our day. In addition, let's ask the LORD to help us reflect Him this Christmas. He is not stressed or in a hurry; His face doesn't turn red because of traffic, shoppers, and the cost of gifts and we shouldn't be stressed either. Let's stay filled with the Spirit this Christmas and there will be no room left for stress. Let the only red we see this Christmas be on the decorations, not in the mirror! Let's enjoy the season as we prepare to welcome Baby Jesus into our hearts.

"Kind hearts are the gardens, Kind thoughts are the roots, Kind words are the flowers, Kind deeds are the fruits. Take care of your garden and keep out the weeds, fill it with sunshine, kind words and kind deeds." (Henry Wadsworth)

"How silently, how silently, the wondrous gift is given! So God imparts to human hearts the blessings of His heaven. No ear may hear His coming, but in this world of sin, where meek souls will receive Him still, the dear Christ enters in." (Rector Phillips Brooks)

December 2
Love Came Down

John 14:6
Jesus answered, "I am the way and the truth and the life. No one comes to the Father except through Me."

Ephesians 3:19
To know this love that surpasses knowledge—that you may be filled to the measure of all the fullness of God.

The love of Jesus is greater than anyone can ever know. He humbly died, gloriously rose, and comes again to us in His Word and Sacraments so that He can prepare us for eternity with Him. We have joy in His restored presence. The promised Messiah came so that His perfect, pure, and innocent love for His Father and others will become our own. Jesus came to die for the sins of humankind but that's not all. He came to show us how to live. He is the truth, the embodiment of all that is real, trustworthy and reliable. He is life itself, the One in whom death meets its end and the Source in whom anyone may find purpose and abundance. He is the way, the incarnation of how we are to live our days. Jesus is our Righteousness and He will fill every aspect of our lives. Love came down so that we can live life to the fullest.

"Jesus is the Savior...Receive Him
He's the Shepherd...Follow Him
He's the King...Serve Him
He's the Lord...Trust Him
He's the Christ...Worship Him
He's the Life...Enjoy Him!" (DaySpring)

"I do not go alone through the hours of this day, for Thou art with me."(Author unknown)

"Jesus not only proclaimed love; HE LIVED LOVE." (Author unknown)

December 3
The Light of Jesus

John 1:1-5
In the beginning was the Word, and the Word was with God, and the Word was God. He was with God in the beginning. Through Him all things were made; without Him nothing was made that has been made. In Him was life, and that life was the light of men. The light shines in the darkness, but the darkness has not understood it.

I enjoy this time of year because each night there are new Christmas lights. It reminds me of the Light of Jesus shining in people who quietly go about giving to others in so many ways. They give of their time, energy, talents and do this naturally, not expecting anything in return. Jesus Christ is the true Light and nothing will ever extinguish His Light. When we follow Jesus, the true Light, we can avoid walking blindly and falling into sin. He lights the path ahead of us so we can see how to live. We need to let Christ guide our lives and we'll never need to stumble in darkness. We have the Christmas Light that will remain with us even after the Christmas season has passed because this Light is eternal. We should let His Light shine in us every day in every way. We must do it quietly, humbly and naturally, not expecting anything in return. We should let the Light of Christmas shine in us for all to see His love and glory.

"The One who is the True Light, who gives light to everyone, was coming into the world. Jesus is...the Light of Christmas, the Joy of our hearts, the Hope of our world." (DaySpring)

"God is using you for His special purpose.
To Shine His light.
To Share His love.
To Shape His People." (Author unknown)

December 4
Starry, Starry Night

Psalm 8:3-5
When I consider Your heavens, the work of Your fingers, the moon and the stars, which You have set in place, what is man that You are mindful of him, the son of man that You care for him? You made him a little lower than the heavenly beings and crowned him with glory and honor.

As we look up to the heavens, the joy that we feel will humble us and relieve the stress all around us. We should take a moment away from the street lights and noise of the night and go to a dark, quiet place to look up at God's sky filled with stars glittering like gemstones on black velvet. We must respect God's majesty when we compare ourselves to His greatness as we look at the vast expanse of His creation. We are valuable to Him. We bear the stamp of the Creator and He cherishes each of us more fiercely than the sum total of His firmament. We should go enjoy a starry, starry night.

"Starry, starry night, shining ever so bright.
Starry, starry night, what peace and delight.
Starry, starry night, God's forever light.
Starry, starry night, oh, what a beautiful sight." (Author unknown)

"Prayer is the exercise of drawing on the grace of God."
(Oswald Chambers)

December 5
The Christmas Heart

Philippians 2:6-11
(Jesus) Who, being in very nature God, did not consider equality with God something to be grasped, but made Himself nothing, taking the very nature of a servant, being made in human likeness. And being found in appearance as a man, He humbled Himself and became obedient to death—even death on a cross! Therefore God exalted Him to the highest place and gave Him the name that is above every name, that at the name of Jesus every knee should bow, in heaven and on earth and under the earth, and every tongue confess that Jesus Christ is Lord, to the glory of God the Father.

Christmas is coming and God's Heart comes in the form of a baby born in a manger. In the birth of Jesus Christ, we celebrate the fullest picture of God the world has ever received. Jesus left His royal throne and came to earth as a baby and grew into a man who ate, walked and slept just as we do. By the life He lived, He revealed the heart of our gracious and loving Father. Our Lord knows our hearts and He came to earth to find us. We can't hide behind our fears and pride because God reaches into the darkest, dirtiest, most fearful places to correct and restore us into the people He means for us to be. Jesus Christ cleanses us from the stains of life with comfort and healing. Let's open our hearts to Jesus, receive His love and celebrate the Christmas Heart and the birth of our Savior.

"God is always trying to give good things to us, but our hands are too full to receive them." (St. Augustine)

"The only true foundation there can be for anything in this world is solid faith." (Author unknown)

December 6
The Christmas Gift

Romans 15:4
For everything that was written in the past was written to teach us, so that through endurance and encouragement of the Scriptures we might have hope.

There is a Christmas gift that all of us have that will get us through the hustle and bustle of the Christmas season. This gift is ours all year long and it is God's Word. God's Word is the gift that can help us keep our perspective during the busyness of this season and every single day of our lives. Let's face it—we are every day not just during a particular season. It's just that we expect a lot from December and we become overloaded with those expectations. When we begin and/or end our days with our Bible, we find encouragement for those times when our expectations go unmet. Think about Mary and Joseph and all that happened to them in their young lives. None of the circumstances that they faced were what they expected, but, despite their difficult situations, they trusted God. They received the gift of God's voice and they followed His directions. God's Word speaks to us and His voice reminds us of what is important. Scripture speaks to our deepest needs and keeps us focused on Him and His will. We should not leave this Christmas gift unopened. The Word of God has the counsel, wisdom and power that we need. Let's take a moment to open God's Christmas gift—His Word. It's amazing.

"The heart that gives ... gathers." (Hannah More)

"Faith is the most powerful of all forces operating in humanity and when you have it in depth nothing can get you down."(Norman Vincent Peale)

December 7
Jesus was No Ordinary Baby

John 1:1
In the beginning was the Word, and the Word was with God, and the Word was God. He was with God in the beginning.

Luke 1:30-35
But the angel said to her, "Do not be afraid, Mary, you have found favor with God. You will be with child and give birth to a son, and you are to give Him the name Jesus. He will be great and will be called the Son of the Most High. The LORD God will give Him the throne of His Father David, and He will reign over the house of Jacob forever; His kingdom will never end." "How will this be," Mary asked the angel, "since I am a virgin?" The angel answered, "The Holy Spirit will come upon you, and the power of the Most High will overshadow you. So the holy one to be born will be called the Son of God."

Jesus was no ordinary baby. His life began before conception because He always existed as the eternal Son of God. He came to earth as a baby, miraculously conceived in a virgin's womb by the Holy Spirit. This was perfect timing, everything was in place, and the world was ready for a Savior. God had the power to create a child in a virgin's womb and Jesus was born holy. Although, He was fully human and fully God, Jesus never ceased to be the eternal God who has always existed as the Creator and Sustainer of all things, and the Source of eternal life. This is the truth about Jesus and the foundation of all truth. He certainly was no ordinary baby.

"The holy child is waiting to be born in every instant, not just once a year." (Marianne Williamson)

"Christmas is a time to mark our progress through this earthly journey. Because of Christmas, this we know: Christ was born for us. He is love, and the plans He has for us always surpass our own." (Karen Kingsbury)

December 8
Christmas Bread

Micah 5:2
"But you, Bethlehem Ephrathah, though you are small among the clans of Judah, out of you will come for me one who will be ruler over Israel, whose origins are from of old, from ancient times."

John 6:48-51
Jesus said, "I am the bread of life. Your forefathers ate the manna in the desert, yet they died. But here is the bread that comes down from heaven, which a man may eat and not die. I am the living bread that came down from heaven. If anyone eats of this bread, He will live forever. This bread is my flesh, which I will give for the life of the world."

Bethlehem means "house of bread." It was God's plan that the One who would claim to be "the living bread that came down from heaven" was born in the "house of bread." This is so appropriate and shows God's perfect plan. In the Old Testament it was prophesied that a Messiah, the King of Kings, would come from Bethlehem. God orchestrated events that would lead Joseph and Mary to Bethlehem just in time for Mary to give birth to the Son of God. This was all preordained by God and He planned the events to bring about the fulfillment of His Word. Jesus is God in the flesh and is the Christmas Bread.

"All that we love deeply becomes a part of us." (Helen Keller)

"Each of us will one day be judged by our standard of life, not by our standard of living; by our measure of giving, not by our measure of wealth; by our simple goodness, not by our seeming greatness."
(William Arthur Ward)

December 9
The Christmas Lamb

John 1:29
"Look, the Lamb of God, who takes away the sin of the world!"

Jesus, the Christmas Lamb, was born in a stable—a smelly, dank, dirty, noisy stable amongst the animals. This is our Lord and we might ask, "Shouldn't He have been born in a better place?" Again, this was God's plan for His Son because Jesus had a role to fulfill. He came to save the world and humbly serve but not to rule as the kings of those days ruled. He was born amongst the livestock and the lambs. Every day a perfect, unblemished lamb was sacrificed in the temple for the sins of the people. Jesus was the Lamb of God who came to take away the sins of the world. Jesus would be the penalty paid for our sins. God, Himself, chose to provide the ultimate and perfect sacrifice—His Son. God's wisdom was displayed in the stable. The manger scene is an illustration of the role Jesus came to fulfill. Jesus was the perfect, sinless, unblemished Lamb who would one day be the Lamb sacrificed for all of us. Jesus is the Christmas Lamb.

"Some people drink at the fountain of knowledge. Others just gargle."
(Author unknown)

"Each day comes bearing its own gifts. Untie the ribbons."
(Ruth Ann Schabacker)

December 10
The Christmas Birth Announcement

Luke 2:8-14
And there were shepherds living out in the fields nearby, keeping watch over their flocks at night. An angel of the Lord appeared to them, and the glory of the Lord shone around them, and they were terrified. But the angel said to them, "Do not be afraid. I bring you good news of great joy that will be for all the people. Today in the town of David a Savior has been born to you; He is Christ the Lord. This will be a sign to you: You will find a baby wrapped in cloths and lying in a manger." Suddenly a great company of heavenly host appeared with the angel, praising God and saying, "Glory to God in the highest, and on earth peace to men on whom His favor rests."

John 10:11
I am the Good Shepherd. The Good Shepherd lays down His life for the sheep.

That is some birth announcement! The Messiah had come and the first group to learn of this baby's birth was a group of shepherds out in the field. This was life-changing news and it came to a group of people who had no prestige or influence. An angel, along with a company of heavenly host, appeared and announced the good news. God had a plan and He chose those humble shepherds to be the first to greet the Good Shepherd, the Lamb of God, who would later take away the sins of the world. At first, the shepherds were terrified but their fear turned to joy when the angel announced the Messiah's birth. The shepherds came to welcome this special Baby and shared this good news with others. What Good News—Jesus comes to all, including the plain and ordinary. He comes to anyone with a heart humble enough to accept Him. Jesus accepts us just as we are, ordinary people, living ordinary lives loved by no ordinary Baby. Jesus, the Good Shepherd, the Lamb of God, came to lay down His life for us, His sheep. Glory be to God!!!

"You don't need all the answers. The teaching isn't in the answers. It's in the question, the conversation, the journey to the answer."
(Author unknown)

"The first principle to making life matter is to value the beautiful people and places in your life. God has given those places to us as gifts and with the understanding that how we treat these things in our journey determines, ultimately, what we value in God." (Author unknown)

December 11
Christmas Grace

Matthew 1:21
She will give birth to a son, and you are to give Him the name Jesus, because He will save His people from their sins.

As we go through the Christmas season, we will at one time or another get frustrated, harried and upset with those around us. We will not be merry at a time when we should be the most joyful. This is when we need Christmas Grace. We have Grace all year long, but we especially need it now as we struggle through the holidays. We need a Savior whose Grace covers us the rest of the year and is there during the most wonderful time of the year when we may be feeling stressed. Christ's love for us is the most important message of Christmas because Christmas Grace is Jesus and the name Jesus means "the LORD saves." Jesus is both God and human and God's plan is perfect and His wisdom is displayed in the name He chose for His Son. The infinite God took on the limitations of humanity so He could live and die for the salvation of all who would believe in Him. Christmas Grace came to earth to save us because we can't save ourselves.

"Grace—God's unconditional loving, unmerited favor is ours because of Jesus. It is truly more than we deserve and greater than we can imagine." (Max Lucado)

"Amazing grace! How sweet the sound
That saved a wretch like me.
I once was lost, but now am found,
Was blind, but now I see." (John Newton)

December 12
Christmas Presence

Acts 17:28
For in Him we live and move and have our being. As some of your own poets have said, 'We are His offspring.'

Romans 11:33
Oh the depth of the riches both of the wisdom and knowledge of God! How unsearchable are His judgments and unfathomable His ways.

God with us—Immanuel. God's plan was perfect because at the time of the birth of Jesus, the Jewish people were expecting a Savior. The Bread of Life was born in Bethlehem which means the "house of bread." The baby born in a stable was no ordinary baby because He was the Son of God, the greatest gift we could ever receive. The Lamb of God, born to a virgin among the livestock, was wrapped not in royal robes but in rough fabric and laid on straw in a manger. He was not attended by doctors, nurses or servants but looked upon by sheep and donkeys. Jesus who left the throne of heaven came not to be served but to serve the lowly, the forgotten and the least—all of us. His birth announcement was made to a ragtag group of shepherds out in the field who had no influence or prestige. What an honor to be those shepherds and to be the first to hear that the Good Shepherd had finally come to lay down His life for His sheep. This was life-changing news and it was shared with those who were not religious and political leaders. Again, this was God's plan. Even His name was planned by God. His purpose was to live among us and to save His people from their sins. Eternal life began at Jesus' birth because the Light of the world had come and remains present with us today. All we need to do is to become lowly in heart and humble ourselves in submission to Him. The Christmas Presence never ends but stretches on forever. This is the greatest story ever told and the greatest gift we could ever receive. God governs the universe and our lives in perfect wisdom, justice and love. The Christmas Presence is with us always and turns real life into Real Life.

"People see God every day. They just don't recognize Him."
(Pearl Bailey)

"In Jesus, God has an "open-door" policy." (Thrivent Financial)

December 13
The Innkeeper

Luke 2:7
… and she gave birth to her firstborn, a son. She wrapped Him in cloths and placed him in a manger, because there was no room for them in the inn.

How do we see Jesus today? Is He still a baby in the manger? Have we made room for Him in our "Inn"—our hearts? We are the Innkeepers and it's up to us as to whether or not we make room for Him. Jesus lived an amazing life in 33 years. He died for us, ascended to heaven and will come back to this earth as the King of Kings. Christ will rule the world and judge all people according to their decisions about Him. We must not underestimate Jesus but open the "Inn" of our hearts to Him to let the baby born in the manger grow up in our lives. He will work in us and through us wherever He is needed and when He does return, we will be ready.

"Each of us is an Innkeeper who decides if there is room for Jesus." (Neal A. Maxwell)

"God isn't concerned with the quality of our voices or even the polished words in our songs. He's looking at our hearts." (Mandisa)

December 14
The Gift

Isaiah 9:6
For to us a Child is born, to us a Son is given, and the government shall be upon His shoulders. And He will be called Wonderful Counselor, Mighty God, Everlasting Father, Prince of Peace.

2 Corinthians 9:15
Thanks be to God for His indescribable gift!

God's indescribable gift is not peace or joy although His gift *brings* peace and joy. His gift is Jesus Christ. When we have Jesus, we have everything God wants to give us.

What a love! What a Savior! What a gift!
May our hearts be open to receive Him,
may our faith be ready to trust Him,
may our wills be surrendered to obey Him,
may our feet and hands be committed to follow Him,
may our faces be anointed to reflect Him,
may our actions and attitudes honor Him,
and may our voices be uplifted to praise Him. (Roy Lessin, DaySpring)

"God answers the mess of life with one word: Grace" (Max Lucado)

December 15
Hope and Waiting

Psalm 18:32
It is God who arms me with strength and makes my way perfect.

Isaiah 40:31
But those who hope in the Lord will renew their strength. They will soar with wings like eagles: They will run and not grow weary, they will walk and not be faint. (NIV)

Hope and waiting seem like opposites. Hope seems so positive and uplifting, while waiting seems horrible and angst—ridden. But hope and waiting go hand in hand. We can wait because we have hope. We wait on Jesus' timing because our hope is in Him and Him alone, and this is the very essence of Christmas. All that waiting and all that hoping for a Messiah was fulfilled at Christmas with the birth of Jesus—God with us. None of us will ever like waiting yet we can be filled with hope for all that tomorrow holds. With the One that arrived so long ago, a babe wrapped in swaddling clothes, hope was revealed and He was worth the wait.

"Remember that faith will lead you through unsteady times."
(Author unknown)

"Love Him in the morning when you see the sun rising. Love Him in the evening cause He took you through the day. And in the in-between times when you feel the pressure coming, remember that He loves you and He promises to stay." (John Fischer)

December 16
Christmas White

1 Corinthians 14:33
For God is not a God of disorder but of peace.

The ground is blanketed with snow and as the snow is falling, it is so peaceful. Everything is white, clean and pure. White lights at Christmas mean "Jesus, the light of the world." Christmas lights, whether they are white or different colors, are a welcome sight in the dark of winter and lift our spirits. Christmas white reminds us to keep Christmas clutter-free by living with simplicity of heart. Christmas white reminds us of the basics of Christmas—love, generosity, worship, service, giving, contemplation and gratitude. We must not let the busyness of Christmas take away from the joy and peace of the season. Let's enjoy the lights of Christmas as we enjoy the "Light of the World"—Jesus.

"I believe God embedded the miraculous in the ordinary, and it is our task to discover it and celebrate it." (Kent Nerburn)

"When in doubt, err on the side of generosity." (Author unknown)

December 17
Christmas Letter

John 17:24-26
"Father, I want those You have given Me to be with Me where I am, and to see My glory, the glory You have given Me because You loved Me before the creation of the world. Righteous Father, though the world does not know You, I know You, and they know that You have sent Me. I have made You known to them, and will continue to make You known in order that the love You have for Me may be in them and that I Myself may be in them."

Whenever I contemplate writing a Christmas letter, I try to express God's greatest gift to us—*His Son, Jesus.* Now, if God were to write a Christmas letter I wonder how it would read:

> Dear Family and Friends, Baby Jesus came to serve and to save you from yourself and your sins. He grew as a little boy should and He loved all those around Him. He was kind, caring, and giving. He shared all that He had with His family and friends and learned lessons well because He always knew the reason for His short life on earth. I AM His Father and I know My Son. It was very hard for Me to let Him leave Heaven to spend 33 years on earth but I could not get through to you. Your sinning and denial of Me would not stop and you complained at every turn no matter what I did. It was a sacrifice that had to be made and My Son, Jesus, courageously accepted this mission. It broke my heart when He prayed to me, "Father, if You are willing, take this cup from Me; yet not My will but Yours be done." (Luke 22:42) Jesus dreaded more than anything the separation from Me that He would endure after dying on the cross for the sins of the world. I could not stop His purpose for coming to you because then you would not have believed in us. The Bible would not have had a New Testament, and a love story would not have been written. We have done this for you because We love you so much. My Son walked the earth and touched peoples' lives by healing, feeding, clothing and teaching them. He became their friend while laughing, dancing, crying and performing miracles. My Son, Jesus Christ, is a man after My own heart because He loves you so much that when He rose from the dead and came back to Heaven He sent the Holy Spirit to live in each of you so that you would know us and not be left alone. Jesus is alive and well and is Grace. He will find you and come to you whenever you need Him and wherever you are. You can trust Us— We will never let you down. Keep Christ in Christmas as you celebrate His birthday. Merry Christmas! Love, God

"Worship is no longer worship when it reflects the culture around us more than the Christ within us." (A.W. Tozer)

December 18
Hallmark Channel

Ephesians 2:8-10
For it is by grace you have been saved, through faith—and this not from yourselves, it is the gift of God—not by works, so that no one can boast. For we are God's workmanship, created in Christ Jesus to do good works, which God prepared in advance for us to do.

Christmas isn't found on the Hallmark channel. The stories are nice and leave us with good feelings, but, after watching a few of them, there is emptiness inside us. The true meaning of Christmas isn't there. Yes, they talk about love, and, Christmas is all about love, but Christmas is about the love of God and what He did for us. Christmas is about the gifts He gave us—the greatest gifts ever, His Son Jesus Christ and our salvation. Christmas is not about what we do but is about His love and grace. We don't need to work our way to God because our salvation and our faith are gifts. We should respond with gratitude, praise and joy. We become Christians through God's grace, not as a result of any effort on our part. However, out of gratitude for this free gift, we will seek to help and serve others with kindness, love and gentleness, not merely to please ourselves. We can enjoy the Hallmark channel for stories of Christmas, but to know the real Christmas Story, we need to go to our Bibles and local churches to learn about the God of Grace who loves us so much that He gave His Son as the greatest gift we could ever receive.

"In the waters of Baptism, through the Bible, and in the bread and wine of Christ coming to us, we come before our Lord guilt-ridden, sin-struggling, fear-filled, and consumed by doubt, to receive His humble Means of Grace. His Grace alone gets all the credit for the faith and joy that now abound in our hearts." (Portals of Prayer)

"It is not my ability, but my response to God's ability that counts." (Corrie ten Boom)

December 19
Christmas Courage

Psalm 1:1-3
Blessed is the man who does not walk in the counsel of the wicked or stand in the way of sinners or sit in the seat of mockers. But his delight is in the law of the Lord, and on his law he mediates day and night. He is like a tree planted by streams of water, which yields its fruit in season and whose leaf does not wither. Whatever he does prospers.

Mary conceived a child through the Holy Spirit. Mary and Joseph faced ridicule and shame for what they were asked to do by our Lord. The baby born to them would also bear contempt and the shame of sin on the cross so that grace and faith might abound for everyone. The story of the Holy family is told so that we realize the courage that it took for them to do what the LORD asked. Christmas courage is doing what our Lord asks us to do, knowing that He will be faithful and that we will have His grace to follow Him amidst ridicule and possible shame. We should not allow those who ridicule God to affect our thoughts and attitudes and separate us from our Source of nourishment. God crowns our crosses (our burdens) with opportunities for His grace so that our faith may become evident to all. Christmas courage is true courage.

"Courage is the decision to place your dreams above your fears."
(Author unknown)

"If you want to see the rainbow, you must first put up with the rain."
(Author unknown)

December 20
Hear Ye, Hear Ye—Good News

Matthew 4:23-24
Jesus went throughout Galilee, teaching in their synagogues, preaching the good news of the kingdom, and healing every disease and sickness among people.

We all want to hear good news, but what we hear is all the bad news and very little good news. The Good News of the Bible is that the Messiah has come—that is Good News. He was born in Bethlehem in a stable and was placed in a manger. He came to save us and to show us God by teaching, preaching and healing. His miracles of healing authenticated His journey, proving that He truly was God. The Good News is that the Kingdom of Heaven has come to live amongst us. Jesus is Immanuel—God with us. He cares for us and can heal us physically and spiritually. There is no problem too big or too small for Jesus to handle. His words are Good News because they offer forgiveness, freedom, hope, love, joy, peace of heart and soul. He offers eternal life with God. We should turn away from the bad news of the world and get into the Bible to read about the Good News of our Lord and Savior, Jesus Christ—*Immanuel.*

"Recognizing who we are in Christ and aligning our life with God's purpose for us gives a sense of destiny...It gives form and direction to our life." (Author unknown)

"Keep still, and He will mold you to the right shape." (Martin Luther)

December 21
We Are God's Ornaments

John 6:37-40
"All that the Father gives Me will come to Me, and whoever comes to Me I will never drive away. For I have come down from heaven not to do My will but to do the will of Him who sent Me. And this is the will of Him who sent Me, that I shall lose none of all that He has given me, but raise them up at the last day. For My Father's will is that everyone who looks to the Son and believes in Him shall have eternal life, and I will raise Him up at the last day."

We are God's ornaments on His Christmas Tree of Life. When we accept Jesus as our LORD and Savior, we are welcomed into God's family, and we have His promise that we will live eternally with Him. Just as ornaments are different shapes, sizes, colors and textures, we, too, are all different. Some ornaments are new and shiny and some have been on the tree for many, many years with memories associated with them. Some members of Christ's family have been believers forever but there are those who, in the last few moments of life, accept Him. We are all His family and adorn His Tree of Life. We have different lives, experiences, educations but we come together in oneness. We become a beautiful family just as a Christmas tree is transformed from a bare, green tree into a beautiful, glorious sight with all its ornaments and lights. The lights of the tree represent the light of Jesus living in us. This year as we look at all the ornaments and lights on our Christmas tree, we should remember that we are part of a bigger tree—*The Tree of Life.* Just as a lit Christmas tree brightens a dark room or shines brightly in the dark night, the light of Jesus lives in us for all to see His Glory in a dark world.

"God never gives someone a gift they are not capable of receiving. If He gives us the gift of Christmas, it is because we all have the ability to understand and receive it." (Pope Francis)

"Faith is salted and peppered through everything at Christmas. And I love at least one night by the Christmas tree to sing and feel the quiet holiness of that time that's set apart to celebrate love, friendship, and God's gift of the Christ child." (Amy Grant)

December 22
Christmas Love

Song of Solomon 2:4
...and His banner over me is love.

John 3:16-17
For God so loved the world that He gave His one and only Son that whoever believes in Him shall not perish but have eternal life. For God did not send His Son into the world to condemn the world, but to save the world through Him.

1 John 4:19
We love because He first loved us.

Christmas love is God's love that reaches out and draws others in. God set the pattern for true love and this pattern is the basis of all love relationships. When you love someone dearly, you are willing to give freely to the point of self-sacrifice. God paid the highest price He could pay with the life of His Son because He loved us. There is no greater love. His Son paid the price for our sins and then offered us the new life. This is Christmas love for us to enjoy and share.

"He loves us not because we are all loveable but because He is love." (Author unknown)

"Look for a little bit of God in everyone." (Author unknown)

December 23
The Christmas Wreath

Isaiah 14:7-8
All the lands are at rest and peace; they break into singing. Even the pine trees and the cedars of Lebanon exult over you ...

Isaiah 60:13
The glory of Lebanon will come to you, the pine, the fir and the cypress together, to adorn the place of my sanctuary; and I will glorify the place of my feet.

The evergreen wreath adorns many homes each Christmas season. In the past, evergreens were an emblem of peace, joy and victory. Early Christians placed them in their windows to indicate that Christ had entered the home. Holly and ivy, along with pine and fir, are called evergreens because they never change color and represent eternal life and strength. They are ever-green, ever-alive, even in the midst of winter. The color green speaks of hope and new life while the red ribbon that adorns the traditional Christmas wreath symbolizes Christ's shed blood. The circular shape means no beginning and no end and this symbolically represents God's eternal and never-ceasing love for us. Wreaths symbolize the unchanging nature of our God, and they remind us of the everlasting life that is ours through Jesus Christ. Isaiah also reminds us that the reign of the Messiah will never end. Our wreaths in the form of a circle, a shape with no beginning and no end, remind us of this as well.

"Everywhere you are—God is." (Babbie Mason)

"God loves each of us as if we were the only one to love."
(Babbie Mason)

December 24
The Christmas Child

Isaiah 9:6
For to us a child is born, to us a Son is given, and the government will be on His shoulders. And He will be called Wonderful Counselor, Mighty God, Everlasting Father, Prince of Peace.

Romans 6:23
The gift of God is eternal life in Christ Jesus our Lord. Romans 6:23

God's gift is still the greatest ever given and the greatest our hearts will ever receive.

Praying the truth of this gift fills our hearts with joy this Christmas!

      A Child
        Has been
     boRn for us,
 A Son Is given
    to uS;
      auThority rests
  upon hiM; and
  He is nAmed
      JESUS. (Author unknown)

God must have said, "I'll know what I'll do, I'll send my love right down there where they are. And I'll send it as a tiny baby so they'll have to touch it and they'll hold it close." (Gloria Gaither)

December 25
Christmas Joy Is Immanuel—*God with Us*

Isaiah 9:6
For to us a child is born, to us a Son is given, and the government will be on His shoulders. And He will be called Wonderful Counselor, Mighty God, Everlasting Father, Prince of Peace.

Christmas Joy is Jesus, the Messiah—Immanuel, God with us. He is called the "Light of the World" and gives us hope. He came to fulfill the messages of the Old Testament which was to save everyone from their sins. He was both human and God, visible and tangible, completely human and completely divine. He was a babe in a manger who came to fulfill God's law. In Christ, God revealed His nature and essence in a way that could be seen and touched. In Christ, God became man who lived and walked the earth. Thank You, LORD, for this wonderful gift. As we celebrate the birth of Immanuel, may we remember that Jesus is with us always and that we have everlasting life with Him. May we sing praises to the LORD and shout with joy because the Holy One of Israel has been born. Merry Christmas—"for to us a child is born."

Four names describing the Messiah.
Wonderful Counselor—*He is exceptional, distinguished, and without peer, the One who gives right advice.*
Mighty God—*He is God Himself.*
Everlasting Father—*He is timeless; He is God our Father.*
Prince of Peace—*His government is one of justice and peace.*

"The good news of Christmas is not found under the tree, but in the hearts of those who worship Jesus." (Thrivent Financial)

"Christmas is for children. What better time could there be to honor and love our children than the time when the King of the Universe was Himself a little child?" (Guidepost)

December 26
It's a Boy! Come See Him!

Luke 2:6-14
While they were there, the time came for the baby to be born, and she gave birth to her firstborn, a son. She wrapped him in cloths and placed him in a manger, because there was no room for them in the inn. And there were shepherds living out in the fields nearby, keeping watch over their flocks at night. An angel of the Lord appeared to them, and the glory of the Lord shone around them, and they were terrified. But the angel said to them, "Do not be afraid. I bring you good news of great joy that will be for all the people. Today in the town of David a Savior has been born to you; He is Christ the Lord. This will be a sign to you: You will find a baby wrapped in cloths and lying in a manger." Suddenly a great company of the heavenly host appeared with the angel, praising God and saying, "Glory to God in the highest, and on earth peace to men on whom His favor rests."

John 3:16
For God so loved the world, that He gave His only Son.

This is the greatest birth announcement ever given because the Lamb of God was born! He came to take away the sins of the world and we are all invited to meet Jesus our Messiah, our Savior. We should come and meet Him in the Word and in prayer every day. We can come because He has come for all of us—no matter who we are, what we do or where we live. He wants to be a part of our lives and accept us. We must come because the greatest gift ever given is Jesus, God's Son. He wants our hearts and all the burdens that we carry. He wants our lives and we should give them to Him. Merry Christmas—*"for to us a child is born."* Christ is Christmas so we should come to meet Him; we will never be sorry or want anything more.

"Live your life while you have it. Life is a splendid gift—there is nothing small about it." (Florence Nightingale)

"God knows the rhythm of my spirit and knows my heart thoughts. He is as close as breathing." (Author unknown)

December 27
CHRISTmas Every Day

Hebrews 13:5
… because God said, "Never will I leave you; never will I forsake you."

Jesus is with us every day not just during the Christmas season. One of His many promises is that He will never leave us. When He left after His death and resurrection, He went back to sit at the right hand of God and sent the Counselor, the Holy Spirit, to be with us to guide and help us to know Him even more. The Holy Spirit teaches us the truth about Jesus and comforts us when we are hurting. CHRISTmas is "Christ with us" every day. He is present with us always and has forgiven ALL of our sins. He came to us in a lowly manger, born in a stable, to live a simple life. No other man has ever affected the life of man on earth as much as Jesus.

"Omniscient Lord, thank YOU for the mercy that pens my life story. Amen" (Portals of Prayer)

"If God is going to do something wonderful, He starts with a problem. If God is going to do something spectacular, He starts with an impossibility." (Author unknown)

December 28
Christmas Wonder

Matthew 18:2-5
He called a little child and had him stand among them. And He said: "I tell you the truth, unless you change and become like little children, you will never enter the kingdom of heaven. Therefore, whoever humbles himself like this child is the greatest in the kingdom of heaven. And whoever welcomes a little child like this in my name welcomes me."

The wonder and excitement of children at Christmas is so heartwarming and joyful. God wants us to be childlike in our faith with humble and sincere hearts that trust and depend on Him for everything. As children of God, we need to move away from our self-centeredness and pride to become like little children, unwrapping the baby Jesus and learning all that we can about Him. Jesus is our greatest gift and there is so much that He wants us to know about Him. Just as the shepherd is concerned about one lost sheep, God is concerned about every human being He has created. As we watch little children this Christmas and see the wonder, joy and excitement in their eyes and on their faces, remember this is how we should be looking with wonder at Jesus in the manger.

"Being defeated is often only a temporary condition. Giving up is what makes it permanent." (Marilyn Vos Savant)

"Spread the love everywhere you go: First of all in your own house. Give love to your children, to your wife or husband, to a next door neighbor ... Let no one ever come to you without leaving happier. Be the living expression of God's kindness; kindness in your face, kindness in your eyes, kindness in your smile, kindness in your warm greeting." (Mother Teresa)

December 29
CHRISTmas Kindness

Jeremiah 31:3
I have loved thee with an everlasting love; Therefore with loving-kindness I have drawn thee.

Proverbs 18:21
The tongue has the power of life and death ...

Proverbs 25:11
A word aptly spoken is like apples of gold in settings of silver.

CHRISTmas kindness doesn't end on Dec. 31. As we begin to wind down from Christmas and are basking in the love and kindness that was shown to us, what do we take with us from this day forward to sustain us throughout the next year? We take CHRISTmas kindness with us. We continue being kind and go forward every day performing simple acts of kindness towards others like a smile, hug, and a helping hand that can turn someone's day around. Wise words are valuable, precious, lovely, uncommon and have immense power. Our words can bless or destroy, heal, help, and encourage. We can make a positive difference by telling others we appreciate them. We should be kind and have CHRISTmas every day.

"Kindness is a language that the deaf can hear and the blind can see." (Mark Twain)

"Kind words can be short and easy to speak, but their echoes are truly endless." (Mother Teresa)

"Be a rainbow in someone else's cloud." (Maya Angelou)

"You never know when a moment and a few sincere words can have an impact on a life." (Zig Ziglar)

December 30
Christmas Love Goes On and On

Ephesians 5:2
Christ loved us and gave Himself up for us.

1 Corinthians 16:14
Let all you do be done with love.

God so loved the world and everyone in it that He gave His Son, a gift we are reminded of every Christmas. We need to take time today and everyday to savor God's great gift of Jesus and show appreciation for Him as we worship, praise, pray to, love, share and thank Him for all that He has brought to us. This is Christmas love going on and on.

"Love was born as a baby, sent to save, died on the cross, and lives eternally. Remember how love lived!
Love that goes upward is Worship
Love that goes outward is Affection
Love that stoops is Grace." (DaySpring)

"Love Came Down
The world was blessed at Christmas
with a miracle of love...
a guiding star and angel choir
rejoicing from above.
They pointed to a tiny babe
within a cattle stall -
a Savior bringing peace on earth—
the greatest gift of all." (DaySpring)

"Christmas is not as much about opening our presents as opening our hearts." (Janice Maeditere)

"Christmas is a special time to thank the Lord for the gift of His love that binds our hearts through every season of the year! The love of Jesus is the light of the world. The love of Jesus is greater than anyone can ever know." (Author unknown)

December 31
Time

Ecclesiastes 3:1-8
There is a time for everything, and a season for every activity under heaven:
A time to be born and a time to die, A time to plant and a time to uproot,
A time to kill and a time to heal, A time to tear down and a time to laugh,
A time to mourn and a time to dance, A time to scatter stones and a time to gather them,
A time to embrace and a time to refrain, A time to search and a time to give up,
A time to keep and a time to throw away, A time to tear and a time to mend,
A time to be silent and a time to speak, A time to love and a time to hate,
A time for war and a time for peace.

Ecclesiastes 3:11
He has made everything beautiful in its time. He has also set eternity in the hearts of men; yet they cannot fathom what God has done from beginning to end.

Today is the last day of the year. It seems as though we were just saying hello to a new year and now we're about to say goodbye. Time is fleeting, and we often say we don't have enough of it to do what we want or what we know we should be doing. Each day is a gift because we are given 24 hours a day, 365 days a year. When broken down, that amounts to 8,760 hours a year, 1440 minutes a day and 525,600 minutes a year. Timing is important because the secret to peace with God is to discover, accept and appreciate God's perfect timing. To do that means that we must set aside time each day to spend with God because He has a plan for us. Without Him, life's problems have no lasting solutions. As we embark on a New Year, we should make time for God because the only way to have everlasting peace and hope is to trust and rely fully on Him. There is a time for everything, and our time is better spent when we start each day with *Jesus*. Let's give Him first place in our lives because it is all about Him. When we put Him first in every area of our lives, we can live the life He has planned for us. He is our Source, our LORD and Savior, our Rock and Foundation—He is Everything. So as we embark on a new year, we should put Him first and trust Him to guide us through every day with its joys and struggles. Jesus is LORD and He is our best friend, and the Source of all that we need and want. Let's be wise as we choose to spend our time with Jesus this New Year!

"Christ was born to bring new Life. May the New Year renew Life in you." (Author unknown)

"Seek to do good and you will find that happiness will run after you." (James Freeman Clarke)

Numbers 6:24-26
"May God bless you and keep you. May God's face shine upon you and be gracious to you. May God's favor be upon you and give you peace."

Made in the USA
Charleston, SC
15 January 2017